武大通识

U0872646

珞珈博雅文库

（通识教材系列）

博雅弘毅

文明以止

成人成才

四通六识

中西民俗文化对比赏析

主　编　邓长慧

副主编　陆　朋　鲁亚侠　刘　莹

WUHAN UNIVERSITY PRESS

武汉大学出版社

图书在版编目(CIP)数据

中西民俗文化对比赏析:英文/邓长慧主编.—武汉：武汉大学出版社,2020.9

珞珈博雅文库.通识教材系列

ISBN 978-7-307-17048-3

Ⅰ.中…　Ⅱ.邓…　Ⅲ.风俗习惯—对比研究—中国、西方国家—高等学校—教材—英文　Ⅳ.K891

中国版本图书馆 CIP 数据核字(2019)第 298848 号

责任编辑:罗晓华　　责任校对:李孟潇　　版式设计:韩闻锦

出版发行：**武汉大学出版社**　(430072　武昌　珞珈山)

(电子邮箱：cbs22@ whu.edu.cn　网址：www.wdp. com.cn)

印刷:湖北恒泰印务有限公司

开本:720×1000　1/16　印张:21.5　字数:339 千字　插页:1

版次:2020 年 9 月第 1 版　2020 年 9 月第 1 次印刷

ISBN 978-7-307-17048-3　定价:55.00 元

总　序

小而言之，教材是“课本”，是一课之本，是教学内容和教学方法的语言载体；大而言之，教材是国家意志的体现，是高校教学成果和科研成果的重要标志。一流大学要有一流的本科教育，也要有一流的教材体系。新形势下根据国家有关要求，为进一步加强和改进学校教材建设与管理，努力构建一流教材体系，武汉大学成立了教材建设工作领导小组、教材建设工作委员会，设立了教材建设中心，为学校教材建设工作提供了有力保障。一流教材体系要注重教材内容的经典性和时代性，还要注重教材的系列化和立体化。基于这一思路，学校计划按照学科专业教育、通识教育、创业教育等类别规划建设自成系列的教材。通识教育系列教材即是学校大力推动通识教育教学工作的重要成果，其整体隶属于“珞珈博雅文库”，命名为“通识教材系列”。

在长期的办学实践和教学文化建设过程中，武汉大学形成了独具特色的融“五观”为一体的本科人才培养思想体系，即“人才培养为本，本科教育是根”的办学观，“以‘成人’教育统领成才教育”的育人观，“厚基础、跨学科、鼓励创新和冒尖”的教学观，“激发教师教与学生学双重积极性”的动力观，“以学生发展为中心”的目的观。为深化本科教育改革，打造世界一流本科教育，武汉大学于2015年开展本科教育改革大讨论并形成《武汉大学关于深化本科教育改革的若干意见》《武汉大学关于进一步加强通识教育的实施意见》等文件，对优化通识教育顶层设计、理顺通识课程管理体制、提高通识教育课程质量、加强通识教育保障机制等方面提出明确要求。

早在20世纪八九十年代，武汉大学就有学者专门研究大学通识教育。进入21世纪，武汉大学于2003年明确提出“通专结合”，将原培养方案的“公共基础课”改为“通识教育课”，作为全国通识教育改革的先行者率先开创“武大通识1.0”；2013年，经过十年的建设，形成通识课程的七大板块共千门课程，是为“武大通识2.0”；2016年，在武汉大学本科教育改革大讨论的基础上，学校建立通识教育委员会及其工作组，成立通识教育中心，重启通识教育改革，以“何以成人，何以知天”为核心理念，以《人文社科经典导引》和《自然科学经典导引》两门基础通识必修课为课程主体，同时在通识课程、通识课堂、通识管理和通识文化四大层次全面创新通识教育，从而为在校本科生逾3万的综合性大学如何实现通识教育的品质提升和卓越教学探索了一条新的路径，是为“武大通识3.0”。

当前，高校对大学生要有效“增负”，要提升大学生的学业挑战度，合理增加课程难度，拓展课程深度，扩大课程的可选择性，真正把“水课”转变成有深度、有难度、有挑战度的“金课”。那么通识课程如何脱“水”冶“金”？如何建设具有武汉大学特色的通识教育金课？这无疑要求我们从课程内容设计、教学方式改革、课程教材资源建设等方面着力。

一门好的通识课程应能对学生正确价值观的塑造、健全人格的养成、思维方式的拓展等发挥重要作用，而不应仅仅是传授学科知识点。我们在做课程设计的时候要认真思考“培养什么人、怎样培养人、为谁培养人”这一根本问题，从而切实推进课程思政建设。武汉大学学科门类丰富，教学资源齐全，这为我们跨学科组建教学团队，多维度进行探讨，设计更具前沿性和时代性的课程内容，提供了得天独厚的条件。

毋庸讳言，中学教育在高考指挥棒下偏向应试思维，过于看重课程考核成绩，往往忘记了“教书育人”的初心。那么，应如何改变这种现状？答案是：立德树人，脱“水”冶“金”。具体而言，通识教育要注重课程教学的过程管理，增加小班研讨、单元小测验、学习成果展示等鼓励学生投入学习的环节，而不再是单一地只看学生期末成绩。武汉大学的“两大导引”试行“8+8”的大班授课和小班研讨，经过三个学期的实践，取得了很好的成效，深受同学们欢迎。我们发现，小班研讨是一种非常有效的教学方式，能够帮助学生深度阅读、深度思考，增加学生课堂参与度，培养学生独立思考、理性判断、批判性思维和团队合作等多方面的能力。

课程教材资源建设是十分重要的。老师们精心编撰的系列教材，精心录制的在线开放课程视频，精心设计的各类题库，精心搜集整理的与课程相关的文献资料，等等，对于学生而言，都是精神大餐之中不可或缺的珍贵元素。在长期的教学实践中，老师们不断更新、完善课程教材资源，并且教会学生获取知识的能力，让学习不只停留于课堂，而是延续到课后，给学生课后的持续思考提供支撑和保障。

“武大通识 3.0”运行至今，武汉大学已形成一系列保障机制，鼓励教师更多地投入到通识教育教学中来。学校对通识 3.0 课程设立了准入准出机制，建设期内每年组织一次课程考核工作，严格把控立项课程的建设质量；对两门基础通识课程实施助教制，每学期遴选培训研究生和青年教师担任助教，辅助大班授课、小班研讨环节的开展；对投身通识教育的教师给予最大支持，在“351 人才计划”教学岗位、“教学业绩奖”等评选中专门设立通识教育教师名额，在职称晋升等方面也予以政策倾斜；对课程的课酬实行阶梯制，根据课程等级和教师考核结果发放授课课酬。

武汉大学打造多重通识教育活动，营造全校通识文化氛围。每月举行一期通识教育大讲堂，邀请海内外一流大学从事通识教育顶层设计的领袖性人物、知名教师、知名学者、杰出校友等来校为师生做专题报告；每学期组织一次通识教育研讨会，邀请全校通识课程主讲教师、主要管理人员参加，采取专家讲座与专题讨论相结合的方式，帮助提升教师的通识教育理念；不定了近代湖北高等外语教育乃至近代湖北高等教育的篇章。

与此同时，在英国国内，英国文学尚未成为一门真正的现代学科。在20世纪之初，英国文学仅仅被视为一门适合女性、工人和帝国殖民者的学科，散发着业余的气息，在牛津大学和剑桥大学始终被看作半瓶子醋学科。第一次世界大战之后，英国打败德国，在民族骄傲和爱国情绪之中，还夹杂一种"精神上的饥渴"，这种渴求恰好在英国文学中得到了满足和振奋。正如伊格尔顿所言，英国文学借着战时民族主义的东风一跃登上了权力的宝座。1917年，剑桥大学成立了英文系。及至20世纪20年代，在利维斯、理查兹和燕卜逊等人的努力下，英国文学最终获得了合法性，成为一门具有科学客观性的严肃学科。

从湖北最初的外语教育到现在，从英国文学被确立为一门严肃独立的学科到现在，百余年的历史光阴倏忽而逝。与其他的学科相比，中国的外国文学研究其实是一个相当年轻的学科。如今，西方的文学批评理论一度高歌猛进并完成了体制化，业已进入了后理论时代；放眼寰球，世界格局已然发生了巨大的变化。在这样的全球化境遇中，中国的外国文学研究者应该怎样理解和研究外国文学与文化，应该有何作为？我们能否在多年紧紧跟随西方理论的动静冷热之后，将西方理论资源转化为自己的学术话语体系并在此基础上完成学术创新？

"新时代外国文学与文化"系列教材便是武汉大学外国语言文学学院同仁们近些年的教学研究和学术思考的结晶，是对上述两个问题的部分解答。本系列教材作为入选"武大通识3.0"的规划教材，具有鲜明的特点，即文学文本（text）与文化语境（context）的相互参照，文学研究与文化研究之间的重叠。举一二例加以说明。《莎士比亚与西方社会》将莎剧文本与社会语境相结合，不仅深入研究莎剧所反映的社会维度，同时探索这一社会维度如何反作用于莎剧。《英语诗歌欣赏》知人论世，在赏析诗歌的文学形式与审美特征之外，将诗歌流派与社会文化思潮勾连起来相互印证，引导读者深入浅出于文学文化之表里。《电影中的俄罗斯文学》则在欣赏经典电影的同时评述俄罗斯文学名著的主题思想、写作技巧、语言风格和时代性意义，并且探究广义上的俄罗斯民族的价值观念和性格情感。

代性的课程内容，提供了得天独厚的条件。

毋庸讳言，中学教育在高考指挥棒下偏向应试思维，过于看重课程考核成绩，往往忘记了“教书育人”的初心。那么，应如何改变这种现状？答案是：立德树人，脱“水”冶“金”。具体而言，通识教育要注重课程教学的过程管理，增加小班研讨、单元小测验、学习成果展示等鼓励学生投入学习的环节，而不再是单一地只看学生期末成绩。武汉大学的“两大导引”试行“8+8”的大班授课和小班研讨，经过三个学期的实践，取得了很好的成效，深受同学们欢迎。我们发现，小班研讨是一种非常有效的教学方式，能够帮助学生深度阅读、深度思考，增加学生课堂参与度，培养学生独立思考、理性判断、批判性思维和团队合作等多方面的能力。

课程教材资源建设是十分重要的。老师们精心编撰的系列教材，精心录制的在线开放课程视频，精心设计的各类题库，精心搜集整理的与课程相关的文献资料，等等，对于学生而言，都是精神大餐之中不可或缺的珍贵元素。在长期的教学实践中，老师们不断更新、完善课程教材资源，并且教会学生获取知识的能力，让学习不只停留于课堂，而是延续到课后，给学生课后的持续思考提供支撑和保障。

“武大通识 3.0”运行至今，武汉大学已形成一系列保障机制，鼓励教师更多地投入到通识教育教学中来。学校对通识 3.0 课程设立了准入准出机制，建设期内每年组织一次课程考核工作，严格把控立项课程的建设质量；对两门基础通识课程实施助教制，每学期遴选培训研究生和青年教师担任助教，辅助大班授课、小班研讨环节的开展；对投身通识教育的教师给予最大支持，在“351 人才计划”教学岗位、“教学业绩奖”等评选中专门设立通识教育教师名额，在职称晋升等方面也予以政策倾斜；对课程的课酬实行阶梯制，根据课程等级和教师考核结果发放授课课酬。

武汉大学打造多重通识教育活动，营造全校通识文化氛围。每月举行一期通识教育大讲堂，邀请海内外一流大学从事通识教育顶层设计的领袖性人物、知名教师、知名学者、杰出校友等来校为师生做专题报告；每学期组织一次通识教育研讨会，邀请全校通识课程主讲教师、主要管理人员参加，采取专家讲座与专题讨论相结合的方式，帮助提升教师的通识教育理念；不定期开展博雅沙龙、读书会、午餐会等互动式研讨活动，有针对性地选取主题，邀请专家报告并研讨交流。这些都是珍贵的教学资源，有助于我们多渠道了解通识教育前沿和通识文化真谛，不断提升通识教育的理论素养，进而持续改进通识课程。

武汉大学的校训有一个关键词：弘毅。“弘毅”语出《论语》：“士不可以不弘毅，任重而道远。”对于“立德树人”的武大教师，对于“成人成才”的武大学子，对于“博雅弘毅，文明以止”的武大通识教育，皆为“任重而道远”。可以说，我们在通识教育改革道路上所走过的每一步，都将成为“教育强国，文化复兴”强有力的步伐。

“武大通识3.0”开启以来，我们精心筹备、陆续推出“珞珈博雅文库”大型通识教育丛书，涵盖“通识文化”“通识教材”“通识课堂”和“通识管理”四大系列。其中的“通识教材系列”已经推出“两大导引”，这次又推出核心和一般通识课程教材十余种，以后还将有更多优秀通识教材面世，使在校同学和其他读者“开卷有益”：拓展视野，启迪思想，融通古今，化成天下。

周叶中

序1

据史料记载，湖北省的高校外语教育最早可以追溯至百余年前的自强学堂和方言学堂（二者皆为武汉大学的前身）。光绪十九年十月（1893年11月），湖广总督张之洞向朝廷奏陈《设立自强学堂片》，力陈创设自强学堂的必要性，并提出了以“讲究实务、融贯中西、研精器数”为办学宗旨。他认为“盖闻经国以自强为本”“自强之道，以教育人才为先”，故取“自强”二字。自强学堂自创立伊始便是两湖最高学府，并效仿西方高等教育模式，进行分门（科）教学，设方言（外语）、格致、算学和商务四个专业，每个专业招生20人，略具综合性学校之雏形。其中，只有学方言或者修外语的学生在学校上课教学。张之洞非常重视外语人才的培养，甚至下令让格致和商务改课方言。到19世纪末，方言专业开设英、法、德、俄、日5国外语，延聘外籍教师8人，成为语种齐全、师资强大的“外语学院”。1902年，张之洞另择校址，成立方言学堂，令自强学堂原有学生移入。从自强学堂到方言学堂，开启了近代湖北高等外语教育乃至近代湖北高等教育的篇章。

与此同时，在英国国内，英国文学尚未成为一门真正的现代学科。在 20 世纪之初，英国文学仅仅被视为一门适合女性、工人和帝国殖民者的学科，散发着业余的气息，在牛津大学和剑桥大学始终被看作半瓶子醋学科。第一次世界大战之后，英国打败德国，在民族骄傲和爱国情绪之中，还夹杂一种“精神上的饥渴”，这种渴求恰好在英国文学中得到了满足和振奋。正如伊格尔顿所言，英国文学借着战时民族主义的东风一跃登上了权力的宝座。1917 年，剑桥大学成立了英文系。及至 20 世纪 20 年代，在利维斯、理查兹和燕卜逊等人的努力下，英国文学最终获得了合法性，成为一门具有科学客观性的严肃学科。

从湖北最初的外语教育到现在，从英国文学被确立为一门严肃独立的学科到现在，百余年的历史光阴倏忽而逝。与其他的学科相比，中国的外国文学研究其实是一个相当年轻的学科。如今，西方的文学批评理论一度高歌猛进并完成了体制化，业已进入了后理论时代；放眼寰球，世界格局已然发生了巨大的变化。在这样的全球化境遇中，中国的外国文学研究者应该怎样理解和研究外国文学与文化，应该有何作为？我们能否在多年紧紧跟随西方理论的动静冷热之后，将西方理论资源转化为自己的学术话语体系并在此基础上完成学术创新？

“新时代外国文学与文化”系列教材便是武汉大学外国语言文学学院同仁们近些年的教学研究和学术思考的结晶，是对上述两个问题的部分解答。本系列教材作为入选“武大通识 3.0”的规划教材，具有鲜明的特点，即文学文本（text）与文化语境（context）的相互参照，文学研究与文化研究之间的重叠。举一二例加以说明。《莎士比亚与西方社会》将莎剧文本与社会语境相结合，不仅深入研究莎剧所反映的社会维度，同时探索这一社会维度如何反作用于莎剧。《英语诗歌欣赏》知人论世，在赏析诗歌的文学形式与审美特征之外，将诗歌流派与社会文化思潮勾连起来相互印证，引导读者深入浅出于文学文化之表里。《电影中的俄罗斯文学》则在欣赏经典电影的同时评述俄罗斯文学名著的主题思想、写作技巧、语言风格和时代性意义，并且探究广义上的俄罗斯民族的价值观念和性格情感。

在武汉大学外国语言文学学院与经管学院之间的郁郁林荫之中，张之洞的雕像稳稳地端坐在那里，日复一日地淡然陪伴着来往穿行的师生。虽然他的“自强学堂”以及一系列的“自强”活动已经成为历史，但他的“自强”精神依然是我们宝贵的精神遗产，时常提醒我们这些外国文学与文化研究者们在与他者文化相遇时自觉保持主体意识和文化自信。

王爱菊

2019 年 6 月于武汉大学湖滨

序 2

武汉大学外国语言文学学院四位老师编写了一本关于中西民俗比较的英文书籍，请我审阅作序，我感到很高兴。目前市场上以中国民俗为主题的著作为数不少，论述西方民俗的图书也比比皆是，但是立足于文化自信，传播中国民俗文化，系统比对中西方民俗的英文教材则屈指可数。

人类文明发展至今，不同国家、不同民族的人民在生产生活中形成了独具特色的风俗习惯，这些风俗习惯成为丰富多彩的人类文明中不可或缺的组成部分。习近平总书记指出："世界是在人类各种文明交流交融中成为今天这个样子的。推进人类各种文明交流交融、互学互鉴，是让世界变得更加美丽、各国人民生活得更加美好的必由之路。"由此可见各国、各民族之间的文化交流的必然性和重要性。中国同世界各国、各民族之间的文化交流历史悠久、源远流长。丝绸之路作为桥梁和纽带，有力地促进了中西方的经济文化交流，至今仍是中西交往的重要渠道。

只有民族的才是世界的。中国民俗文化是中华文化的瑰宝。在坚持中华民族文化自信的新时代，我们既要学习借鉴国外先进文化，做好吸收引入国外民俗文化工作；更要重视推动中国文化走出去，做好传播推介中国民俗文化的工作，引导大学生从比较角度增进对中西民俗文化的认识，增强对中华民族文化的热爱，培养学生的跨文化鉴赏与交流能力和对中华文化的传播能力。

中西民俗文化博大精深，内容广泛多样，编写以大学生为主要读者的这方面的教材实非易事。四位英语教师以跨文化教育者的责任激励自己，做出这种探索和尝试，他们的工作值得肯定和称道。

在我看来，这本教材不仅可以作为高校大学生的传统文化普及读本，亦可成为传统文化爱好者和留学生们的入门读物。

鉴于此，乐以为序。

桂胜

武汉大学社会学院

2019年11月

前言

民俗文化凝聚着民族的性格、民族的精神、民族的文化创造和民族的真善美，是宝贵的文化遗产。世界文明高度发展，文化交融日渐频繁，但中西方民众历代沿袭的民俗文化由于生存环境、历史渊源和宗教信仰等不同因素的影响依然存在很大差异且各具特色。

习近平总书记指出，文明因多样而交流，因交流而互鉴，因互鉴而发展。中外文化交流是对等的、双向的，在全球化、国际化的时代，我们既要大胆吸收世界各国文化，又要积极推动中国文化走向世界；大学生要以开放的胸襟学习国外先进的文化，更要增进对中国文化的认知，肩负起传承和传播的责任。中国民俗文化是中国文化的重要组成部分，但目前我国大学开设的中国民俗文化课程多以汉语讲授，大多数学生还不具备用英语讲述本土文化的能力，也很少有英语课程涉及中西民俗文化的对比分析，英文版的相关教材更是寥寥无几。为使中国民俗文化更好地走向世界，同时让世界民俗文化为大学生熟知，编写英语版中西民俗文化教材尤为重要和迫切。

本教材以英语为媒介，以比较为手法，从中国和西方英语国家文明的起源入手，选取饮食、民居、人生礼仪、民间信仰等中西方民众在长期的生产生活实践中创造和发展起来的风俗习惯和生活智慧进行历时和共时的比对，促使学生全面了解中西方在物质民俗、社会民俗、精神民俗和语言民俗方面的差异及特色；通过探究和分析中西方民俗文化的渊源、发展和现状，引导学生学会用英语赏析中西民俗文化，激发学生对本民族文化的热爱，增强民族文化自信，提高跨文化交际能力。

本教材主要特色如下：

1. 立足弘扬中国民俗精粹

中国民俗蕴涵着丰富、深邃的人文内涵，是炎黄子孙共有的精神财富。但随着社会的发展、生活方式和价值观的改变，人们对传统文化的认同感不再强烈，曾历经千年而不衰的民俗文化积淀濒临流失。在坚定中华文化自信和推进中华文化走出去的新时代，弘扬中国民俗精粹是本教材编写的立足点。

2. 突出中西民俗文化对比

本教材对四类民俗中最具代表性的话题信息进行精心挑选整理，从多个视角重点阐述比对中西民俗的差异及特色，将标志性的民俗事象进行宏观和微观的比较分析，每个单元设置反思题，以引导学生进行跨文化思考，培养学生的文化鉴赏能力和批判性思维能力。

3. 凝练中西民俗主题词汇

中西民俗文化的用语广博且内涵丰富，为有助于学生辨识和把握，本教材将大量有关民俗文化的常用主题词汇以彩色字体显现，并随行附有准确的注释，以利于学生快速融入民俗文化，有效接受民俗文化的熏陶。

4. 拓展中西民俗文化知识

中西民俗文化的内容和话题多样，为促进学生对民俗的全面了解，在专题讲解核心民俗事象要点的基础上，每单元末尾都设置了民俗文化小百科，拓展该主题的相关知识，以方便学生自主学习。

我们深知中西民俗文化博大精深，要编撰一本好教材实非易事。但编者本着“不忘初心，牢记使命”的担当，勉力而为。本教材的编撰工作由邓长慧（负责第 1 单元、第 2 单元、第 3 单元及第 12 单元）、陆朋（负责第 4 单元、第 7 单元、第 10 单元和第 11 单元）、鲁亚侠（负责第 5 单元和第 6 单元）、刘莹（负责第 8 单元和第 9 单元）四位老师合作完成。

本教材在编写中参阅和引用了国内外民俗文化领域的专家和学者的大量研究成果及资料，武汉大学社会学院的民俗学专家桂胜教授对此书的编写提出了宝贵的专业建议，我们在此深表感谢！对本书的欠缺之处，我们诚恳希望读者给予批评指正。

本教材系“武大通识 3.0”的阶段性成果，可供高校大学生使用，亦可作为普通读者（尤其是有一定英语水平且对民俗文化有兴趣的读者）提高人文素养的大众读本，更可作为来华留学生和爱好中国传统文化的国际人士的入门读物。

编者

2019 年 11 月于珞珈山

目 录

Contents

Unit 1
An Introduction to Folklore

Chinese Couplets

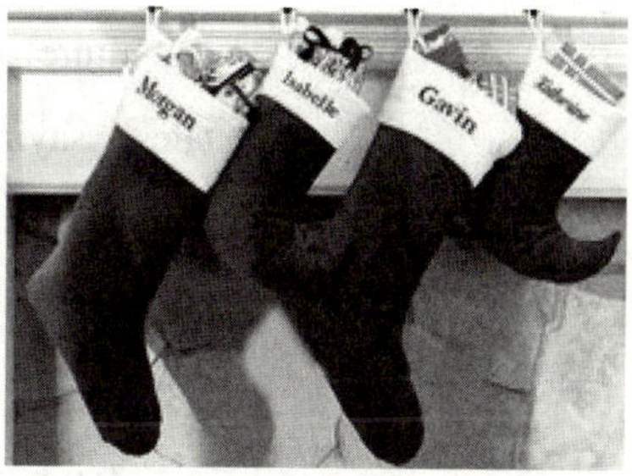

Christmas Stockings

Learning Objectives

- To be familiar with the definition and classification of folklore
- To get a better understanding of the foundations of Chinese and Western civilizations
- To compare and contrast the similarities and differences about Chinese and Western philosophies

Lead-in Questions

- How do you define folklore and culture? How is folklore related to culture?
- What do "yellow civilization" and "blue civilization" stand for respectively? Why?
- Do you know Confucius and Socrates? What are their main teachings or philosophical ideas? How do their doctrines influence people's way of life?

Part I What Is Folklore?

1. Definitions

folklore 民俗

The term "**folklore**" was coined in 1846 by the Englishman William Thoms. Put it simply, folklore is part of culture which focuses mainly on traditional customs, tales, sayings, dances, or art forms preserved among a people, usually passed through generations by word of mouth or by performance. Here are detailed explanations of folklore.

(1) Zhong Jingwen, a famous Chinese folklorist, defines folklore as culture about life created, enjoyed and inherited by people in a country or an ethnic group. Folklore originates from the needs of the collective life of human beings, constantly formed, expanded and evolved in specific regions, times and nations to serve people's daily life. It includes not only folk customs, rural or urban, ancient or newly-produced, but also folk literature inherited orally, as well as material, spiritual and social folk customs inherited in the form of matter, behavior and mentality.

(2) According to Wikipedia, folklore is the expressive body of culture shared by a particular group of people; it includes the traditions common to that culture, subculture or group. To be specific, oral traditions (such as tales, proverbs and jokes), material culture (ranging from

traditional building styles to handmade toys), customary lore, the forms and rituals of celebrations (like Spring Festival and weddings, folk dances and **initiation rites**) all belong to the scale of folklore. Not only the forms but also their **transmission** are essential parts of folklore, for these traditions are not taught in a formal school curriculum or studied in the fine arts but passed along informally from one individual to another either through verbal instruction or demonstration.

initiation rites 成人仪式

transmission 传播

(3) Folklore and folklife (including traditional arts, beliefs, traditional ways of work and leisure, **adornment** and celebrations) are cultural ways in which a group maintains and passes on a shared way of life.

adornment 装饰品

As New York folklorist Ben Botkin wrote in 1938:

Every group bound together by common interests and purposes, whether educated or uneducated, rural or urban, possesses a body of traditions which may be called its folklore. Into these traditions enter many elements, individual, popular, and even "literary", but all are absorbed and ***assimilated*** *through repetition and variation into a pattern which has value and continuity for the group as a whole.*

assimilated 同化的

These traditional forms of knowledge are learned informally within a one-to-one or small group exchange, through performance, or by example. In all cases, folklore and folklife are learned and ***perpetuated*** *within the context of the "group", for it is the shared experience which shapes and gives meaning to the exchange.*

perpetuate 持续

2. Features

Folk cultures in different regions or countries share similarities as well as differences. Here are some typical features common to various kinds of folklore.

2.1 Collectivism

The human possesses natural, mental and social characteristics, among which sociality is the most fundamental. Folk culture is inseparable from human group activities. Once formed, folk customs become collective habits, which is why **collectivism** is the most important feature of folklore.

collectivism 集体性

2.2 Hereditability

hereditability 传承性

The **hereditability** of folklore refers to its continuity in time. In either traditional or modern society, one's growth is inseparable from education and enlightenment of folklore, which takes place **imperceptibly**. Folk customs pass down from generation to generation either orally or by demonstration so that they persist forever.

imperceptibly 潜移默化地

2.3 Transmissibility

transmissibility 传播性

The **transmissibility** of folklore refers to its extension in space. With its formation and perfection, a new folk custom will gradually display its function and value, becoming acceptable to local people and probably permeating to other ethnic groups. It is often the case that folk customs with a longer history and more functions enjoy a wider transmission.

2.4 Stability

Folklore is a series of folk customs that people create, inherit and enjoy in long-term social practice. Once created, those customs become stabilized together with people's way of production and living, unless dramatic changes happen. With the given political, economic, social and cultural background, folklore keeps its **stability** as long as the economic base remains unchanged.

stability 稳定性

2.5 Variability

The stability of folklore is relative while its **variability** is unavoidable, referring to spontaneous and gradual change in the process of its inheritance and transmission. As internal **impetus** for preservation and development of folklore, variability actually implies its adaptation and vitality.

variability 变异性

impetus 动力

2.6 Service

Folklore is a huge knowledge system as well as an inexhaustible cultural treasure, containing rich cultural connotations and embodying collective wisdom and creation. Its **service** plays a vital role in the development of a society. Its main functions go as follows.

service 服务性

2.6.1 Education

Folklore is a **pedagogic** device which reinforces morals and values and builds wit.

pedagogic 教育的

2.6.2 **Regulation**

regulation 规范

It's widely accepted that folklore helps control people's

thoughts and behaviors by exercising social pressure and setting restrictions.

sustainment 维系，支撑

2.6.3 **Sustainment**

Folklore confirms culture, justifying its rituals and institutions to those who perform and observe them, keeping the society stable.

adjustment 调节，调整

2.6.4 **Adjustment**

Folklore lets people escape from repressions imposed upon them by society, satisfying their psychological and spiritual needs.

2.6.5 Entertainment

A variety of folk art (like folk songs, folk dance), folk tales, festivals and so on can entertain people on special occasions and ordinary days as well, freeing them from tiring labor.

3. Classification

According to Zhong Jingwen, there are mainly four categories of folklore.

3.1 Material Folklore

Material folklore refers to those repetitive and stereotyped activities conducted by people in the process of creating and consuming material wealth, and their products, mainly involving such aspects as production, trade, food, costumes, residence, transportation and medical care, etc.

3.2 Social Folklore

institutional 制度的，机构的

Social folklore, or social structural and **institutional**

folklore, is the socially related routine formed under given conditions. It is also a collective behavioral mode that people apply and pass on from individual to family, to clan, village, ethnic group, even abroad, mainly consisting of social structural folklore (blood relations, geographical relations and occupational relations), social institutional folklore (customary law, life rituals), festival folklore, and entertaining folklore.

3.3 Spiritual Folklore

Spiritual folklore means those folk customs related to **ideology** formed on the basis of material culture and institutional culture. Put in another way, it refers to psychological experience developed in the process of understanding and transforming nature, including folk beliefs, magic, philosophy, **ethics** and art, etc.

ideology 意识形态

ethics 伦理

3.4 Verbal Folklore

Verbal folklore is an information exchange system established by way of oral convention and collective inheritance. It consists of two parts—folk language and folk literature, the former mainly referring to folk sayings, proverbs, riddles and so on, and the latter folk myths, legends, tales, etc.

The above four categories are closely related by mutual restriction and promotion, and they change with the times.

Part II Foundations of Chinese and Western Civilizations

It is common sense that civilization does not come all of a sudden from nowhere. This is true of Chinese and Western civilizations.

As a broad generalization, the Chinese civilization is based on the ethical culture of Confucianism, Buddhism and Taoism, and takes harmony between man and nature as the foundation of its traditional culture. On the contrary, the Western civilization, rooted in ancient Greek and Roman civilizations, is deeply influenced by Christian culture and characterized by contract culture, which emphasizes the opposition between man and nature and the conquest of nature. With justice and legal system as the premise, the Western civilization attaches more importance to equality, self-confidence, science and religion.

It goes without saying that knowledge of ancient philosophies and religions is indispensable to the understanding of folklore as part of culture.

1. Foundations of Chinese Civilization

Legalism 法家思想
Mohism 墨家思想
Warring States Period 战国时期

In the late Spring-Autumn Period, different schools of thought, such as **Legalism**, Taoism, Confucianism, **Mohism**, and yin-yang school of thought, had emerged with considerable social influence. By the middle of the **Warring States Period**, many schools of thought and various theories had laid a sound foundation for the development of Chinese culture.

1.1 Confucianism

Confucianism 儒家思想

Confucianism is a mainstream cultural ideology,

philosophy and religious system founded by China's most famous philosopher Confucius, developed by Mencius, and collected by Xunzi, which has been continuously developing, spread to foreign countries (especially east Asian countries) and still enjoys vitality.

Confucianism was originally one of **the Hundred Schools of Thought**, founded by Confucius in the Pre-Qin Period. During the reign of Qin Shihuang, Confucianism suffered a heavy blow. Later, in order to maintain the feudal autocracy, Emperor Wudi of the Han Dynasty followed Dong Zhongshu's advice of "**dethroning** other schools of thought and respecting Confucianism", leading to its revival.

the Hundred Schools of Thought 诸子百家

dethrone 废黜

Confucianism takes **benevolence**, **forgiveness**, **sincerity**, **filial piety** as the core values, with an emphasis on the gentleman's moral cultivation, enlightenment and benevolent governance, which has exerted a profound influence on Chinese culture. The following are some deeply-rooted ideas.

benevolence 仁
forgiveness 恕
sincerity 诚
filial piety 孝

1.1.1 Responsibility

Confucianism takes the world as one's duty.

1.1.2 Loyalty and Filial Piety

There are five key elements: benevolence, **righteousness**, **propriety**, wisdom and faith.

righteousness 义
propriety 礼

1.1.3 Forgiveness

The golden rule is "do not do to others what you do not want others to do to you".

1.1.4 Ethics

The basic ethics covers self-cultivation, family regulation, state governance and bringing peace to all under Heaven.

Confucius stressed harmonious human relationships as well as man-nature harmony. Humans should listen to the voice of nature, respecting and loving it as the world of life.

Confucius was the first figure in Chinese history to initiate private education. In his eyes, education should take **lofty** ideals, great virtue, love of people, and the **six arts** as the general principles. His focus was not only on increasing knowledge but also on broadening horizons and seeking the greater meaning of life.

lofty 崇高的

six arts 六艺（礼，乐，射，御，书，数）

As one of the greatest and most influential thinkers of China and humanity as a whole, Confucius has been recognized as the chief representative of traditional Chinese culture and philosophy although some of his ideas are outdated.

1.2 Taoism/Daoism

Taoism, a primary school of thought in the Pre-Qin Period, represented by Lao Tzu and Chuang Tzu, is a philosophical, ethical or religious tradition that stresses living in harmony with nature.

Taoism 道家学说

The ***Tao Te Ching***, written by Lao Tzu (571-471BC), consisting of 5,162 Chinese characters, reflects the core Taoist concept in terms of *Tao* and *Te*. *Tao*, the way, or the truth, is the essence and origin of everything in the universe, and everything develops from *Tao*; *Te*, virtue, is what an individual thing receives from *Tao* and it embodies *Tao*. The book has been one of the most translated philosophical works of ancient China.

Tao Te Ching (*The Scripture of Ethics*)《道德经》

Taoism advocates naturalness and **non-action**. The former means a natural state of being, an attitude of following the way of nature. Namely, humans should not try to change anything natural but follow. The latter is the guarantee of naturalness, meaning human creativity should be in accordance with the ways of nature.

non-action 无为

The ideas like "**Tao follows nature**", "**the greatest virtue is water**" and some political and military strategies such as "governing by doing nothing that goes against nature", "overcoming the strong by being weak" , produce great influence on the Chinese and world culture. In addition, Taoism has left a huge impact on traditional Chinese medicine, Chinese Kung Fu and tea ceremony.

Tao follows nature 道法自然

the greatest virtue is water 上善若水

With its profound influence on Chinese philosophy, literature, science and technology, art, music, health preservation, religion and so on, Taoism is regarded as the cornerstone of Chinese culture.

1.3 Buddhism

The founder of **Buddhism** was Siddhartha Gautama, a prince in ancient India who gave up the royal life and **meditated** under the **pipal** tree on human sufferings, getting enlightened and becoming **Buddha**.

Buddhism 佛学

meditate 冥想

pipal 菩提树

Buddha 佛陀

Buddhism was introduced into China about 67 AD. There are two major branches of Buddhism in China: Chinese Buddhism and Tibetan Buddhism.

The foundation of Buddhism is the **Four Truths** centering around the point of human life:

Four Truths 四谛

—Human life is characterized by dissatisfaction.

—The dissatisfaction arises within people.

—People can realize the source of dissatisfaction, ending its most existential forms.

—Buddha displays a path by which people can understand and deal with the actual world.

The Four Truths express the basic orientation of Buddhism: people long for and cling to temporary states and things that cause pain, keeping them caught in the endless cycle of repeated rebirth and dying again. But there is a way to liberation from this endless cycle to the state of **nirvana**, namely following the **Noble Eightfold Paths**.

nirvana 涅槃

Noble Eightfold Paths 八正道

Chinese Buddhism incorporates elements of traditional Buddhism and Taoism. The common practices include: praying with **incense**; paying respect to dead ancestors during Tomb-sweeping Day and **Hungry Ghost Festival**; recognizing the existence of ghosts and hell realm; believing in **reincarnation** and **retribution**; performing religious ceremonies to help the soul find peace; etc.

incense 香

Hungry Ghost Festival 中元节

reincarnation 转世

retribution 报应

Chinese Buddhism or Han Buddhism has shaped Chinese culture in a wide variety of areas including art, politics, literature, philosophy, medicine and material culture.

2. Foundations of Western Civilization

Western civilization traces its roots back to Europe and the **Mediterranean**, closely linked to ancient Greece and **Medieval Western Christendom**.

Mediterranean 地中海

Medieval Western Christendom 中世纪西方基督教国家

Ancient Greek culture has made brilliant achievements

in many aspects, such as religious mythology, philosophy, literature, art and science, etc., which have exerted a huge and far-reaching influence on the development of Western civilization and even the world culture today.

Christianity has played a prominent role in the shaping of Western civilization, which throughout most of its history, has been nearly equivalent to Christian culture.

2.1 Ancient Greek Philosophy

Classical Greek culture, especially philosophy, had a powerful influence on ancient Rome and many parts of the Mediterranean Basin and Europe. For this reason, classical Greece is generally considered the cradle of Western civilization.

Ancient Greek philosophy formulated the basic subject and knowledge category of modern Western philosophy research, such as **metaphysics**, logic, philosophy of language, theory of knowledge, ethics, political philosophy, and philosophy of art. The following three famous Greek philosophers established the foundations of Western philosophy.

metaphysics 形而上学

Socrates (469-399 BC), one of the founders of Western philosophy, was known for his contribution to the field of **ethics**. He made no writings but his theories of virtue and justice have survived through the writings of Plato, his student.

Socrates 苏格拉底

ethics 伦理学

Socrates made his most important and enduring contribution to Western thought by his **dialectic** method of inquiry, known as the Socratic method, which he largely

dialectic 辩证的

applied to the examination of key moral concepts such as the Good and Justice.

Politically, Socrates believed that the wise, or the philosophers are the only type of person suitable to govern others.

In terms of virtue, Socrates expected people to attach more importance to self-development rather than the pursuit of material wealth.

When it comes to knowledge, one of the best known sayings of Socrates is "I only know that I know nothing". He used a term "midwife" to create a vivid image of his question-and-answer method of teaching to achieve knowledge. The Socratic method is still used in classroom to this day.

Socrates occupies a unique position in the history of human civilization not only because of his academic contributions to Western philosophy but also because of his dedication to the pursuit of truths at the cost of his life.

Plato 柏拉图

metaphysical 形而上学的

epistemological 认识论的

theory of Forms 形式论

The Republic《理想国》

Plato (427-347 BC), a follower of Socrates and a teacher of Aristotle, was best known for his **metaphysical** and **epistemological** ideas. He wrote many books in the form of dialogues and conversations, answering various problems about philosophy. But his main concerns are the **theory of Forms** and of the just state.

The Republic is a Socratic dialogue, written by Plato around 380 BC, concerning the definition of justice, the order and character of the just city-state and the just man. It also discusses the theory of Forms, the immortality of the soul and the roles of the philosopher in society.

Plato made a fundamental distinction between appearance and reality. Appearance implies the world of something particular perceived by the senses, whereas reality consists of the unchanging **Ideas** or Forms understood by pure intellect.

Idea 理念

In his great dialogue (*The Republic*), Plato created an ideal state which consists of three classes: the highest is the ruling class, made up of the wisest men in society; then the military class who can protect the state; and the working class who provide material things required by society.

Plato founded the Academy in Athens in 386 BC, the first institution of higher learning in the Western world.

The philosophical base laid by Socrates was developed in depth by Plato, who built the philosophical building of the idea on the basis of Socrates' **conceptualism**. Plato's Theory of Ideas completes the criticism of the **Sophist philosophy** and reestablishes the authority of thought in philosophy.

conceptualism 概念论

Sophist philosophy 智者哲学

Aristotle (384-322 BC) was a logician, scientist, and author of works on logic, metaphysics, ethics, natural science, politics and poetics, which profoundly influenced Western thoughts.

Aristotle 亚里士多德

Aristotle derived his inspiration from his teacher but developed his thought in a different direction.

He considered logic as the basic tool of philosophy and science. With his work on **deductive reasoning**, Aristotle is credited with the earliest study of formal logic, and his conception of it was the dominant form of Western logic until advances in mathematical logic occurred in the 19th century.

deductive reasoning 演绎推理

Aristotle's epistemology is based on the study of things

that exist or happen in the world, and rises to knowledge of the universal, whereas for Plato epistemology begins with knowledge of universal forms (or ideas) and descends to knowledge of particular imitations of these.

For Aristotle, "form" is still what phenomena are based on, but is represented in a particular substance. Aristotle uses **induction** from examples alongside deduction, whereas Plato relies on deduction from a **priori** principle.

induction 归纳
priori 先验的

It is Aristotle who coined the term "metaphysics". He also called it "first philosophy", distinguishing it from mathematics and natural science (physics) as the **contemplative** philosophy which studies the divine.

contemplative 沉思的

Aristotle was the leading expert of his time in almost all fields of knowledge, and his **encyclopedic** writings had been the source of scientific thinking in the West for almost two thousand years.

encyclopedic 百科全书式的

2.2 Christianity

Originating from Palestine in Rome in the 1st century AD, Christianity is founded on the birth, preaching, death and **resurrection** of Jesus Christ. It takes Jesus Christ as the **savior** and the *Bible* as the blueprint. The core idea is the **Gospel**—the **salvation** of god Jesus Christ, which fully demonstrates god's selfless love for the mankind and the whole universe. God loved the world so much that he gave his one and only son, Jesus Christ, to the mankind and whosoever believes in him shall get an eternal life.

resurrection 复活
savior 救世主
Gospel 福音
salvation 拯救

The major branches of Christianity include: (Eastern)

Orthodox, (Roman) **Catholicism**, and **Protestantism**.

The core beliefs of Christianity go as follows:

2.2.1 Ten **Commandments**

Ten commandments, the foundation of Christianity, means ten regulations God had given to the people of Israel through Moses, the prophet of Israel. After the resurrection of Jesus, the commandments apply to the whole Christianity world.

2.2.2 Trinity

The **trinity** is a basic doctrine of Christianity, which indicates the attribute of god — the only true god, but in the form of three persons (father, son and holy spirit). The father is creator and ruler of all creation, as well as creator of salvation; Son — Jesus Christ, is the **executor** of salvation. The Holy Spirit is God's power in action, or his active force. God sends out his spirit by projecting his energy anywhere to accomplish his will.

2.2.3 Original Sin and **Redemption**

This is the basis of Christian ethics and morality. It is believed that the sins of Adam and Eve, the ancestors of human beings, were passed down and became the root of all human sins. People are born with this original sin, and can only rely on the salvation of Jesus Christ.

2.2.4 Heaven and Hell

Christians believe in heaven and eternal life as well as hell and eternal punishment. People's life is limited, but the soul of people will gain rebirth because of faith, getting an eternal life in heaven. Without faith or **repentance**, they will be punished forever by God and suffer in hell.

Orthodox 东正教
Catholicism 天主教
Protestantism 新教
commandment 戒律
trinity 三位一体
executor 执行者
redemption 救赎
repentance 悔过

Enlightenment 启蒙运动

Until the Age of **Enlightenment** (around the 17th-18th century), Christian culture guided the course of philosophy, literature, art, music and science. A lot of them were preserved in the teachings of the Church, in an environment that, otherwise, would have probably got lost.

Part III Comparison and Contrast

1. Holistic Chinese Philosophy VS Dualistic Western Philosophy

Ancient Chinese philosophy places great emphasis on unity between nature and man. In other words, the ancient Chinese philosophers stressed the "one" and harmony, identifying man with nature rather than separating the two. Chuang Tzu proposed that man is part of nature. Confucianism, the dominant ideology in China, sought to teach all people to behave properly in order to promote harmony. Mencius was the first philosopher who proposed the idea of the integration of heaven/nature with man in a complete sense. Lao Tzu of the Taoist School was also an advocate of harmony.

Some iconic practices are closely linked to the holistic philosophy. A **TCM** doctor with **synthetic** thinking treats his patients by looking, listening, feeling and eliciting their complaints in order to form a correct judgment of their general physical condition. The Chinese painting is often a combination of different art forms: calligraphy, painting, poetry, and so on. Chinese people give top priority to collectivism and enjoy group identity, leading to the popularity of values such as harmony, face-saving, humility, courtesy, group loyalty and interdependence.

holistic 整体的	dualistic 二元的	TCM 中医
synthetic 综合的	dichotomy 二分法	demarcation 划分，界限
divine 神圣的	secular 世俗的	analytic 解析的

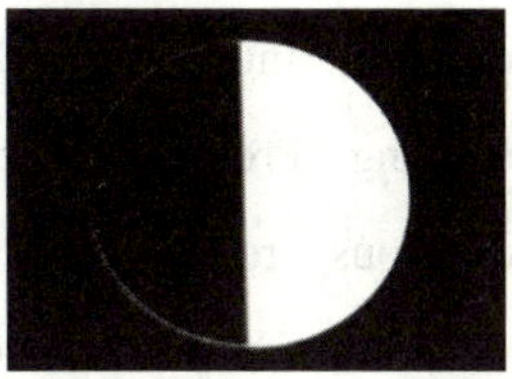

The notion of subject-object **dichotomy** has been popular since Ancient Greek Age in Western philosophy. The ancient Greek philosophers, whose ideas exerted great influence over the whole Europe, tended to believe that the universe was divided into two opposites and there was a clear-cut **demarcation** between man and nature, subject and object, mind and matter, the **divine** and the **secular**, God and man. The dividing worldview is the starting point of Westerners' initiative in exploring and transforming nature.

As a result, Westerners belong to "I" culture or they are individually-centered, valuing things like self-reliance, critical thinking, independence, equality, fairness, privacy and competition. A Western doctor with **analytic** thinking will examine parts of the body through tests before making a diagnosis. A Western artistic work separates painting from poetry instead of integrating both.

Actually, both Western and Chinese cultures recognize opposing elements in the universe, and the difference is that Western culture emphasizes their co-existence and opposition while Chinese one stresses their interdependence and integration.

2. River (Yellow) Civilization VS Marine (Blue) Civilization

Ancient Asian-African civilizations are referred to as river Civilization. There are four of them: the **Tigris-Euphrates River Civilization** in the Middle East in 3500 BC; **the Nile Valley** Civilization in Egypt around 3100 BC; **the Indus River** Civilization around 2600 BC and the Yellow River Civilization in China around

1700 BC.

The Yellow River is the second longest river in China, after the Yangtze River. Originating in Qinghai Province of western China, it flows through nine provinces into the Bohai Sea in Shandong Province. Being the most prosperous region in early Chinese history, the Yellow River basin served as the birthplace of ancient Chinese civilization. A river civilization or river culture is an agricultural nation or civilization situated beside and drawing **sustenance** from a river. With abundant irrigation water, flat **terrain**, relatively fertile land, mild climate, the areas along the river are suitable for human survival and crop cultivation, thus meeting the basic needs of people. People take farming as its basic form and rely on the natural environment. Agricultural economy is one of peace and self-preservation, leading people to be defensive rather than aggressive.

marine 航海的	
Tigris-Euphrates River Civilization 底格里斯河和幼法拉底河的两河文明	
the Nile Valley 尼罗河谷	the Indus River 印度河
sustenance 食物，营养	terrain 地形
Mediterranean 地中海	city-state 城邦

Besides the four ancient civilizations, the Greek Civilization and the Roman Civilization together constitute the **Mediterranean** Civilization. Greece is home to the first advanced civilization in Europe and is considered as the birthplace of Western civilization.

Mountainous Greece consisted of many smaller regions, or several hundred relatively independent **city-states**, each with its own dialect, cultural peculiarities,

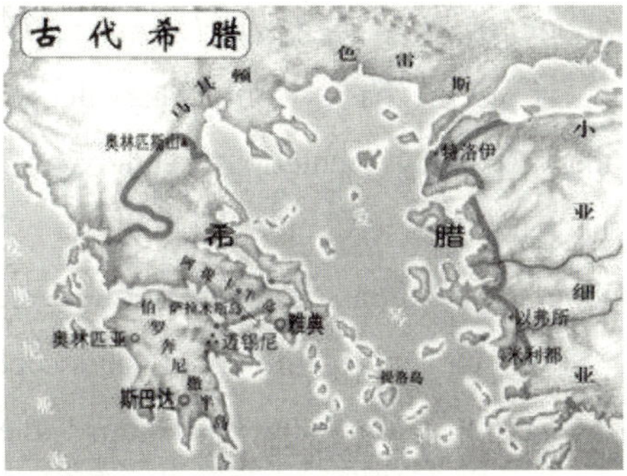

and identity. Regionalism and regional conflicts were a prominent feature of ancient Greece. With poor-quality soil and limited crop production, its economy largely depended on imported goods. As a result, ancient Greeks could only maintain their survival and development through overseas commercial trade. Greek position in the Mediterranean gave its provinces control over some of Egypt's most crucial seaports and trade routes.

Ancient Greek commercial and maritime trade followed the principle of "equal exchange". In addition, the development of commercial trade required a free environment, which in turn promoted the formation of "equality" and the establishment of democratic politics in ancient Greece. Navigation helped the ancient Greeks develop the national character of being open and brave to explore.

3. *The Analects* VS The *Bible*

Confucius (551-479 BC), born in Qufu, Shandong Province, was a sage, philosopher and educator. *The Analects* (*Lun Yu*), a collection of notes of Confucius's discourses, conversations and travels, compiled by his **disciples**, is the earliest and most reliable source embodying the basic values of the Confucian tradition: learning, morality, ritual and filial piety. Confucius put the greatest emphasis on the importance of study in the book. *The Analects* also offers valuable insights into successful governance and the ideal organization of society. Together with the other three volumes of the

"Four Books" (*The Great Learning*, *The Doctrine of the Mean* and *The Mencius*), it teaches the basic Confucian values including propriety, righteousness, loyalty and filial piety, centering around **humanity**. For thousands of years, especially in the feudal society, the "Four Books" and the "Five Classics" had enjoyed popularity and passed down from generation to generation.

As the most influential philosophical work in the Chinese history, *The Analects* of Confucius has shaped the thought and customs of China and of neighboring countries for centuries and plenty of his ideas are still shining in today's society.

disciple 弟子，信徒	humanity 仁慈，人道	scripture 经文
testament 圣约	aphorism 格言	prophetic 预言的
canon 真经	Hebrew 希伯来语	epistle 书信体
Revelation《启示录》	apostle 信徒	

The *Bible* is a collection of sacred **scriptures**, a product of divine inspiration and a record of the relationship between God and humans by Christians, Jews and so on. Consisting of the *Old* ***Testament*** and *New Testament*, with various literary types (like myth, legend, novel, fable, drama, prose, poetry, proverb, **aphorism**, as well as original **prophetic** literature), the *Bible* is widely accepted as a literary masterpiece. Different religious groups include different books in their **canons**. Christian *Bible* ranges from 66 books of the Protestant canon to 81 books of the Orthodox canon.

The *Old Testament* is a collection of 39 Jewish books, written in ancient **Hebrew**, containing the books of law, history, poetry and prophecy, which describes the history of the Jewish nation, belief and its development. The

27-volume *New Testament*, written in Greek, is a classic of Christianity, containing the gospels, the history books, the **epistles** and the ***Revelations***, recording stories of Jesus and his **apostles** and the early church, etc.

With different contents, the *Old Testament* and *New Testament* are intrinsically linked in that both Judaism and Christianity believe that God (Jehovah) is the only true god in the universe. According to Judaism, God promises a savior to his people while Christians believe that Jesus' birth is the coming of the savior, and that Jesus' birth, death and resurrection are the fulfillment of God's promises.

The *Bible* has been translated into thousands of different languages and is widely considered as the most influential and best-selling book in the world.

Part IV Reflection and Presentation

1. Some people think Chinese philosophy takes more of a spiritual approach while Western philosophy of a hands-on one. Does that mean Western philosophy is more logical, scientific and rational? Think critically and illustrate your point of view by examples.

2. What influences do the different origins of Chinese and Western civilizations exert on people's mode of thinking and way of life? How do they affect our economic development and daily life?

3. As a kind of historical and cultural accumulation, folklore is regarded as the concentrated embodiment of national character and culture, as well as the soul and symbol of national culture. Please use specific examples to illustrate the argument.

4. In both Chinese and Western cultures, the golden rule for treating others is "do unto others what you would have them do unto you". Do you think this is a good rule to guide interaction between people of different cultures? Why?

Part V Mini-pedia

1. Mencius

Mencius or Meng Tzu (372-289 BC) was a Chinese philosopher, great thinker, educator and one of the principal interpreters of Confucianism. He was born in the city of Zoucheng, Shandong Province, not far away from Qufu, Confucius' birthplace.

The doctrine of "benevolent government" is the core of Mencius' political thoughts, which is inherited from Confucius' thought of "benevolence". Mencius developed it into an administrative program covering ideology, politics, economy, culture, etc. The basic spirit of "benevolent governance" is to have deep sympathy and love for the common people. Mencius emphasized the important role of the common citizens in the state. Confucius generally thought highly of rulers whereas Mencius argued that the common people were more important than rulers. Mencius also claimed the innate goodness of the individual.

Like Confucius, Mencius traveled around various states, lobbying the monarchs to promote his political ideas, but in vain. He then retired, working with disciples on his book *The Mencius*, recording his thoughts and political strategies. This book is grouped as one of the "Four Books" and considered as one of the classics of Confucianism.

Mencius' ideas have produced great influence throughout the history of China and that's why he has been described as the "second sage", second only to Confucius.

2. *School of Athens*

School of Athens is a famous fresco painted by Raphael, born as Raffaello Sanzio (1483-1520), Italian painter and architect, and known as one of the three greatest painters (together with Leonardo Da Vinci and Michelangelo) in the Italian Renaissance.

Painted in 1510-1511 in the Vatican, and based on the Athens Academy founded by the ancient Greek philosopher Plato, the fresco is set against the backdrop of the arch of the tall building, including over 50 distinct scholars engaged in free and enthusiastic discussion, representing seven liberal schools of ancient civilization (grammar, rhetoric, logic, mathematics, geometry, music and astronomy). With Plato and Aristotle in the center, whose doctrines would dominate the Western thought from Antiquity up to the late 17th century, the former holds his book *Timaeus* and gestures to the heaven, representing The Forms while the latter holds his *Nicomachean Ethics* and gestures to the earth, representing empirical observation.

By blending Plato and Aristotle, Christianity with paganism, and scholars from different fields, the masterpiece creates a harmonious scene full of a hundred schools of thought, depicting Raphael's interpretation of philosophy as a branch of knowledge and his recognition of human's pursuit of wisdom and truth, embodying the theme of worshiping the Greek spirit and pursuing the highest ideal.

References

1. 梁鹤年. 西方文明的文化基因[M]. 北京:生活·读书·新知三联书店, 2014.
2. 刘春芳, 杜晓, 杨银玲. 中西文化对比教程[M]. 北京:中国人民大学出版社, 2017.
3. 史仲文, 陈桥生. 中国文化(*China's Culture*)[M]. 王国政, 译. 北京:五洲传播出版社, 2010.
4. 王焱, 赵牟丹. 中西文化比较(英文版)[M]. 北京:清华大学出版社, 2017.
5. 徐行言. 中西文化比较[M]. 北京:北京大学出版社, 2004.
6. 叶朗, 朱良志. 中国文化读本(英文版)[M]. 北京:外语教学与研究出版社, 2008.
7. 张立玉, 陈珞瑜. 中西民俗对比研究[M]. 北京:中国社会科学出版社, 2016.
8. 张晓立. 世界文化史(英文版)[M]. 北京:对外经济贸易大学出版社, 2014.
9. 钟敬文. 民俗学概论(第二版)[M]. 北京:高等教育出版社, 2010.
10. Ellen McHale. Fundamentals of Folklore[A].In:John Suter, ed. *Working with Folk Materials in New York State: A Manual for Folklorists and Archivists* [M]. Ithaca, NY: New York Folklore Society, 1994: 21.
11. Jan Bronvand. The Study of American Folklore: an Introduction[M]. Norton Press, 2000.
12. https://baike.so.com.
13. https://baike.so.com/doc/5350236-5585692.html.
14. https://baike.so.com/doc/5382272-5618626.html.
15. https://en.wikipedia.org/wiki.
16. http://il.go2yd.com/image.php? url=0k8G5XVAms.
17. https://image.so.com/view? q=孔子论语图片.
18. https://www.chinesefolklore.org.cn/forum/viewthread. php? tid=926.
19. https://www.iep.utm.edu/greekphi/.
20. http://www.visual-arts-cork.com/famous-paintings/school-of-athens.htm.

Unit 2
Chinese and Western Cuisine

On-boat Dim Sum in Suzhou

European Bread

Learning Objectives

- To be familiar with the different characteristics of Chinese and Western cuisine
- To get a better understanding of the different traditional beliefs about diet in China and Western countries
- To compare and contrast the similarities and differences about some typical foods/drinks in different countries and analyze reasons in terms of folklore

Lead-in Questions

- What do we Chinese eat everyday and what do the Westerners have for meals?
- What are the main differences between Chinese and Western cuisine?
- What are the philosophical beliefs implied in Chinese and Western cuisine?
- Do you know any other philosophical ideas or common practices related to our/Westerners' dietary habits? How are these contrasting ideas related to the different cultures?

Part I Chinese Cuisine

1. Eight Chinese Cuisines

Chinese cuisine enjoys a world-wide reputation for its complete presence of color, aroma, taste and shape as well as its abundance. We Chinese greatly value culinary arts and develop an extensive study of them based on traditional medical beliefs. Just as the old saying goes, "food is the first necessity of the people". Food is indispensable to our culture so that it becomes multifunctional. People eat not only to fill their stomach and keep fit, but also to foster relations and solve problems. In other words, eating can serve as a means of socializing, a psychological therapy and an essential means of developing business connections. Probably no other place in the world puts so much emphasis on food or has such a great variety of delicacies as China does. A number of different cooking styles contribute to our rich dietary culture. There are mainly eight influential cuisines in China, which are distinctive from one another due to various factors such as availability of resources, climate, geography, history, cooking techniques and lifestyles.

Eight Famous Chinese Cuisines

Cooking Style	Characteristics	Specialties
Shandong Cuisine 鲁菜	light, fresh, crisp, tender 清、鲜、脆、嫩	Yellow River common carp in sweet and sour sauce 糖醋鲤鱼 braised abalone 红烧鲍鱼
Sichuan Cuisine 川菜	hot, tongue-numbing, sour and delicious 麻、辣、酸、鲜	spicy diced chicken with peanuts (kung pao chicken)宫保鸡丁 sliced beef and ox tongue in chili sauce 夫妻肺片

Continued

Cooking Style	Characteristics	Specialties
Jiangsu Cuisine 苏菜	strong but not greasy, light but delicate 浓而不腻，淡而不薄	Yangzhou meatball 扬州狮子头 crystal meat 水晶肴蹄
Fujian Cuisine 闽菜	fine cutting technique; mainly using seafood and emphasizing color 重刀工，擅长海鲜佳肴，重色	salted shrimps 盐水虾 Buddha jumps over the wall 佛跳墙(made of 18 pricey ingredients, including shark fin 鱼翅, abalone 鲍鱼, sea cucumber 海参, ginseng 人参, scallops 干贝,etc.)
Anhui Cuisine 徽菜	stressing oil, soy color and fire control 重油,重色,重火工	braised turtle with ham 火腿炖甲鱼 smelly mandarin fish 臭鳜鱼
Guangdong (Cantonese) Cuisine 粤菜	fresh, crisp and light 鲜脆清淡 seasonal dishes 时令菜 original flavor 本味	roast suckling pig 烤乳猪 steamed sea bass 清蒸鲈鱼
Hunan Cuisine 湘菜	smoked, piquant, tasty 熏制，辛辣，入味	smoked bacon and rice-field eel 腊肉鳝鱼 steamed fish head with diced hot red peppers 剁椒鱼头
Zhejiang Cuisine 浙菜	fresh and delicate 食材新鲜，清淡可口	West Lake fish in vinegar gravy 西湖醋鱼 Dongpo pork 东坡肉

2. Peculiarities of Chinese Culinary Culture

(1) All Chinese chefs strive for harmony of sight, smell, color and texture. In other words, their culinary arts rely on the standard of color, aroma, taste and shape, and missing any one element would not make a good dish.

(2) Food and medicine share the same roots. Based on the **yin-yang theory**, medicinal food combines food and Chinese herbal medicine, providing an efficient way to prevent illnesses, maintain health and prolong life

yin-yang theory 阴阳学说

expectancy.

I Ching《易经》

"Four Natures" "四性"

pungent 辛辣的

(3) According to the ***I Ching*** (or *The Book of Changes*) and traditional Chinese medicine, a good meal is expected to balance the " **Four Natures**" (hot, warm, cool and cold) and the "Five Tastes" (**pungent**, sweet, sour, bitter and salty).

(4) Chinese dietary culture originates from crop farming, which means Chinese food structure relies more on vegetables than on meat. A combination of meats and non-meats makes dishes more nutrition-balanced. Seasonings such as fresh ginger root, garlic, **scallion**, **cilantro** and sesame are widely used in many regional cuisines.

scallion 大葱

cilantro 香菜

staple food 主食

(5) Rice is a **staple food** for people from rice farming areas in southern China while in wheat-farming areas in northern China, people largely rely on flour-based food, such as noodles, *bing* (pancakes), *jiaozi* (dumplings) and *mantou* (steamed buns).

(6) Chinese cuisine is famous for its wide variety in raw materials. Most Chinese are not confined to religious taboos and that is why Chinese dishes enjoy very extensive choices. Most kinds of meat from domestic animals and fish can be used as cooking ingredients.

slicing 切片

shredding 切丝

flaking 切薄片

dicing 切成丁

mincing 切碎

filleting 切柳

grinding 磨碎

(7) Cutting, the foundation for cooking, is essential in Chinese cuisine, influencing tastes and shapes. Nearly 40 ways of cutting in practice transform raw materials into different sizes and shapes by **slicing**, **shredding**, **flaking**, **dicing**, **mincing**, **filleting**, **grinding** and the like.

(8) There are about 50 cooking methods to make

Chinese food into various **delicacies**, among which the basic ones include boiling, **simmering**, **stewing**, **braising**, **frying**, baking, steaming, smoking and **scalding**.

One perfect dish usually needs more than one method in cooking with the addition of seasoning or adjustment of heating at appropriate time.

(9) Alcoholic drinks in China are consumed together with food rather than on their own. Chinese *baijiu*, pure alcohol or **hard liquor** made from grain, is the most widely-consumed **distilled** spirit in the world. The famous brand within China is the "**sauce-scented**" Moutai produced in Guizhou. Other common brands include *wuliangye* and varieties of *erguotou*. Besides *Baijiu*, there are also *huangjiu* (yellow rice wine), *mijiu*(rice wine), wine, beer and so on.

(10) The Chinese fondness of eating contributes to many colorful and popular expressions like *chikui* (be taken advantage of), *tiefanwan* (a secure job).

It seems that not only humans who like to eat, but **deities**, for people always offer them food **sacrifices** on special occasions like Tomb-sweeping Day and **Hungry Ghost Festival**.

delicacies 佳肴
simmering 煨
stewing 炖，煲
braising 烧
frying 煎
scalding 白灼
hard liquor 烈性酒
distilled 蒸馏
sauce-scented 酱香
deity 神灵
sacrifices 贡品
Hungry Ghost Festival 中元节

3. Chinese Tea Culture

3.1 History

China was the earliest country to cultivate and drink tea, enjoyed by people from all social classes. Tea processing began after the Qin and Han Dynasties. Tea as a drink flourished during the Tang Dynasty and tea houses have been popular since then. A major event of this time was the completion of ***Tea Classics***, the cornerstone of Chinese tea culture, by Lu Yu (733-804), Tea Sage of China. Tea is still consumed regularly, both on casual and formal occasions. In addition to being a popular beverage, it is used in traditional Chinese medicine as well as in Chinese cuisine. One of the most essential accessories in modern China, especially for the middle-aged and elderly, is a double-walled insulated glass **thermos** with tea leaves in the top behind a **strainer**.

Tea Classics《茶经》，世界第一部茶叶专著，为唐代茶圣陆羽所著

thermos 保温杯

strainer 滤网

3.2 Classification

Chinese tea is classified into different types, among which are green tea, *oolong* tea, black tea, **scented tea**, white tea, and **compressed tea** according to the species of plant from which it is sourced, the region in which it is grown and the method of production used. China is the world's largest exporter of green tea. Well-known types of green tea include Xihu *Longjing*, Huangshan *Maofeng*, Dongting *Biluochun*, Putuo Buddha Tea and Liu'an *Guapian*.

scented tea 花茶

compressed tea 砖茶

3.3 Tea-brewing

Tea-brewing in China depends on variables like the formality of the occasion, the kind of tea being brewed and so on. For example, green tea is usually brewed with cooler water since it is more delicate than *oolong* tea or black tea; the most informal method of brewing tea is to simply add the leaves to a pot of boiling water, which is commonly found in households and restaurants. The popularity of tea results in a

tea-brewing 沏茶

lot of by-products like tea houses and tea ware.

Kungfu tea, which is quite popular in China, makes use of small **Yixing purple clay teapots** to enhance the **aesthetics** and better the taste of the tea. Brewing tea in a Yixing purple clay teapot can be done for private enjoyment as well as for welcoming guests. In different regions of China, differences may occur in the steps of brewing as well as the tools used in the process. For example, Taiwanese-style *Kungfu* tea makes use of several additional instruments including **tweezers** and a **tea strainer**. The procedure is mostly applicable to oolong tea, but it is sometimes used to make *pu'er* and other **fermented** teas.

Yixing purple clay teapots 宜兴紫砂壶
aesthetics 美感
tweezers 镊子
tea strainer 滤茶器
fermented 发酵的

It is customary for Chinese to drink tea with snacks such as nuts, plums, dried fruit, small sweets and melon seeds, as well as **dim sum**.

dim sum 点心

3.4 Functions

Tea drinking is multi-functional in that it not only makes people relaxed and refreshed but also serves many other needs. For example, in traditional Chinese society, younger people or the people of lower social status show their respect to the older generation or the superior by offering a cup of tea. In addition, going to tea houses becomes a popular activity to develop ties at family or friend gatherings. And tea may be offered as part of a formal apology. Most important of all, in the traditional Chinese marriage ceremony, the bride and groom kneel in front of their respective parents, serve them tea and then thank them, which is a devout way to express their gratitude for being raised. This process symbolizes the joining together of the two families.

Part II Western Cuisine

1. Peculiarities of Western Culinary Culture

Western cuisine, or alternatively European cuisine, is a generalized term referring to the cuisines of Europe and other Western countries. Four categories are characteristics of European food: meats, sugar, cereals and fats.

(1) A formal Western dinner consists of several courses, including an **appetizer**, soup, the **side dish**, the main dish, salad, a dessert and coffee. The proper Western dinner at a fine restaurant is one of manners, focusing on communication. The atmosphere will be filled with light music serving as background for conversation.

appetizer 开胃菜
side dish 副菜

(2) Cereals (flour, bread, wheat, oats and other grains) are the most important ingredients in European cuisine. The most used fats are olive oil and butter. Salads are an integral part of Western cuisine. Steak and **cutlet** in particular are common dishes across the West. **Internal organs** of animals are usually thrown into dustbins in the West for their excessive addition of **cholesterol** and calories.

cutlet 肉饼
internal organs 内脏
cholesterol 胆固醇

(3) Western cuisines put emphasis on grape wine and sauces as **condiments**, seasonings, or accompaniments (in part due to the difficulty of seasonings penetrating the often larger pieces of meat used in Western cooking). Many dairy products are utilized in the cooking process.

condiments 调味品

(4) Wheat-flour bread has long been the most common source of starch, along with **pasta**, dumplings and **pastries**, although the potato has become a major starch plant in the diet of Europeans.

pasta 面食
pastry 糕点

(5) In the Western countries, water was not considered as a safe **beverage** for a long time since it was not purified in the past. Instead, wine, brandy, beer, ale, gin and whiskey were the most popular drinks.

beverage 酒水，饮料

Wine is an alcoholic beverage made from fermented grapes while brandy is a spirit created by distilling wine. Wine has long played an important role in religion. Red wine was associated with blood by the ancient Egyptians. Brandy may be added to other beverages to make several popular cocktails.

2. British Cuisine

People in Britain have a wide variety of foods based on the cuisines of Europe, India and other parts of the world. In addition to the influence of the Romans and the French, British cuisine has absorbed the culinary influence of those who have settled in Britain, especially Indian cuisine with its strong spices and herbs. A case in point is **hybrid dishes**, such as **chicken tikka masala**. Food rationing policies, put in place by the British government during wartime periods of the 20th century, are said to have been responsible for the poor international reputation of British cuisine. Just as the rumor goes, in Britain there is no chef but cook.

hybrid dishes 混合菜
chicken tikka masala 咖喱鸡

Well-known traditional British dishes include full

breakfast, fish and chips, the Christmas dinner, the Sunday roast, **steak and kidney pie**, **shepherd's pie**, and **banger and mash**.

steak and kidney pie 牛肉腰子派

shepherd's pie 羊肉馅饼

banger and mash 香肠土豆泥

2.1 Regional Cuisines

British cuisine has many regional varieties within the broader categories of English, Scottish and Welsh cuisines and Northern Irish cuisine. Each has developed its own regional or local dishes, many of which are geographically indicated foods such as **Cornish pasties**, the Yorkshire pudding, Cumberland Sausage, **Arbroath Smokie** and Welsh cakes.

Cornish pasties 康沃尔馅饼

Arbroath Smokie 阿布罗斯熏鱼

English cuisine shares much with wider British cuisine, partly through the importation of ingredients and ideas from North America, China and India during the time of the British Empire and as a result of post-war immigration. In Ireland, the **Ulster Fry** is particularly popular. Traditional Scottish dishes such as **haggis** and **shortbread** exist together with international foodstuffs brought about by migration. Scotland is known for the high quality of its beef, lamb, potatoes, oats and sea foods. In addition to foodstuffs, Scotland produces a variety of whiskies. Wales is best known for its sheep, and thus lamb is the meat traditionally associated with Welsh cooking.

Ulster Fry 乌斯特炸饼

haggis 羊杂布丁，肚包羊杂碎，苏格兰国菜

shortbread 酥饼

2.2 British Tea Culture

Since the eighteenth century, the United Kingdom has been one of the world's greatest tea consumers. Tea is a prominent feature of British culture and society. While it is usually served with milk, it is not uncommon to drink it black or with lemon, with sugar being a popular addition to any of the above. Strong tea, served in a mug with milk and sugar, is a popular combination known as builder's tea.

- Tea as a Break

British workers by law, have the right to a minimum of a twenty-minute break in a shift of six hours; government guidelines describe this as "a tea or lunch break". More informally, this is known as **elevenses**, i.e. a couple of hours before the midday meal, traditionally served at 11 am. Builder's tea in a mug is typical of a quick tea break in the working day.

elevenses 午前茶点，上午茶

- Tea as a Meal

Tea is not only the name of the beverage but also of a light meal to prevent hunger between luncheon and dinner. The tradition began in 1840 and continues to this day in tea rooms in the UK. While these establishments have declined in popularity since World War II, there are still many to be found in the countryside. In the West Country, cream teas are a speciality: scones, clotted cream and jam accompany the drink. Afternoon tea, in contemporary British usage, usually indicates a special occasion, perhaps in a hotel dining room, with **appetizing** snacks (tea sandwiches) as well as small sweet pastries.

appetizing 开胃的

A tea party means a social event to enjoy tea together, usually in a private home.

"Tea" or "high tea" can also mean the appetizing, hot early evening meal. This usage is common in working-class British English and in Northern England, Scotland and Ulster.

2.3 British Pubs

Pubs are relaxed, social drinking places and a prominent part of British culture. In many places, especially in villages, a pub is the focal point of the community. British pubs are social centers of British society with home-like qualities; 80% adults are pub-goers and 1 in 4 Britons meets their future wife or husband in a pub.

sociality 社交

buying the rounds 轮流做庄买酒

lock-in 关门后不能进人但里面的人还可接着喝

British pubs enjoy some confusing hidden rules: there are no TVs or waiters' service in order to promote **sociality**; there are no queues but an invisible line exists when buying drink: customers just use eye contact with a barman; tipping is unnecessary but you can buy staff a drink; **buying the rounds** is a popular practice; pubs usually close at 11 pm, but you can experience a **lock-in**; not only beverages (beer, wine, cider, ale, lager, tea, soft drinks) but also food and entertainment are provided. Games are played in pubs, ranging from the well-known darts, pool table, a stand-up comedy performance and so on.

cocktails 鸡尾酒

mocktails 无酒精鸡尾酒

Drinking wine is a pleasant pastime for both American and British people but their wine cultures are different. For example, American bars provide TV and music; there is a wide selection of liquid, **cocktails** (made of spirits, mixed with fruit juice or cream) and **mocktails**; beer and wine are included but not as wide a selection as in pubs.

3. American Cuisine

3.1 Eight Popular Cuisines in America

The United States is a land of immigrants. American

cuisine reflects the history of the United States, blending the culinary contributions of various groups of people from around the world. Its basis is formed by blending cooking methods of early native Americans with early Europeans. One characteristic of American cooking is the fusion of multiple ethnic or regional approaches into completely new cooking styles.

American diet is rich in red meat, dairy products, processed and artificially sweetened foods and salt, with minimal intake of fruits, vegetables, fish, legumes and whole grains. The Western Pattern Diet (WPD) or Standard American Diet (SAD) is a modern dietary pattern that is generally characterized by high intakes of processed meat, **pasteurized** butter, fried foods, high-fat pasteurized dairy products, eggs, refined grains, potatoes and high-sugar drinks. Fast food is a typical example of food consumed in Standard American Diet.

pasteurized 巴氏消毒的

Eight Popular Cuisines in America

Name	Areas	Typical food
Pacific Food 太平洋菜系	States along the Pacific coast, like California	seared ahi tuna 煎金枪鱼 California roll 加州寿司卷 barbecue chicken pizza 烧烤鸡肉披萨 smoked salmon 熏三文鱼 San Francisco sourdough bread 三藩市酵母面包
Southwest Food 西南菜系	States along the Mexican border such as Arizona, New Mexican and Texas	fish tacos 烤鱼卷饼，墨西哥鱼肉卷 grilled spareribs with Texas sweet chili sauce 得州甜辣酱烤排骨 guacamole 牛油果酱

Continued

Name	Areas	Typical food
Cajun Food 法国后裔菜	Louisana	cornbread 玉米面包 jambalaya 什锦红烩饭 gumbo 秋葵虾汤饭
Soul Food 南方黑人菜系	American South	pulled pork 手撕猪肉三明治 fried chicken 炸鸡
New York Food 纽约菜系	New York	bagel 贝果，百吉饼 thin crust pizza 薄底披萨 Reuben sandwich 鲁宾三明治
New England Food 新英格兰菜系	New England	roasted turkey 烤火鸡 baked beans 焗豆 pumpkin pie 南瓜派 lobster roll 龙虾三明治 clam chowder 奶油蛤蜊汤
Classic Food 经典菜系	Whole America	German hamburger, French fries, Italian pizza, steak, fried chicken, hot dogs IPA — India Pale Ale 印度麦酒 lager 拉格啤酒
Chinese Food 中餐	Whole America	Chuan Food 川菜 Yue Food 粤菜 Xiang Food 湘菜

3.2 American Coffee Culture

The history of coffee dates back to the 9th century. Since its accidental discovery in Ethiopia, coffee has been a **catalyst** for social interaction across cultures and eras.

catalyst 催化剂

Coffee is a brewed drink made from roasted coffee beans which must be **ground** and brewed to create a beverage.

ground 研磨(grind 的过去式)

Various ways may be used to serve coffee. **Drip-brewed**, **percolated**, or French-pressed coffee may be served as white coffee with a dairy product such as milk or cream, or as black coffee without such addition. It may be sweetened or iced.

drip-brewed 滴漏(咖啡)
percolated 过滤(咖啡)

Espresso-based coffee is served in a variety of forms. The most basic form is an espresso served alone as **a short black**, or with hot water added, when it is known as **Caffè Americano**. A **long black** is made by pouring a double espresso into an equal portion of water, retaining the **crema**, unlike Caffè Americano. Milk is added in various forms to an espresso: steamed milk makes a caffè **latte**, equal parts of steamed milk and **milk foam** make a **cappuccino**, and a dollop of hot foamed milk on top creates a caffè **macchiato**. A **flat white** is prepared by adding steamed hot milk (microfoam) to espresso so that the flavour is brought out and the texture is unusually soft.

espresso 意式浓缩咖啡
short black 清咖啡
Caffè Americano 美式咖啡
long black 澳式黑咖啡
crema 咖啡油脂
latte 拿铁咖啡
milk foam 奶泡
cappuccino 卡布奇诺
macchiato 玛奇朵咖啡
flat white 咖啡奶泡浓缩

American's obsession with coffee is real. American modern coffee shop is modeled on the espresso and pastry-centered Italian coffeehouses arising with the establishment of Italian-American immigrant communities in major cities of the U S. It is the Seattle-based Starbucks—the largest coffee chain in the world—that brought the model into mainstream culture. It is said that about 400 million cups of coffee are consumed daily in the US. There were about 24,000 shops and sellers specializing in coffee in 2004. Seattle is called "American Capital of Caffeine". With 2.5 coffee shops for every 1,000 citizens, Seattle has the greatest concentration of coffee houses in the country. To encourage the creativity to make better coffee, a yearly competition is held.

It's true that coffee houses today continue to serve traditional purposes as lively social centers in many communities, but they have obviously adapted to the new times. For example, as **hubs** of information exchange and communication, many coffee houses provide Internet access and newspaper for their customers. It's common to see some people sitting in a Starbucks listening to music and surfing on Internet. The decorations are also changed to give customers a cozy feeling like home.

hubs 中心

Part III Comparison and Contrast

1. Sensory Chinese Diet VS Rational Western Diet

Cuisine in China is a harmonious integration of color, aroma, taste, shape and texture. Chinese food satisfies people's senses like taste, smell and sight; and top priority is given to people' sensory feeling.

Chinese dietary culture originates from crop farming, which means the food structure relies more on vegetables instead of meat. Based on the yin-yang theory in traditional Chinese medicine, **medicinal food** combines food with herbs and stresses balance of meats and non-meats, of yin food and yang food, which people believe is beneficial to health.

Eating usually begins in order of **seniority** to show respect for the elder or senior. Drinking is essential for a gathering, where people always urge guests to drink more with a lot of **toasting** rules for politeness and hospitality. Chinese value of **collectivism** is also reflected in the dietary culture. Diners share all **delicacies** from the communal plates at a round table and fight to pay the bill at restaurants, symbolizing hospitality, unity and harmony.

medicinal food 药膳	seniority 资历	toasting 敬酒
collectivism 集体主义	delicacy 佳肴	pragmatic 实用的
animal husbandry 畜牧业	rectangle 长方形	

Generally speaking, Western cuisine places great emphasis on nutrition and scientific structure of dieting. Original flavors and natural nutrition are preserved as much as possible in cooking. Vegetables are eaten raw and cooking methods are relatively simpler and fewer. Their dieting conception highlights **pragmatic** value in accordance with their rational thinking pattern.

Western dietary culture originates from **animal husbandry**, leading to its food structure with more meat and dairy products. Food mainly serves to satisfy hunger and probably that's why meat is served in a larger size. Westerners value individualism and freedom, which suggests why they enjoy their separate portion of food at a **rectangle**-shaped dining table and split the bill at gatherings. In Western cultures, good news is often celebrated by a group of people having a few alcoholic drinks but Westerners prefer to taste wine itself and how much they drink is their own choice.

In religious households, a family meal may begin with making prayers, or at dinner parties the guests might begin the meal by offering some favorable comments on the food and thanks to the host.

2. Fermented Beancurd VS Yorkshire Pudding

Fermented beancurd is a Chinese form of *tofu* with a strong odor. It is usually consumed as a side dish or appetizer put in a small saucer rather than in a plate. According to a Chinese legend, a scholar named Wang Zhihe from Anhui Province invented smelly *tofu* during the Qing Dynasty. After failing the **imperial examination**, Wang Zhihe stayed in Beijing and relied on selling *tofu* to make a living. One day, having a huge quantity of unsold *tofu* on his hands, he cut it into small cubes and put them into an earthen jar. After several days, he opened up the jar and found out that the *tofu* had turned greenish, extremely smelly and surprisingly delicious. He decided to start selling it at his store. The smelly *tofu* that Wang Zhihe invented gained popularity and was later served at the imperial Qing Dynasty palace. The Empress Cixi later named the delicacy "**imperial green cubes**".

Fermented beancurd is usually used as a spread on steamed buns or paired with **rice congee**. It's different from hard **stinky *tofu*** in terms of processing and eating. The latter is often deep-fried and paired with soy sauce or salty spice, sold at night markets or roadside stands as a snack.

fermented beancurd 豆腐乳	imperial examination 科举考试
imperial green cubes 御青方	rice congee 稀饭
stinky *tofu* 臭豆腐，臭干子	batter 糊状物
onion gravy 洋葱肉汁	banger and mash 香肠土豆泥

Yorkshire pudding is a common English side dish consisting of a baked pudding made from **batter** consisting of eggs, flour and milk or water. It is a diversity food that can be served in numerous ways depending on the choice of ingredients, the size of the pudding and the accompanying components of the dish. As a first course it can be served with **onion gravy**. For a main course it is often served with beef and gravy and is part of the traditional Sunday roast, but can also be filled with foods such as **banger and mash** to make a meal. It's said that the pudding got the name "Yorkshire" in that Yorkshire was associated with coal and the higher temperatures produced by coal helped to make the batter crispier. National Yorkshire Pudding Day has been celebrated on the first Sunday in February in Britain since 2007 while Americans' celebration falls on 13 October.

3. Beijing Roast Duck VS The Sunday Roast

Roast Duck is a famous Beijing dish with a world reputation, developed by the Han People in the Ming Dynasty. It is made of high quality meat duck, roasted with charcoal fire. The dish is characterized by its ruddy color, thin, crisp skin and tender meat, the duck skin sliced in front of the diners by the cook. Ducks bred specially for the dish are slaughtered after 65 days and seasoned before being roasted in a closed or hung oven. The skin and meat are often eaten with **spring onion**, cucumber and sweet **bean sauce** or **hoisin sauce** with pancakes rolled around the fillings.

spring onion 大葱	bean sauce 豆瓣酱	hoisin sauce 海鲜酱
Anglicans 圣公会信徒	break the fast 结束斋戒	Lent 大斋节

The Sunday Roast is a traditional British main meal that is typically served on Sunday, consisting of roasted beef, roast potato and Yorkshire pudding with other vegetables, stuffing and gravy added. Other names for this meal are Sunday Dinner, Sunday Lunch and so on. The meal is often considered second only to a traditional Christmas dinner.

The Sunday Roast originated in England as a meal to be eaten after church on Sunday. It is traditional for all Europeans to eat a large meal following church services as with other Christian countries, but the Sunday Roast variant of this meal is uniquely English. On Sundays, all types of meat and dairy products are allowed to be eaten, unlike on Fridays where many Roman Catholics and **Anglicans** traditionally quitted meats and ate fish instead. Likewise, it is common for Anglicans and English Catholics to fast before Sunday services, with a larger meal to **break the fast** afterwards. These religious rules resulted in several traditional dishes in the United Kingdom.

—Only eating fish on Friday created a British tradition of "fish Fridays", still popular in fish and chip shops and restaurants across the whole country on Fridays, particularly during **Lent**.

—Fasting before church in Britain and the "breaking" of that "fast" afterwards created the British tradition of breakfast which later evolved into the full breakfast.

—To mark the end of not being able to eat meat, the Sunday Roast was created as a symbol of celebration.

Part IV Reflection and Presentation

1. In 1949, the Hungarian George Mikes famously declared that: "On the Continent people have good food; in England they have good table manners." How do you understand and support this argument? Why was George Mikes not impressed by English food? What do you know about British table manners?

2. There are varieties of desserts and snacks in different regions of China (e.g. stinky *tofu*, *bingtanghulu*). Choose one of your favorite ones to talk about and analyze why it is popular.

3. Ordering dishes in a Chinese restaurant is quite different from that in an American one. Try to find the different sequences, related customs and table manners.

4. Compare two typical snacks/dishes from China and America/Britain and explore their origins and related folk customs.

Part V Mini-pedia

1. Significant Chopsticks

Apart from being used as tableware in China, chopsticks are given as a blessing or present. The Standard Chinese term for chopsticks is *kuaizi* (筷子), which resembles the pronunciation of *soon* and *son*, and that's why in our tradition people give chopsticks as a gift to the newly-weds wishing them to have a baby soon. Chopsticks are also a good choice as a token of love between lovers. A pair of chopsticks represents the wish of living as a couple forever without separation. Chinese people also send pairs of chopsticks to their business partners since chopsticks should be used in pairs, which stands for close cooperation between two parties. More interestingly, the two ends of chopsticks are of different shapes. One end is round symbolizing heaven while the other is square representing earth, which embodies the yin-yang theory—the cornerstone of Chinese traditional culture.

2. Dinner, Supper or Lunch?

In Britain, it is a working-class hallmark to use dinner to refer to the midday meal, which should be called "lunch". Calling an evening meal "tea" is also a working-class indicator for the upper classes call this meal "dinner" or "supper". Tea, for the higher classes, is taken at around 4 pm, which consists of tea and cakes or scones and perhaps little sandwiches. The lower classes call this "afternoon tea". The implications of these words help us identify the social status of people.

References

1. 何其亮, 张晔. 英释中国传统文化[M]. 杭州:浙江大学出版社, 2006.
2. 刘春芳, 等. 中西文化对比教程[M]. 北京:中国人民大学出版社, 2017.
3. 束定芳. 中国文化英语教程[M]. 上海:上海外语教育出版社, 2016.
4. 王焱,等. 中西文化比较[M]. 北京:清华大学出版社, 2017.

5. 张捷，李悦. 中西饮食文化比较[M]. 上海:上海交通大学出版社，2017.
6. Bao Dengyu. *A Study of C-E Menu Translation in Light of Skopostheorie—Taking Shaanxi Province as an Example.* 万方数据:硕士论文摘选.
7. Fox, K. *Watching the English: the Hidden Rules of English Behavior* [M]. Hodder & Stoughton, 2005.
8. Liu Junru. *Chinese Food Adventures in the World of Eating* [M]. Willian W. Wang trans. Beijing: China Intercontinental Press, 2010.
9. https://baike.so.com/doc/5398497-5635905.html.
10. https://en.wikipedia.org/wiki/.
11. https://g. pclady.com.cn/168/1680229.html.
12. https://image.so.com/view? src=360pic_strong&z.
13. https://lohas. pclady.com.cn/168/1680229.html.
14. http://www.huangye88.com/techan/12049.html.
15. https://www.icourse163.org/course/HUBU-1002981005(英语畅谈中国).
16. https://www.icourse163.org/course/HZNU-1001957005(印象英美——穿越时空之旅).

Unit 3
Chinese and Western Vernacular Dwellings

Chinese *Siheyuan*

British Thatched Cottage

Learning Objectives

- To be familiar with the different characteristics of Chinese and Western vernacular dwellings
- To get a better understanding of the different traditional beliefs about dwelling in China and Western countries
- To compare and contrast the similarities and differences between some typical dwellings in different countries and analyze their origins and developments from the perspective of folklore

Lead-in Questions

- What are the main factors influencing vernacular architecture? What are the typical types of folk dwellings like in China and Britain?
- What are the different beliefs and traditions implied in Chinese and Western folk dwellings?
- Do you know any other special types of folk dwellings in the world? How are these dwellings related to their local cultures?

Part I Traditional Chinese Architecture

1. Peculiarities of Traditional Chinese Architecture

Architectural works, or buildings, are often recognized as cultural symbols and works of art. Traditional Chinese architecture enjoys some unique features, contributing much to our everlasting civilization.

1.1 Bilateral Symmetry

Chinese architecture places emphasis on **bilateral symmetry** to show balance, either in royal palaces or in humble farmhouses.

For example, plans for **renovation** and **extension** of a house will often try to maintain symmetry by placing secondary elements on either side of main structures as two wings to maintain overall balance. The buildings are typically designed to contain an even number of columns in a structure to produce an odd number of **bays**. A main door to a building is usually included in the center bay to maintain symmetry.

bilateral symmetry 两边对称

renovation 整修

extension 扩建

bay 隔间

1.2 Enclosure

Traditional Chinese buildings occupy an entire land but **enclose** open spaces within themselves in the form of courtyard and sky well.

enclose 围住

veranda 走廊

The use of open courtyards is common in many types of northern Chinese buildings. This is especially true of *Siheyuan*, which consists of an empty space surrounded by buildings connected with one another either directly or through **verandas**. These courtyards are usually open, facing the south to allow the maximum exposure of the building windows and walls to the sun while keeping the cold northern winds out.

prevalent 流行的

intersection 交叉

Large open courtyards are **prevalent** in the northern Chinese architecture whereas small sky wells in the south. The structure of sky well is relatively enclosed shaped from the **intersections** of closely spaced buildings and offers small opening to the sky through the roof space from the floor up.

enclosure 围墙

building complexes 建筑群

These **enclosures** fulfill practical functions—temperature regulation and venting the **building complexes**. Southern sky wells serve to collect rain water from the roof tops and to block the amount of sunlight so as to keep cool inside.

1.3 Hierarchy

hierarchy 等级制度

plaque 牌匾

Traditional Chinese architecture shows obvious **hierarchy** by placing different levels of importance on rooms. South-facing buildings in the rear and more private location of the property with more exposure to sunlight are reserved for elder members of the family or ancestral **plaques**. Buildings facing east and west are generally for junior members of the family, while those near the front are usually for servants.

1.4 Horizontal Emphasis

Classical Chinese buildings, especially those of the wealthy, are built with an emphasis on breadth and less on height. This forms a sharp contrast with Western church architecture, which tends to grow in height and depth. Chinese architecture stresses the visual impact of the width of the buildings.

1.5 Cosmological Concepts

Chinese architecture from early times used concepts from Chinese **cosmology** such as *fengshui* (**geomancy**) and Taoism to organize construction and layout from common residences to imperial and religious structures. The following are typical examples.

cosmology 宇宙学
geomancy 风水

Screen walls (also called spirit screen or spirit wall) face the main entrance of the house to ward off evils and help keep privacy. It's widely believed that evil things travel in straight lines.

screen wall 屏帷墙，幕墙

Door gods are displayed on doorways to prevent evil and encourage the flow of good fortune.

The structure is oriented with its back to elevated landscape, ensuring that there is water in the front.

Water sources like ponds, pools and wells are usually built into the structure due to the belief that water can gather wealth.

Buildings usually integrate with the surrounding rivers and mountains, without spoiling the natural beauty.

1.6 Wood Material

Ancient Chinese buildings are made of wood rather than stone because of the Chinese belief that wood symbolizes spring, green and new life and therefore is used to build houses for the living. Stones, however, are usually used for graves.

2. Typical Chinese Vernacular Dwellings

geomorphic 地貌的

China is a country with vast territory, varied **geomorphic** features and diversified climates. Together with 56 nationalities and cultures, it creates a rich variety of settlements and buildings of traditional vernacular dwelling. There are different classifications for various types of dwelling. The following list focuses on typical folk dwellings in existence across China and their main features.

2.1 *Siheyuan* in the North

quadrangle 四合院

Siheyuan or **quadrangle** is a typical form of ancient Chinese architecture, especially in the north of China. It usually faces the south to get enough sunshine and resist cold wind from the north. The name derives from the layout of the entire construction, that is, a house built in each direction. The four houses encircle the courtyard on all four sides forming a central courtyard. The design follows rules of *fengshui* and hierarchy.

roof beams 屋顶梁

A big *Siheyuan* of high-ranking officials and wealthy merchants is specially built with **roof beams** and pillars beautifully carved and painted, each with a front yard and a back yard.

A small or medium-sized *Siheyuan* usually has its main or only entrance gate at the southeastern corner with a screen wall just inside to protect privacy.

The elders or master live in the sunny **main houses** and their children live in the side houses or **wing rooms**. The **opposite houses** nearest to the entrance are usually used as the study, reception room or the male servant's dwelling.

main house 正房
wing room 厢房
opposite house 倒座房

Beijing's *Siheyuan* is typical of the courtyard dwelling. This mode is characterized by its **solemnity**, elegance, reasonable arrangements, as well as peaceful environment.

solemnity 庄严

The dwellings in the countryside are simplified and not as complete as the typical quadrangle courtyard in an urban setting. They retain the basic structure of a gate, wall, courtyard, central room and wing room.

2.2 Cave Dwellings on Loess Plateau in the Northwest

Loess Plateau 黄土高原

Cave dwellings are mainly distributed in central and west provinces like Henan, Shanxi, Shaanxi, where the loess is of great depth. The loess (yellow earth) is quite **compacted** and has a very strong **vertical** nature, which provides a very good precondition for the development of cave dwellings. There are two main types.

compacted 压紧的
vertical 垂直的

One type is called **cliff cave dwelling**, which is an earth cave dug horizontally along the vertical earth cliff. They are often south-facing, whose **facades** are sometimes faced with bricks or stone.

cliff cave dwelling 崖庄窑
facade 建筑物的正面

The other type is called **pit dwellings**, built where there

pit dwellings 土坑窑

sunken 凹陷的

are no hills. People create **sunken** courtyards. After digging a courtyard that is usually about 10 meters deep, rooms are dug off the main courtyard. A large sunken courtyard complex, or pit dwelling, can have a courtyard as large as one hundred square meters. But they are usually smaller than cliff cave dwellings, because the latter are easier to create.

topography 地势，地形

Cave dwellings save raw materials and require less complicated technology. They help maintain local **topography** and save farmland by making use of space that would have been otherwise left unused. In addition, they are cool in summer and warm in winter.

2.3 Huizhou Dwellings in Anhui and Jiangxi Provinces

ancestral halls 宗祠，祠堂

archway 牌坊

There are three kinds of well-preserved Hui-style architecture—ancient dwellings, **ancestral halls** and **archway**.

alleyways 小巷，通道

gable 山墙

Hui-style dwelling belongs to courtyard dwelling, but with unique features which are different from those in the north. It features high stone walls which encircle the dwellings to form courtyards. The dwellings are built against the hills and have ponds in front. They are connected by more than 20 **alleyways** that run through the village. Inside the houses are wooden pillars and boards as substitutes for **gable** walls.

The following are main features of Hui-style dwellings.

rectangular 长方形的

ventilation 通风

skylight 天窗

Firstly, sky well or patio, which is **rectangular** open space on the roof for light and **ventilation**. Hui merchants believe that water can gather wealth and **skylight** can not only prevent rain from flowing to the outside but also achieve unity between man and nature.

Secondly, **horse-head wall**, used at the top part of gable walls above the roof top to prevent wind, fire and burglars.

horse-head wall 马头墙

Thirdly, grey or black tiles and white walls, forming a harmonious contrast and showing respect for nature.

Besides, Hui merchants use rich decorations to show wealth and position. Three types of Hui carving are popularly used: stone, wood and brick. Deeply influenced by Confucianism, those merchants value traditional virtues by choosing carvings symbolizing loyalty, **filial piety**, honesty and integrity. Both the buildings and decorations embody a perfect harmony between man, nature and resources.

filial piety 孝顺

With a history of over 950 years, Xidi Village in Yixian County, known as "the ancient treasure of the vernacular architecture", is a site typical of Hui-style residences, listed as the World Cultural Heritage Site by UNESCO.

2.4 Earth Buildings (*Tulou*) in Fujian

Tulou, made from **rammed earth**, is a traditional, rural, fort-like, group-oriented dwelling for the **Hakka** and Minnan people in Fujian Province.

rammed earth 夯土

Hakka 客家人

Preferring to live together in remote mountainous and forested regions, Hakkas built strong houses to defend themselves against fierce animals and thieves. Built on a stone base, the *Tulou*'s thick walls were packed with earth and internally **fortified** with wood.

fortified 加强的

Tulou falls into many shapes: rectangular, square, semi-circular, round (the most popular one) and so on.

Multi-storied, it has three to four floors on average, and the largest one can hold more than 50 families. With only one main entrance, *Tulou* has a large central courtyard, which is the place to organize community activities. Halls, storage houses, domestic animal houses, wells and other public houses are in the yard. Bedrooms are usually on the third or upper floor.

The first *Tulou* appeared during the Song Dynasty (960-1279). The Hakka or the "guest people" migrated around 1,500 years ago from the Central Plains to the South because of war, **persecution** or famine. They tried to maintain their own culture and way of life by building earthen complexes to guard against invasion from the local bandits and protect their children from the influence of local communities. All the families of a Hakka clan lived together in an enclosed earth building.

persecution 迫害

Hakka earth buildings are fire-proof, quake-resistant and defensive, with good ventilation and lighting, warm in winter and cool in summer. The structure also reflects the Hakka tradition of solidarity, harmony and love passed down from generation to generation. *Tulou* was listed as the World Cultural Heritage Site by UNESCO in as early as 2008 and is still in use now.

Other defensive residences in China include Kaiping Diaolou, castle-like towers in Guangdong Province and Tibetan stone houses.

2.5 The Mongolian Yurts in Inner Mongolia

Mongolian yurts 蒙古包

A tent-like structure made from a wooden frame and

covered by wool **felt**, the yurt is the traditional, portable dwelling of the **nomads** in Inner Mongolia. Traditional yurts easily collapse, assemble and are transported by animals like horses and camels.

felt 毡
nomads 游牧民

The construction and structure of the **Mongol** yurt have changed little since **Genghis Khan**'s times. The wooden **wattles** are fastened with leather **thongs** and **studs** to form a fence-like structure. Each part of the yurt is quite convenient to assemble and carry. The diameter of a small yurt is about four to six meters, with no pillar inside, while the bigger one needs two to four poles for support. There are thick felts on the ground of yurts to avoid humidity. Every yurt has an opening on the top to let in light, and there's usually a stove under it. The assembly of a yurt can be finished within two or three hours with little difficulty.

Mongol 蒙古族(人)的
Genghis Khan 成吉思汗
wattle 编条
thong 皮条
stud 大头钉

The yurt was and is a very simple dwelling for the nomads, who relocate several times over a year.

2.6 *Ganlan* or Bamboo Houses of the Dai People in the Southwestern China

Ganlan houses, made of wood or bamboo, usually two-storied, are widely distributed in the mountains of minority nationalities in the southwest semi-tropical **climes** (humid, hot and rainy climate), mainly in Yunnan, Guizhou, Guangdong and Guangxi. It is the residence for Dai, Jingpo, Zhuang and other ethnic minority groups, also called tropical **loft** in the rainforests.

Ganlan 干栏式
clime 气候
loft 阁楼

A *Ganlan* usually stands alone, separated from other *Ganlan* houses. Supported by poles, the living sector of

Ganlan is usually on the second floor high above the ground, while the first storey is reserved for raising domestic animals and storing, avoiding moisture as well as the attack of insects, snakes and other animals.

stilted houses 吊脚楼

There is another kind of house called **stilted houses** (*Diaojiaolou*), similar to *Ganlan*, but not completely hung in the air, thus named semi-*Ganlan* style. Stilted houses are the most representative traditional residences for the ethnic minority groups like Tujia, Miao, Yao and Dong. They are typically built along rivers or in steep mountainous areas. These houses feature a bamboo or wood structure partly suspended above the ground and raised on timbered **stilts**, according to the local topography. They are widely distributed in the southeast of Chongqing, the northwest of Guangxi, the west of Hunan and of Hubei and the southeast of Guizhou.

stilt 支柱

There are also some other kinds of residential houses like Xinjiang's *Ayiwang* (**Uygur** residence) and Yunnan's *Yikeyin* (seal-shaped courtyard), which are not covered here.

Uygur 维吾尔族

Part II Western Vernacular Dwellings

1. Introduction to Western Vernacular Dwellings

Ancient Greece is the cradle of European or Western culture and also a pioneer of European architecture, with great achievements mainly in memorial buildings like temples. Folk residences in the West share some of the Greek architectural ideas but have changed a lot according to different physical and social environments in different regions or countries. The following is a general introduction to traditional Western dwellings in terms of material widely used.

1.1 Timber-framed Dwellings

In ancient times, a lot of countries in Europe were covered with forest, which played a vital role in people's life as hunters. They learned how to make simple shelters by using wood. **Batten** and **barrack** dwellings with small windows appeared as a result, the former being smaller than the latter. Both were simply and crudely constructed for limited techniques. These wood dwellings were quite popular for their heat preservation, especially in northern European countries.

batten 木条房

barrack 木板房

With the improving techniques, a **truss**-framed wood dwelling came into being. Truss frame means beams and columns are made of wood, usually durable oak; between trusses are infills such as brick and clay, which is probably the earliest form of wall in Europe.

truss 桁架

1.2 Stone-framed Dwellings

Stone-framed dwellings are widely spread in hilly and mountainous countries, like Italy, France, Greece and Spain, for the rich natural material. Stone architecture in the countryside in western Europe makes great contribution to preserving the traditional local architecture forms and techniques.

Take Italy as an example. Italian farmers developed economical ways to make full use of stone in building

dry-stone masonry 干石砌筑
mortar 砂浆
cement 水泥
casting 浇铸
trulli 圆锥顶石屋

houses. Three ways of laying stones were used: **dry-stone masonry** (without using **mortar**), **cement** stone masonry and **casting** stone wall. Italian stone houses are well-preserved and still in use today. The famous dry-stone **trulli** in Italian historic town Alberobello attract countless tourists every year.

2. Typical British Vernacular Dwellings

Generally speaking, British vernacular dwellings take two frames: timber and brick. The prominent chimney is positioned in the center for the two-storied wood house while the chimneys are at both sides of the brick house. Each floor has got several rooms for different functions. The whole house doesn't cover a large space since it is developed vertically rather than horizontally. The roof tends to be steeply triangular. Windows of grids are popular.

Other English-speaking countries like Canada and America follow British styles in folk residence but with changes based on local environments.

reigning monarch 在位的君王

According to the British and French custom, British housing styles are named after a **reigning monarch**. Here are some of the most popular home styles built up from the late 15th century to the early 20th century.

2.1 Tudor Architecture Style

Medieval 中世纪的

The Tudor architectural style is the final development of **Medieval** architecture in England, during the Tudor Period (1485-1603). It is a blend of Gothic style and Renaissance style.

Tudor-style houses and buildings of ordinary people are timber-framed, **half-timbered**, filled with **wattle and daub**, sometimes with brick. The dark painted wood contrasts strongly with the pale walls, displaying the distinctive features of Tudor style.

Tudor-style houses use square or **rectangular** floor plans in towns or cities but usually H-shaped for farmhouses. The roof is **steeply** pitched, **thatched** or covered with tiles of slate. There are **dormer windows** on the roof. The houses have prominent cross gables, chimneys as well as tall, narrow doors and windows with diamond-shaped **window panes**.

The top floor is jetted to increase interior space in cities.

Open floor fireplaces were a feature during the time of Henry VII. Positioned in the back of the home were **outhouses**, especially beyond cities in market towns since there were no flushable toilets at that time.

A small herb garden lies behind the house, with little landscaping.

In a word, Tudor houses appear **rustic**, featuring steeply pitched roofs, half-timbering, **casement** windows and often **herringbone** brickwork.

half-timber 半木(砖木)结构

wattle and daub 抹灰篱笆墙

rectangular 长方形

steeply 陡的

thatch 用茅草覆盖屋顶

dormer window 老虎窗，屋顶采光窗

window pane 窗格

outhouses 户外厕所

rustic 粗糙的

casement 门式窗，窗框

herringbone 人字形

2.2 Queen Anne Style

The Queen Anne style in Britain refers to either the English Baroque architectural style approximately of the reign of Queen Anne (reigned 1702-1714), or a revived form that was popular in the last quarter of the 19th century and the early decades of the 20th century (when it is also known as Queen Anne revival).

The Queen Anne style is largely associated with Richard Norman Shaw (1831-1912), British architect and urban designer famous for his residential architecture and for his role in the English Domestic Revival Movement. His picturesque country houses derive from a study of regional developments in the English manorial style of the 16th century.

manor house 庄园

In British architecture, the Queen Anne style houses are mostly domestic buildings up to the size of a **manor house**, designed elegantly but simply by local builders or architects. They are featured by strongly bilateral symmetry with a **pediment** on the facade.

pediment 山形墙，山墙饰

door-case 门框

sash windows 推拉窗

quoins 隅石

hipped roof 四坡屋顶

Other defining features of this style are as follows:

—a sweep of steps leading to a carved stone **door-case**

—rows of painted **sash windows**

—stone **quoins** emphasizing corners

—a central triangular pediment set against a **hipped roof** with dormers

Anne-style houses gain great popularity in America but it means differently in some aspects. For example, asymmetry is American Anne style while symmetry is British.

2.3 Georgian Architecture

Georgian architecture refers to the set of architectural styles widely used between 1714 and 1830 in most English-speaking countries.

Palladian 帕拉第奥式的建筑风格

This style is mainly influenced by revived **Palladian**

architecture with a focus on symmetry and **exquisite** decoration, and common among the upper and middle classes. Houses are located in grand landscaped settings, generally wide and relatively shallow, in order to look more impressive from a distance. The front door is typically centred as the main focal point of the exterior. There are classical porches on the **front elevation**. The windows are also symmetrical up and down, divided into many small grids. The whole wall is decorated into three parts — **dado**, **metope** and **eave**. The fireplace is also a focus of decoration.

exquisite 精美的

front elevation 正立面

dado 墙裙

metope 墙面

eave 屋檐

2.4 Victorian Architecture

Victorian architecture is a series of architectural revival styles in the mid-to-late 19th century. Victorian refers to the reign of Queen Victoria (1837-1901), called the Victorian Era. However, many elements of what is typically termed "Victorian" architecture did not become popular until later in Victoria's reign. The styles often include interpretations and **eclectic** revivals of historic styles.

eclectic 折中的

2.5 Edwardian Architecture

Edwardian architecture is an architectural style popular during the reign of King Edward VII of the United Kingdom (1901-1910). Architecture up to the year 1914 may also be included in this style.

Edwardian-style houses are generally less **ornate** than late Victorian architecture. Their designers use lighter colors, without much concern for the need to hide or decorate **soot** formation on walls thanks to the use of gas and later electric

ornate 华丽的

soot 烟尘

lights. The decorative patterns are less complex with more plain wallpaper and curtain designs. Ornaments tend to be grouped rather than everywhere.

3. Distinctive Houses and Cottages in British Countryside

The charm and romance of the English rural landscape has aroused countless people's yearning for the rural life in England. Chinese famous scholar and translator Lin Yutang once said: "the universally ideal life is to live in the English countryside house with American hydroelectric facility and a Chinese cook..." His witty and humorous tone intrigues us to explore more details of British houses in the countryside.

3.1 The Cotswold Stone Cottages in England

The Cotswold style of architecture is a unique style based on houses from the Cotswold region of England. Typical features are roofs made with **pseudo-thatch**, steep **arch** gables and arched doorways. Walls are usually made of brick, stone or **stucco**. Cotswold houses often have small and irregularly shaped rooms, with a prominent chimney often near the front door. Buildings made in this form are also referred to as Tudor cottages.

pseudo-thatch 仿茅草顶
arch 拱形
stucco 灰泥

The Cotswold region contains the Cotswold Hills, famous for attractive small towns and villages built of the underlying Cotswold stone, a yellow **limestone**.

limestone 石灰石

In 2006, Kingham, a village in the Cotswold region, was voted as "England's Favourite Village". With rows of limestone cottages and an open village green, Kingham attracts numerous tourists and does live up to the dream image people read about in a story book.

3.2 English Country Houses

An English **country house** is a large house or mansion in the English countryside, where those who also own a town house can enjoy life in the country and in the city at will.

country house 乡村别墅

In England, the terms "country house" and "**stately home**", despite their similar meaning, may mean differently in terms of construction. Many country houses were deliberately designed not to be stately in order to be in harmony with the landscape, while some of the great houses were built as "power houses" to dominate the landscape and be impressive.

stately home 豪宅

Today, many country houses have become hotels, schools, hospitals, museums and prisons, while others have survived as conserved ruins. Most of the houses that survived destruction are now listed as Grade I or II buildings of historic interest, only the most faithful and most accurate restoration and recreation being permitted.

The English country houses can be described as "the most incomparable house in Britain, the one which created the greatest impression and summarizes so exquisitely English country life qualities".

3.3 Thatched Cottages

In most of England, thatch remained the only roofing material available to people living in the countryside until the slate 石板

late 1800s. Around 1820, Welsh **slate** began replacing thatch as another choice for roof material thanks to easier and cheaper transport like canals and later railways. By the late 19th century, with mechanization in place of agriculture, people began to migrate to cities and work in factories, thatch became a symbol of poverty.

vegetation 草木

insulator 隔热体

flammable 易燃的

Thatching is the craft of building a roof with dry **vegetation** such as straw, water reed, sedge and rushes, layering the vegetation so as to shed water away from the inner roof. The dry and densely packed plants can trap air and so thatch is a natural **insulator**, ensuring that a house is cool in summer and warm in winter. Good thatch does not require frequent maintenance and is not as **flammable** as many people believe.

aristocratic 贵族的

affinity 亲近

With the revival of historic buildings in the past decades, thatched huts or cottages are now symbols of wealth rather than poverty. With their hand-rubbed mud walls and little wooden windows, the old thatched cottages in the English countryside are surrounded by flowers, with green vines and rose-branches climbing over the walls. Britons' **aristocratic** feeling, sense of gentlemanliness and natural **affinity** to the old or traditional culture make them far more enthusiastic about the old than the new, leading to the revival of thatched cottages.

3.4 Half-timbered Houses (Black-and-white Houses)

By the 15th and 16th century timber framing began to be exploited for its decorative qualities. Timber buildings in England were developed to a very high level due to an abundant supply of oak and European techniques. There are four types of traditional timber buildings in Britain — **cruck frame**, **box frame**, **half timber** and **hammer beam roof**.

Half timbering became popular in Britain from the late Medieval ages to the 19th century. It is a structure with a frame of load-bearing timber, creating spaces between the timbers called **panels**, which are then filled in with some kind of nonstructural material like wattle and daub, laths and plaster, or bricks. The exposed, dark wood and the whitewashed wall form a sharp contrast, enhancing the decorative effect.

Large and small houses alike have half-timbering in their upper stories and gables are constructed with tall ornamental chimneys, appearing simple and rustic.

Half-timbered houses in the countryside, their blackened oak beams showing the fissures and cracks of great age, the floors tilting **slantingly**, these images compose an important part of the charm of Medieval and Tudor England for visitors.

cruck frame 曲木结构
box frame 箱形结构
half timber 半木结构
hammer beam roof 锤式屋架
panel 嵌板
slantingly 倾斜地

Part III Comparison and Contrast

1. Ethical Chinese Quadrangle VS Religious British Residence

Quadrangle courtyards (*Siheyuan*) are most widely-used residences in China which fully embody the traditional **ethics** of Chinese people. Enclosure comes first, for there are no windows in the four walls of *Siheyuan*, with the main gate as the

only opening to the outside. The second is its **patriarchal** or **hierarchical** system, since there are strict rules for the layout of *Siheyuan* and fixed room arrangement of family members. The main room for the elder is higher than the **wing rooms** or side rooms for the children. Thirdly, every *Siheyuan* has a **hall house** used for some important rites like worshiping, praying, weddings and funerals. In some way, it incorporates the national cultural spirit into family life and makes a family sacred. The last but not the least is kinship integration. The corridors under **eaves** and the sky-well or yard provide very good places for families' communication.

In a word, ancient Chinese architecture like *Siheyuan* is a miniature of the long-standing ethical ideas of Chinese people.

ethics 伦理观	patriarchal 家长的	hierarchical 按等级划分的
wing room 侧房，厢房	hall house 堂屋	eaves 屋檐
Gothic 哥特式的	secular 世俗的	intersection 交汇
yearning 向往		

Traditional British residence is quite religious, mainly influenced by **Gothic** and Roman church architecture.

Gothic architecture originated from France in the second half of the 11th century, spreading its influence from church to **secular** buildings. The following four aspects of traditional British residence reveal Gothic trace: the **intersection** of central gable and the steep side gable, with elaborately-decorated eaves; the facade wall going directly into the central gable; the beam on the window being of pointed-arch shape; the porch supported by Gothic pillars.

Roman architecture was popular in the Christian areas during the 10th to 12th century. Residence of this style is made of stone with a rough and simple beauty. The solid wall provides a sense of security while the small window causes mystery.

Roman and Gothic styles are two representatives of British traditional residence under the influence of Christian culture; the former' gloom embodying the mysterious religion while the latter's pointed arch implying people's **yearning** for heaven on high.

2. Chinese Courtyard-style Temples VS Western Gothic Churches

Chinese temples are used as places of worship for Chinese Buddhism, Taoism or Chinese folk religion. They not only represent the long history and culture of China, but also preserve the historical **relics** of each dynasty.

Following the integration of man and nature in site selection, Chinese temples are often located in famous mountains with a good view, suggesting the spirit of **serenity**. For example, Baima Temple is located in the east of Luoyang City, backed by Qishan Mountain in the north and facing the Luoshui River in the south.

The courtyard-style temples follow the north-south **longitudinal** axis to organize the space and creates a symmetrical, solemn and orderly appearance. The middle road of the temple **facade** goes to the gate hall, on the left and right of which stand the bell tower and the drum tower. Then comes the Tianwang Hall, where there are the Four Guardians' statues. The next is the main hall called

Daxiongbaodian followed by the **depository of scriptures**, with the monk room and the monastic dinning hall on the two sides. The temple pattern shows that man and God live in the same **plane** and the paradise is on the earth, implying the harmony between man and heaven.

relic 遗迹	serenity 宁静	longitudinal 纵向的
facade 正面	depository of scriptures 藏经楼	plane 平面
vertical 垂直的	skeletal 骨瘦如柴的	pointed arch 尖形拱门
spire 尖顶	sublimity 崇高	flying buttress 飞扶壁
beam column 束柱	stained glass 彩绘玻璃	

Gothic churches can be seen everywhere in the Western countries, mostly in busy downtown areas. They are of **vertical**, almost **skeletal** stone structures with a **pointed arch**, great expanses of glass, clustered columns and sharply pointed **spires**, suggesting the spirit of **sublimity**. Milan Cathedral in Italy is a typical Gothic-style church.

The plane layout of the church is usually in the shape of a Latin cross. All four sides of the church are designed as closed space, with curved dome and straight passage of spire, implying the existence of the upper space or heaven. Ribbed arch, **flying buttress**, slender **beam column** are used to create a feeling of flying. Flying buttress also helps share the pressure on the main wall. Glass windows not only show stories from the *Bible* or from the lives of saints but also reduce weight and let light in. The **stained glass** is mainly of blue and red, which symbolizes the heaven or the blue sky and the blood of Christ respectively.

Gothic churches are tall, solemn and spacious, with every detail producing a feeling like heaven, where believers' aspiration to heaven and worship to God come spontaneously. The world is suffering, and only heaven is the paradise.

3. Minnan Red-brick Residence VS British Red House

Minnan red-brick houses are of courtyard style with some palace features, mainly distributed in Xiamen, Zhangzhou and Quanzhou in Fujian Province. Their beauty can be expressed by a vivid description in Chinese characters here: 红砖白石双坡曲, 出砖入石燕尾脊, 雕梁画栋皇宫式.

Two simple views can help people appreciate its charm from the outside. One is the red-brick wall, a very festive color. It's said the red bricks in Quanzhou are most bright-colored and gorgeous. Since most houses in China are of black tile and white wall, Minnan red-brick residence is considered a miracle of Chinese traditional folk dwellings. Usually the whole wall is made of red bricks, with white stones only at the bottom, forming a sharp contrast. The facade wall is more gorgeous with **floral** bricks or **cross-masonry** bricks of different **color shades**.

The other is the double-pitch roof with a curved ridge. The red-tile roof is eye-catching enough, but it's only part of the story. More attractive is its swallow-tailed ridge and *wuxing* (five-element) gable, which are culture-specific. Swallow tail not only appears very animating but also implies flying high or promotion. *Wuxing* gable is an **auspicious** symbol as well as a distinctive decoration.

The red-brick houses become an important carrier of Minnan culture by taking in the essence of traditional Chinese culture, Minyue culture and marine culture.

floral 带花纹的	cross-masonry 交错砌筑	color shade 颜色深浅
auspicious 吉利的	high-pitched 陡的	drawing-room 会客室
casement 门式窗	hipped 斜脊	dormers 老虎窗，屋顶采光窗

sash windows 推拉窗 bull's eye windows 小圆窗

The Red House is the designer William Morris' family home, located in the town of Bexleyheath in Southeast London, England. It is made of red tile and brick without decoration on the wall. It is an influential Arts and Crafts building, co-designed in 1859 by the architect Philip Webb and William Morris.

The Red House takes a luxurious L-shape, two-storied, with a **high-pitched** roof made of red tile. On the ground floor lie the large-hall, the dining room, the library, the morning-room, and the kitchen while on the first floor the main living-rooms, the **drawing-room**, the studio and the bedrooms.

The Red House is featured by its various windows, **casements**, **hipped dormers**, round-headed **sash windows** and **bull's eye windows**, which are positioned to suit the design of the rooms rather than to fit an external symmetry.

The architectural style of the Red House is a perfect combination of British Gothic architecture and traditional rural architecture.

Part IV Reflection and Presentation

1. How do you describe a typical English cottage in terms of architecture characteristics and culture?

2. *Fengshui* (geomancy) is a Chinese philosophical system of harmonizing with the surrounding environment. Discuss the *fengshui* practice (the Eight

Trigrams or yin-yang principle) in architecture in China with specific examples.

3. Introduce one of the vernacular dwellings in China in terms of its architectural features and connection to folklore.

4. What are the key features of classical Chinese garden architecture? Suzhou Museum, designed by the world-famous architect I. M Pei (a Chinese-American), is a perfect embodiment of traditional Chinese garden architecture. How do you understand the statement?

Part V Mini-pedia

1. The Grand Courtyard of Family Qiao

Owned by Qiao Zhiyong, a famous financier in the Qing Dynasty, the courtyard of Family Qiao is located in the central part of Qiaojiabao Village, Qixian County, Shanxi Province. The entire courtyard covers an area of 4,175 square meters, consisting of 6 main courtyards and 20 smaller ones, with 313 rooms in total, decorated with various carvings and murals. The bird's-eye view of the entire complex appears very much like the Chinese character *shuangxi*(囍).

With Chinese classical architectural design and exquisite decorations, the courtyard is representative of Chinese northern folk residences, not only showing the fortune and prosperity of the family, but also the folk customs of Shanxi in that period. Now it is also a museum of folk and business customs, housing 2,000 pieces of cultural relics like porcelains, silk embroidery, furnishings, paintings and calligraphy.

2. Italian Trullo

A trullo is a traditional Apulian dry stone hut with a conical roof in southern Italy. Constructed as temporary field shelters and storehouses or, as permanent dwellings by small proprietors or agricultural laborers, trulli are made of only stones without mortar or cement. They take a round form, with self-supporting domed roof, like mushroom. The town of Alberobello witnesses a dense concentration of trulli, thus nicknamed as beautiful "mushroom village", and has been designated as a UNESCO World Heritage Site since 1996.

Local residents still live there because they make a living by providing bed and board for tourists in their trulli.

References

1. 蔡燕歆. 中国建筑[M].[新加坡]李(Lee. A)等,译. 北京:五洲传播出版社, 2010.
2. 单德启,等.中国民居(*Chinese Vernacular Dwellings*)[M].王德华,等,译. 北京:五洲传播出版社, 2017.
3. 施维琳, 丘正瑜. 中西民居建筑文化比较[M]. 昆明:云南大学出版社, 2007.
4. 束定芳. 中国文化英语教程[M]. 上海:上海外语教育出版社, 2016.
5. 王焱,等. 中西文化比较[M]. 北京:清华大学出版社, 2017.
6. 王其钧. 中国民居[M].北京:中国电力出版社, 2012.
7. 叶朗, 朱良志. 中国文化读本(英文版)[M].北京:外语教学与研究出版社, 2008.
8. 张勃. 中西建筑比较(英文版)[M]. 许华锋,译. 北京:五洲传播出版社,

2008.

9. 张立玉，陈珞瑜. 中西民俗对比研究[M].北京:中国社会科学出版社，2016.
10. Lawrence Wodehouse & Marian Moffett. *A History of Western Architecture* [M]. California: University of Tennessee, Mayfield Publishing Company, Mountain View, 1989.
11. https://baike.so.com/doc/1379481-1458275.html.
12. https://baike.so.com/doc/5352292-5587750.html.
13. https://baike.so.com/doc/5376890-5613017.html.
14. https://baike.so.com/doc/8491104-8811334.html.
15. http://blog.sina.com.cn/s/blog_641343bc0102wy66.html.
16. http://depts.washington.edu/chinaciv/3rcave.htm.
17. http://en.ce.cn/Life/travel/201209/21/t20120921_23703158_3.shtml.
18. https://en.wikipedia.org/wiki.
19. http://english.anhuiews.com/system/2010/08/02/003324826.shtml.
20. https://wenku.baidu.com/view/c5ad457a168884868762d6bd.html.
21. http://www.bambubuild.com/en/the-traditional-houses-in-china/.
22. https://www.britainexpress.com/History/half-timber.htm.
23. http://www.china.org.cn/index.htm.
24. http://www.chinadaily.com.cn/culture/2016-04/19/content_24668078.htm.
25. https://www.mongolyurt.com.
26. https://www.travelchinaguide.com/attraction/fujian/fuzhou/earth_tower.htm.

Unit 4

Chinese and Western Folk Costumes

Dress of Miao Ethnic Group

American Western Wear

Learning Objectives

- To be familiar with some particular functions and styles of regional costumes
- To get a better understanding of the different cultural connotations of different regional costumes
- To compare and contrast the origins and functions of different clothing accessories (such as Chinese Archer's Ring and Greek Ring)

Lead-in Questions

- The traditional Chinese costumes have regained popularity recently. How do you explain it?
- Which regional costume do you like most? What distinguished features does it have?
- Chinese people used to say "wearing gold shows you are rich, wearing jade brings you good luck". What is the cultural message conveyed by the saying?

A regional costume which expresses an identity is usually associated with a particular geographic area, an ethnic group or a period of time in history. The main functions of clothing include helping protect people from various types of harsh weather and improving safety during risky activities such as dueling, hunting and riding. Costumes also serve the social and cultural functions of expressing modesty, status, age, occupation, region, gender and ethnicity. If the costume is used to represent the culture or identity of a specific ethnic group, it is usually known as ethnic costume. Today's regional costumes often come in two forms: one for tourist attraction, the other for traditional festivals and formal wear.

Part I Chinese Regional Costumes

1. Traditional Clothing

In ancient Chinese society, people's rank and social status could easily be recognized from their daily clothing, especially for the ordinary people and the upper class. There were strict restrictions on the styles and colors people could wear. Traditional ideas of clothing color are greatly affected by **Five-Element Theory**. **Cyan**, vermilion, yellow, white and black which represented the five elements were viewed as **pure colors** while the others were **secondary colors**. In most dynasties pure colors were used by the upper class. In the Zhou Dynasty black was the color of high prestige used by the king when he did sacrifice to the heaven. The Emperor Wu of Han Dynasty adopted the suggestion of esteeming the Yellow Emperor. From then on yellow

Five-Element Theory 五行
cyan 青色
pure color 正色
secondary color 间色

gradually became the royal color. Even though Confucius didn't like purple, others regarded purple as a noble color. There is an idiom "朱衣紫绶" which indicates government officials usually wear red clothes with purple ribbons in ancient times.

The earliest materials used in making clothes were **kudzu** cloth, **ramie** cloth and **hemp** cloth. According to tradition, silk weaving technology was invented by **Leizu** about 4,700 years ago, and silk gradually became a very popular material among the upper class. The famous Silk Road which is seen as the commercial communication between the Orient and the Occident was inspired by the trade of silk, tea and ceramics. By the time of the Yuan and Ming Dynasties, cotton was introduced into China from India which became popular quickly.

kudzu 葛

ramie 苎麻

hemp（用于制纤维的）大麻

Leizu 嫘祖，传说中黄帝的妻子，发明了丝绸的制作方法

One common technique in traditional Chinese costume making is embroidery. The four most famous types in China are Su Embroidery, Yue Embroidery, Xiang Embroidery, and Shu Embroidery, each having its own style and different themes. A rare subset of Su Embroidery is double-sided embroidery which has different designs on both sides. The other distinguished feature of Chinese costumes is **knot button**. A knot button is a bulge of thread which functions as button.

knot button 盘扣

Chinese people prefer to express good wishes by using auspicious **patterns**. This is echoed in the art of clothes making, from silk dress to kudzu clothing. The patterns used on clothes can be animals, plants, mountains, geometrical patterns, or other auspicious designs. They are not only

pattern 图案，花样

beautiful, but also meaningful. For example, dragons on an emperor's robe are saying that the emperor is the "son of the heaven", **pythons** on the robe of a senior official and phoenixes on a queen's robe are symbols of their social status.

python 蟒

2. Traditional Costumes in Modern Society

In modern times, some elements of traditional costumes are inherited and applied in modern clothing, like knot button, embroidery, particular pattern, etc. Besides, there are several modified styles which are popular among Chinese, even Westerners. They are *Hanfu*, Tang Suit, Zhongshan Suit and Qipao.

2.1 *Hanfu*

Some say that *Hanfu* appeared in China more than four thousand years ago and it was clothing of the legendary Yellow Emperor, a great sage king of ancient China. Actually, what is called *Hanfu* nowadays is a new invention by people who want to evoke the traditional Han culture.

Even though modern *Hanfu* changes and evolves with the fashion, it basically consists of a *Yi* and a *Chang*. *Yi* is a knee-length **tunic** tied with a **sash**, and *Chang* is a narrow skirt. Sometimes *Yi* and *Chang* are sewed together while sometimes they are separated. The tunic can be replaced by a blouse called *Ru*.

Yi 衣
Chang 裳
tunic 宽松外衣
sash 腰带，绶带
Ru 襦

2.2 Tang Suit (Tangzhuang)

Tang Suit often refers to a type of Chinese jacket. The word of "Tang Suit" was created by the overseas Chinese people. As the most prosperous and powerful dynasty in the history of China's feudal society, the Tang Empire was so famous in the world that foreigners used to call the overseas Chinese people "Tang People", the places where they lived "Chinatowns" (literally meaning "Tang People Streets") and the clothes they wore "Tang Suit".

Tang Suit has two varieties which are strikingly different from each other in style. One refers to the authentic Tang-era clothes whereas the other refers to male jacket evolving from ***Magua*** of the Qing Dynasty, which is made by absorbing a Western-style suit cutting method, featuring a Mandarin collar, a **frog** (a knob made of intricately knotted strings) and a *duijin* (a kind of Chinese-style jacket with buttons down the front).

Magua 马褂

frog 纽扣和纽袢

2.3 Zhongshan Suit

Zhongshan Suit is a type of male **attire** designed by Sun Zhongshan which combined the Western-style suit and Chinese clothes. It has become extremely popular among the Chinese people since its **inception**, especially during the Republic of China (1912-1949). Later, after Chairman Mao had been seen wearing it in public numerous times, this outfit gained another name "Mao Suit".

attire 服装;盛装

inception 成立,创立

The suit has four pockets, five bigger central buttons in the front and three smaller cuff-buttons on either sleeve. The four pockets represent **four virtues (benevolence, loyalty, probity and shame)**. The five bigger buttons symbolize the separation of **five powers (administration, legislation, jurisdiction, examination and supervision)**. The three smaller cuff-buttons on either sleeve represent **Three**

four virtues (benevolence, loyalty, probity and shame) 四维(即礼、义、廉、耻)

five powers (administration, legislation, jurisdiction, examination and supervision) 五权(行政权、立法权、司法权、考试权、监察权)

People's Principles (Nationalism, **Democracy and the People's Livelihood**, as put forward by Sun Zhongshan). The two inverted pen-rack-shaped pocket flaps symbolize flourishing the state with culture rather than with military power. The turn-down closed collar represents the meticulous attitude towards managing state affairs, and the one-piece suit represents the unity of China.

Three People's Principles (Nationalism, Democracy and the People's Livelihood) 三民主义(民族、民权、民生)

2.4 *Qipao*

The cheongsam (*Qipao*) evolved from the long gowns worn by Manchu women of the Qing Dynasty. The Manchu ethnic people were also called Qi people by Han people; hence this long gown was named *Qipao* (Qi gown). *Qipao* is a body-hugging one-piece female dress, which features a frog and two big openings at either side of the hems for convenient movement, and it is often buttoned on the right side. *Qipao* can perfectly display a woman's graceful figure. *Qipao* has various styles based on differences in the shapes of collars, the length of dresses, the width of sleeves and even the positions of *kaijin*.

Qipao became very popular in the first half of the 20th century, favored by women of different ages and social status. Fans of *Qipao* include Song Qingling and her younger sister, Song Meiling.

3. Ethnic Costumes

China is a country with 56 ethnic groups and each group has its own costumes. For example, Hui people are famous for their white caps with delicate patterns,

Uighur people for their colorful caps, Miao people for their refined silver jewellery, Tujia people for their Lushui wedding dresses and Oroqen for their leather gowns. In modern times, Han people don't have their ethnic costumes, but many people view *Hanfu* and Zhongshan Suit as their costumes.

Hezhe 赫哲族
Oroqen 鄂伦春
Ewenki 鄂温克
Mongolian 蒙古族人
Kazakh 哈萨克族人
Yugur 裕固族

Traditional Chinese ethnic costumes varied in raw materials, textile technology, fashions and decoration according to their living environment and their living styles. The **Hezhe** people used to make a living on fishing, so their clothes were made of fish-skin. The **Oroqen** and the **Ewenki** were hunting ethnic minority groups, so they preferred leather of wild animals. Nomads like the **Mongolians**, Tibetans, **Kazakhs**, **Yugur** people made their costumes mostly from domestic animal hide. In addition, farming ethnic minority groups usually took the local plants like hemp and silk as raw materials.

pleated skirts 百褶裙
tube skirts 筒裙

Chinese ethnic costumes can be classified into two types: long gowns and short clothes. As for short clothes, they fall into two types: trousers and skirts. There are **pleated skirts**, **tube skirts**, short skirts and so on. Even though women of the Li, the Dai, the Jingpo, the De'ang ethnic minority groups all wear tube skirts, the Li wear brocade skirts made of cotton, the Dai wear skirts made of common cloth, the Jingpo wear woolen multicolored skirts, and the De'ang wear skirts with horizontal stripes.

In a vast country like China, with so many ethnic groups and an unbalanced social development, styles of clothes vary a lot due to different economic lives, cultural levels, natural environment, geographical conditions and climatic conditions.

3.1 Lushui Wedding Dress

Lushui wedding dress 露水衣，土家族女子婚服

The girl of Tujia used to wear Lushui dress on her wedding day. Lushui dress consists a bright-colored smock, a skirt, a handkerchief and an umbrella. The **smock** is decorated with patterns of dew which contribute to the name Lushui. Usually Lushui dress was not made by the bride herself. Lushui dress was borrowed from others. It is said the older the dress is, the better the wish it carries. By wearing Lushui dress, the newly married couples will never betray each other.

smock 女用宽松上衣

3.2 Maiden Caps of the Bai

The movie *Five Jinhua* (*Fairy Maiden*) made the Bai costume well known among Chinese. One of the most prominent is Jinhua headdress which demonstrates the beautiful scenery of Dali—"**flower of Shangguan, wind of Xiaguan, snow of Cangshan, moon of Erhai**". The embroidered headscarf under the hairpin is like the camellia and rhododendron on the top of the mountain, representing the flowers blooming in the four seasons of Dali; the fluttering and swaying tassels symbolize the wind blowing all the year round; the embroidered cap vividly shows the snow on the top of Cangshan and the round bending symbolizes a bright moon rising from the sea.

flower of Shangguan, wind of Xiaguan, snow of Cangshan, moon of Erhai 上关花，下关风，苍山雪，洱海月

Another cap of the Bai is the **phoenix cap**. It is made of two pieces of cloth and looks like a flying phoenix with its tail slightly slanting upward. Its middle part is **beset** with a red "flower" surrounded by silver and jade, and therefore

phoenix cap 凤凰帽

beset 镶嵌

the cap looks brilliant. Girls in such caps look extraordinarily pretty. There is a folk story about the origin of the phoenix cap. Once upon a time, there were two girls who were diligent, pretty and kind-hearted. One day after harvest, birds came to greet them and a phoenix gave two beautiful caps to the girls. A vicious king was attracted by their incomparable beauty in the caps, and forced them to marry him. The king captured the elder sister. She chose to commit suicide instead of marrying the king. The younger sister then tried to find a chance to kill the king. To commemorate them, the Bai girls developed the custom of wearing phoenix caps which stand for pureness and beauty.

3.3 Silver Ornaments of the Miao

exquisite 精美的

The Miao costume is known for its **exquisite** silver ornaments. Traditionally after a girl was born, her parents started to make fancy silver ornaments for her. On her wedding day, the girl would wear these beautiful silver ornaments, adding a joyful atmosphere to the happy event. The Miao people have been deeply enamored with silver since ancient times. Silver takes special importance in their culture. The craft of making silver ornaments has developed into a unique art form and a carrier of the culture. The fancy Miao silver ornaments include hats, horns, combs, earrings, necklaces, bracelets, etc.

Part II Western Costumes

Different areas in UK have their own regional costumes. Scotland is known for the man's kilt made from clan tartans. The Celts in Ireland and Scotland used to wear shirts and plaid mantles, which they arranged on their bodies in various ways. Some of the Welsh and Irish costumes are recently invented traditions. As their language and culture faded in the early nineteenth century, intellectuals promoted the preservation of customs and traditions. This extended to dress. England did not suffer the same crisis of identity as them, so there is no particular folk dress in England.

1. Kilts (Scottish)

Originating from the traditional dress of Gaelic men and boys in the Scottish Highlands, a kilt is a particular type of knee-length **non-bifurcated** skirt with pleats at the back. In the 16th century the great kilt was a full-length garment whose upper half could be worn as a **cloak**. Gradually the bottom half of the great kilt turned into the small kilt or modern kilt. Since the 19th century, kilts were associated with the glorious culture of Scotland, and more broadly with Gaelic or **Celtic** heritage. A kilt is most often made of woolen cloth in a **tartan** pattern.

A kilt covers the body from the waist down to the center of the knees. The overlapping layers in front are called "**aprons**" and are flat; the single layer of fabric around the sides and back is pleated. A kilt pin is fastened to the front

non-bifurcated 不分叉的

cloak 斗篷

Celtic 凯尔特人的

tartan 格子呢(尤指苏格兰格子呢)

apron 围裙

apron on the free corner. The pin does not pass through the layer below, as its function is to add weight. Traditionally, it was believed that a "true Scotsman" should wear nothing under his kilt, but the Scottish Tartans Authority warned that the practice could be "childish and **unhygienic**".

unhygienic 不卫生的

The typical kilt as seen at modern Highland game events is made of **twill** woven worsted wool. The twill weave used for kilts is a "2-2 type", meaning that each **weft thread** passes over and under two **warp threads** at a time. When woven according to a given **sett** or written color pattern, this kind of twill is called tartan. Tartan is one distinctive feature of the authentic Scots kilt. In contrast Irish pipers don't wear tartan kilts, theirs are made from solid-color cloth, with **saffron** or green being the most widely used colors.

twill 斜纹织物
weft thread 纬线
warp thread 经线
sett 格子呢图案，(图案中)方格
saffron 藏红花(色)

2. Traditional Welsh Costume

The traditional Welsh costume refers to the costume worn by rural women in Wales. It gradually became recognized as a traditional costume by the women of the better-off families, who wore it for special occasions or when went to market to sell their products. The costume included a version of the gown, originally worn by the **gentry** in the 17th and 18th centuries. The unique Welsh hat, which made its first appearance in the 1830s, was used as an icon of Wales from the 1840s.

gentry 社会地位高的人

Selected elements of traditional Welsh costume were adopted as a national costume when it had gone out of general use from the 1880s. From then on it was worn by women at events such as royal visits, by **choirs** at church and chapel, for photographs and occasionally at **eisteddfodau**. It was first worn by girls as a celebration on Saint David's Day just before the First World War. The costume is now recognized as the national dress of Wales.

choir 唱诗班
eisteddfodau 威尔士全国诗歌音乐比赛大会

Other than the hat, the most distinctive feature of the Welsh costume might be the gown and bedgown. Although both have often been referred to as bedgowns, the term "gown" is now used for the long-tailed, tailored **garment**. The skirt and underskirt were normally of heavy **flannel** with **vertical** or occasionally **horizontal** stripes in bold colors, often reds and dark blue or black and white. The cape or mantle were long and often had large hoods (to cover the Welsh hat). Blue woolen cloaks were far more common than red ones in most places of Wales until the 1860s.

garment (一件)衣服
flannel 法兰绒
vertical 竖直的
horizontal 横的

Sometimes now referred to as a **fichu**, the handkerchief was a square piece of fabric, normally of printed cotton or linen, worn around the neck and tucked into the top of the gown, or worn over the head like a head scarf. The apron worn by Welsh woman was often of natural colors (white through cream and grey to black) in **chequered** patterns. Before about 1850 many rural women walked barefoot to and from market, or wore footless stockings. Many women spent a lot of time knitting stockings but most were sold for export.

fichu 三角领巾
chequered 双色方格图案的

The distinctive features of Welsh hats are the broad, stiff, flat **brim** and the tall **crown**. There are two main shapes of crown: drum shaped crowns which were worn in northwest Wales and slightly **tapering** crowns which were

brim 帽檐
crown(帽)顶
taper 逐渐变窄

felt 毡，毛毡
plush 长毛绒
buckram（作里衬的）硬棉布

found in the rest of Wales. They were made of **felt** or silk **plush** on a stiffened **buckram** base. A third type of hat, known as the cockle hat, was worn in the Swansea area.

3. American Western Wear

Western wear is a category of male and female clothing which derives its unique style from the clothes worn in the 19th century Wild West. Western wear can be a very informal combination like a T-shirt and blue jeans, or tailored formal garments. At minimum, western wear generally incorporates a cowboy hat, a leather belt, and cowboy boots.

Boss of the plains 牛仔帽的一种

The first western model of hats was the open-crowned "**Boss of the Plains**", and after that came the front-creased Carlsbad, destined to become the cowboy style.

ranch 牧场
ranchero 牧场工人，牧牛工
rodeo 牧马骑术表演
apparel 衣服，衣着

The cowboy hat is a high-crowned, wide-brimmed hat known as the defining piece of attire for the North American cowboy. The cowboy hat was influenced by 19th century Mexican culture and is popular among **ranch** workers in the western and southern United States, western Canada and northern Mexico. Many country-western singers and **ranchero** singers in Mexico, participants in the North American **rodeo** circuit wear it now. It is recognized around the world as part of old west **apparel**.

Cowboy boots refer to a specific style of riding boot, historically worn by cowboys. There are two basic styles of cowboy boots, western (or classic) and roper. The classic style is featured by a tall boot shaft, going to at least mid-

calf, with an angled "cowboy" heel, usually over one inch high. Another common "walking" heel is slightly lower, still angled. The toe of western boots was originally rounded or squared in shape. The narrow-pointed toe design appeared in the early 1940s.

calf 小腿肚

Cowboy boots are normally made from cowhide leather but are also sometimes made from "exotic" skins such as **alligator**, snake, lizard, eel, elephant, elk, buffalo, and the like.

alligator 短吻鳄

Part III Comparison and Contrast

1. Chinese Archer's Ring (Thumb Ring) VS Greek Ring

Manchu people valued hunting skills, especially horsemanship and **archery**. When hunting, the **bowstring** was pulled back with the thumb of the right hand, making a thumb ring essential both to protect the thumb and to ensure a smooth release of the arrows. In addition to their practical functions, thumb rings gradually became personal adornment. The earliest archer's rings were made of deer bone. In hunting and warfare, most Manchu archers, even the highest-ranking **aristocrats**, favored plain thumb rings of bone or antler for use. At other times, however, they wore luxurious thumb rings that were highly decorated and made of fragile or precious materials, such as jade, amber or ivory.

Traditionally, Chinese rings were used to warn or remind somebody of something, so there were moral words curved inside them. Besides, it could also be used to express people's friendship or love, so rings of the same style were worn by friends or couples.

Manchu 满族的，满族人	archery 箭术
bowstring 弓弦	aristocrat 贵族
sovereign 拥有最高统治权的	engrave 在……雕刻字或者图案

The early Greek rings were mostly used as seals by the king or men of the royal court. Soon their use for highlighting prestige and authority was recognized. Yet, the rise of democracy spread the wearing of rings in men of all social status. Public officials, generals, even philosophers started wearing rings as a sign of both power and pride. Gradually, it became a necessary accessory of the **sovereign** citizen of the Greek city.

Another purpose that was fulfilled with this custom, was the memory of a happy or prideful event. To celebrate the rescue of his son, Telemachus, by one of the dolphins of the sea, Odysseus ordered a ring **engraved** with a dolphin. Victories in the Olympic Games or on the battlefield also became favorite themes that were engraved on Greek's rings.

Moreover, due to their widespread use, the art of crafting rings bloomed in the wealthiest of the ancient Greek cities. The ancient Greek rings were made of various materials, such as gold, silver, iron, ivory and amber. Additional themes were inspired by Greek mythology, religion and nature.

2. *Baijiayi* VS Patchwork

Baijiayi is made by sewing scraps of fabric together to form design art. This technique is still used in modern Chinese **quilting**. Silk or cotton is used to make the **patchwork**. *Baijiayi* is a symbol of good luck in China. In the past, due to the lag in health care and education, infant **mortality** was relatively high. After the birth of a baby, the family would use cloth blocks begged from neighbors and made a piece of clothing for the baby. Every patch represented the blessing of people towards the baby. At that time, people believed that an infant's death was due to a ghost, so the blessing from the neighbors could help to protect him. The **scraps** must be from the families with healthy family members, or it would be a disaster. It's said that Emperor Qianlong's son was killed after wearing a *baijiayi* because the robe was from a child who had smallpox.

baijiayi 百家衣	quilting 绗缝	patchwork 拼布
mortality 死亡率	scrap 碎片	geometric 几何的
bicentennial 两百周年纪念		

Patchwork is often used in making quilts. It is a form of needlework that involves sewing together pieces of fabric into a larger design. The larger design is usually based on repeating patterns built up with different fabric shapes (which can be different colors). These pieces are carefully measured and cut into basic **geometric** shapes that can be easily sewed together. Patchwork enjoyed a

widespread revival during the Great Depression as a way to recycle worn clothing into warm quilts.

Although crafters today use brand new cotton fabrics as the basis for their designs, there was a time that even small and worn pieces of material were adopted. In the US, patchwork declined after World War II, but was again revived during the American **bicentennial**. In the past, hand quilting was often done in a group around a frame. When the pieces were sewed together, the shapes, colors and patterns can be arranged repeatedly or randomly. Traditional patchwork has identifying names based on the arrangement of colors and shapes.

3. Chinese Phoenix Crown VS British Crown

Phoenix crown is a traditional type of Chinese **headgear** for women. It was worn mainly by noblewomen for ceremonies or official occasions. Girls from common families had a chance of wearing phoenix crown on their wedding days.

The name originates from its adornments: phoenixes made of inlaid **kingfisher** feathers, as well as gold dragons, beaded pheasants, pearls and other gemstones. One of the earliest phoenix crowns that has been excavated belonged to Empress Xiao of the Sui Dynasty.

There were strict restrictions on the numbers of phoenixes, dragons and precious gems on each crown. For example, there are 6 dragons, 3 phoenixes, 5,449 pearls, 71 rubies and 57 **sapphires** on the phoenix crown of Ming Empress Xiaoduan; 9 phoenixes, 12 dragons, more than 3,500 pearls and more than 150 gemstones are found on the phoenix crown of Empress Xiaojing. The pearls, gemstones and kingfisher feathers were made into ornamental flowers, leaves, clouds and **temple ornaments**. The weight of the entire crown can be 2-3 kilograms.

headgear 头饰	kingfisher 翠鸟	sapphire 蓝宝石
temple ornaments 两博鬓	coronation 加冕典礼	heraldry 纹章，纹章学

A crown is a traditional symbolic form of headgear worn by a monarch or by a deity, for whom the crown traditionally represents authority, legitimacy, victory, honor and glory, as well as immortality, justice and resurrection. Apart from the traditional form, crowns also may be in the form of a wreath and be made of flowers, oak leaves, or thorns and be worn by others, representing what the **coronation** part aims to symbolize with the specific crown. In religious art, a crown of stars is used similarly to a halo. Crowns worn by rulers often contain jewels. A crown is often a symbol of the monarchy, a monarch's government, or items endorsed by it. The word itself is used, particularly in Commonwealth countries, as an abstract name for the monarchy itself, as distinct from the individual who inhabits it. A specific type of crown is employed in **heraldry** under strict rules. Indeed, some monarchies never had a physical crown. What they had was just a heraldic representation, as in the constitutional kingdom of Belgium, where no coronation ever took place.

Part IV Reflection and Presentation

1. Choose one costume of Chinese ethnic minority group and analyze the relationship between the costume and the local geographic features.

2. Compare traditional Chinese wedding dress with Western wedding dress and explore the cultural connotations behind them.

3. Design one dress by combining traditional Chinese clothing culture with fashions. Try to use as many elements as you can.

Part V Mini-pedia

1. Chinese Knot Button

Chinese knot button is essentially a diamond knot where the lanyard loop is shortened to a minimum, tightened to the knot itself. There emerges only two lines next to each other from the knot: the beginning and the end. As a distinctive feature of traditional Chinese apparel, Chinese knot buttons are highly visible nowadays, especially on garments like *Qipao* and Tang Suit. The history of knot buttons dates to the prehistoric era, when ropes were first used as a primitive form of belts. Knot buttons are usually made of cords woven from cotton, so compared with common buttons, they are more comfortable to lie on and to rest against, and they are not easy to be broken even by the laundry. A skilled Chinese tailor can tie the knot without guide, flat on his table.

There are two main types: linear knot and figure knot. One of the basic figure knot buttons is *panxiangkou* which adopts the shape of coiled incense.

2. Lace

Lace was used by clergy of the early Catholic Church as part of vestments in religious ceremonies but did not come into widespread use until the 16th century in the northwestern part of the European continent. In 1840, Britain's Queen Victoria married in lace, influencing the wedding dress style until now. Catherine of Aragon was said to have supported the lace makers there by burning all her lace and commissioning new pieces. This may be the origin of the lace maker's holiday — St.Catherine's Day, or Cattern's day. On this day (25 or 26 November) lace makers were given a day off from work, and Cattern cakes—small dough cakes made with caraway seeds, were used to celebrate.

References

1. 何其亮，张晔. 英释中国传统文化[M]. 杭州：浙江大学出版社，2006.
2. 刘春芳，等. 中西文化对比教程[M]. 北京：中国人民大学出版社，2017.
3. 沈从文. 中国古代服饰研究[M]. 上海：上海世纪出版集团，2002.
4. 束定芳. 中国文化英语教程[M]. 上海：上海外语教育出版社，2016.
5. 王焱，等. 中西文化比较[M]. 北京：清华大学出版社，2017.
6. Catherin Richardson. *Clothing Culture, 1350-1650*. London & New York: Routledge, Taylor and Francis Group, 2016.
7. Kelly Olson. *Dress and the Roman Women*. London & New York: Routledge, Taylor and Francis Group, 2008.
8. https://baijiahao.baidu.com/s?id=1581036867243333490&wfr=spider&for=pc.
9. https://dianying.fm/movie/pocket-money/.
10. https://en.wikipedia.org/wiki/Chinese Clothing.

11. https://en.wikipedia.org/wiki/crown.
12. https://en.wikipedia.org/wiki/folk costume.
13. https://en.wikipedia.org/wiki/kilt.
14. https://en.wikipedia.org/wiki/knot button.
15. https://en.wikipedia.org/wiki/welsh costume.
16. http://pngimg.com/imgs/clothing/cowboy_hat/.
17. http://www.chinadaily.com.cn/life/2011-02/28/content_12089492.htm.
18. https://www.chinahighlights.com/travelguide/traditional-chinese-clothes-zhongshan-suit.htm.
19. http://www.historyofclothing.com/clothing-history/hanfu/.
20. http://www.metmuseum.org.
21. https://www.topchinatravel.com/china-guide/costumes-of-ethnic-minorities.htm.
22. https://www.travelchinaguide.com/intro/clothing/feature.htm.

Unit 5

Chinese and Western Birth Customs

First Birthday Celebration (*Zhuazhou*)

The Infant Baptism

Learning Objectives

- To be familiar with some pregnancy and childbirth-related traditions in China as well as in Western countries
- To get a better understanding of the different birth customs and rituals in China and Western countries
- To compare and contrast different views on life and death as well as on childbirth in the East and West

Lead-in Questions

- Do you know any customs or traditions related to childbirth in China or in a Western country?
- How do you get your name? Is there any symbolic meaning attached to your name?
- What do you think of life and death? Do you know any philosophy about life and death? How are these ideas related to different cultures?

Part I Chinese Birth Customs

1. Traditional Chinese Beliefs About Pregnancy and Childbirth

Every culture has its own traditions about pregnancy and childbirth that are strongly driven by its faith, beliefs and ancient wisdom. Chinese people are no exception and have a long list of customs that may sound strange to an alien.

Here are some notable pregnancy and delivery-related beliefs.

1.1 During Pregnancy

(1) Putting sharp objects on the bed such as knives and scissors will result in the baby born with a **cleft** lip or **palate**.

(2) "Cooling" foods should be avoided as they may lead to the reduction of heat or vitality, thus weakening the **womb**. At the same time, it is believed that certain foods should be taken to help strengthen the womb and ensure a smooth delivery.

(3) No construction work should be done in the house where there is a pregnant woman. Expectant mothers are discouraged from moving furniture or moving to a new house during their pregnancy, because it could lead to a miscarriage or **fetal deformities**.

(4) Pregnant women are not allowed to attend funerals as well as wedding ceremonies.

(5) Traditionally pregnant women in China are advised

cleft 裂缝，裂口
palate 腭
womb 子宫
fetal 胎儿的
deformity 畸形

to take much rest and not to do any heavy work, whereas in Western countries proper exercise is advised to expectant mothers. In China, mothers are fed only well-cooked food. There are many food taboos associated with pregnancy. Pregnant Cantonese women avoid mutton as the Cantonese word for the meat has the same pronunciation as the word for **epilepsy**. Pregnant women in Fujian avoid crab as they believe that doing so will result in the birth of a naughty child.

epilepsy 癫痫

(6) It is believed that what a pregnant woman does, sees, listens to, eats and even thinks affects the child in some manner. It is for this reason that they are encouraged to read pleasant works of literature, eat well-cooked food, think positively and keep a good temper. Improper behavior and mannerisms are supposed to affect the child negatively. Women are discouraged from criticizing others for it is believed that the baby will look and act like the person criticized.

1.2 During Labor and Delivery

(1) Chinese women can drink a potent herbal potion or eat certain food to help them have a less painful labor. Women are told not to fear the process but embrace it. In ancient times, the delivery of the child traditionally happened in a tub, an armchair like furniture or even a futon in some cases, so in Chinese there are idioms like ***linpen***, ***luocao*** to refer to child delivery. Prayers and sacrifices are offered to the Goddess of Fertility Bodhisattva Guan Yin and Jin Hua

linpen 临盆
luocao 落草，指婴儿出生

Fu Ren (Lady Golden Flower) after a successful delivery.

(2) Traditionally the ideal position for labor is squatting. The mother will not have enough energy to deliver if she is lying on her back.

(3) The father is not present during delivery, but he is expected to give the baby its first bath.

The Chinese believe that all celebrations for the baby should happen only after the delivery. The expectant mother's own mother buys the child's entire layette. A month before the baby is due, the maternal grandmother sends a package of clothing for her daughter called ***cuisheng***, or hastening the delivery. There is a white cloth inside the package with which to wrap the newborn. The maternal grandmother waits three days after the baby arrives before she visits the newborn bringing all the clothes and baby equipment.

cuisheng 催生

2. Birth Rituals

2.1 Baby Bathing on the Third Morning

baby bathing on the third morning 三朝洗儿，又称洗三

It is the birth ceremony held on the third morning after a baby is born. Traditionally parents send red eggs (eggs dyed red representing fertility and good luck) to close family members and friends— usually an even number for a girl, odd for a boy. Later, a ceremony of baby bath is performed, and baby is bathed in warm water (with herbal medicine), a blessing to drive off evil spirits and stay healthy all his life.

This custom dated back long time ago, and it became

popular in the Tang Dynasty. Si Maguang's ***History as a Mirror*** recorded this custom of baby bathing on the third morning. Great men of letters like Ou Yangxiu, Fan zhongyan in the Song Dynasty wrote poems in honor of this custom when their friend Mei Yaochen got his youngest son at the age of 58.

History as a Mirror 《资治通鉴》

This ceremony was presided over by a **midwife**. First, incense was burned and candles were lit. Prayers and sacrifices were offered to the Goddess of Delivery and other deities for child protection. Then the families and friends gathered and poured the hot water with herbal medicine into the bath tub. Sometimes people added **shallots** and **ginger** to the water because shallots denoted intelligence and ginger sounded similar to the Chinese character for "strong". During the baby bathing, people scattered multicolored coins, **red dates**, chestnuts, peanuts and **longans** into the water.

midwife 接生婆

shallot 葱

ginger 姜

red date 枣

longan 桂圆，龙眼

2.2 Naming

Usually children are given a nickname or "milk" name before they have a formal name. According to ancient tradition, parents named the children after a humble animal or something ugly to trick evil spirits to stay away from the children, hoping they could be alive and healthy. These names may stay with children throughout childhood. Most Chinese are very cautious when giving a formal name. They will study the birth time of the child (**Eight Characters**) or check the dictionary before they could name a child formally.

Eight Characters 八字

2.3 The Cultural Values of the Names

2.3.1 Worshiping Ancestors

The Han ethnic group prefers to use "华, 夏, 中, 汉, 唐" as names, in order to pay tribute to the ancestors. They want to bring glory to the ancestors, as showed in the names such as "光宗, 耀祖, 祖英, 祖荣".

2.3.2 Worshiping Confucianism

"Benevolence, loyalty, righteousness, wisdom and courtesy" are the moral principles advocated by Confucius. Under the influence of the doctrine, people like to choose "仁, 义, 礼, 智, 信, 忠, 孝, 恭, 敬, 贤, 善", etc for names.

2.3.3 Extolling Determination and Achievement

eulogize 称赞, 颂扬

Chinese culture **eulogizes** heroic deeds and encourages people to fight for their dreams. For this reason, men usually choose the characters to express "bravery, diligence, ambition and success", etc. for their names such as "勇, 武, 胜, 强, 志, 雄, 威, 才, 奋, 进, 勤, 杰", etc.

2.3.4 Extolling Good Virtues

For men, they value the virtues or spirits such as persistence, justice, honesty, impartiality, so they often choose "坚, 毅, 清, 柏, 明, 亮, 辉, 鹏, 诚, 正", etc. for their names.

Women, on the other hand, like to have names to show their "charm, beauty, virtue and elegance", such as in the names "淑, 静, 慧, 秀, 娥, 婷, 凤, 娜, 娟, 娇, 雅, 娴, 丽, 艳, 芬, 芳, 媛, 薇, 香", etc.

2.3.5 Longing for Well-being

Chinese people hope to have a happy, healthy and

prosperous life, so they tend to choose relevant expressions for men's names, usually including "吉祥，兴旺(隆)，昌盛，发达，安康，长寿，松鹤，吉利，福禄寿喜", etc.

prosperous 富足的，兴旺的

2.3.6 Emphasizing the Family Bonds

Within a clan or a family system, besides the common family name, descendants often have another common character in their given names for each generation. This common character in given name is called the "Spreading Character", which is an indication of the person's generation within the family system. For example, **Kong Xiangxi** is the name of a famous person who lived in the last century. Kong is the family name. Xiang is the Spreading Character of his generation. Xi is his unique given name to identify himself.

Kong Xiangxi 孔祥熙

2.3.7 Worshiping the Theories of *The Book of Changes*

The Book of Changes says everything in the universe is made up of five elements— metal, wood, water, fire and earth. By studying the birth time of the baby (Eight Characters), the fortune-teller can tell whether the baby is lacking in an element, then the missing element is needed to be incorporated into his name.

The Book of Changes 《易经》

2.3.8 Names of the Time

Some names mirror a certain period in history. For example, people born in the 1950s often have such names as "建国，振华，建华，卫华，爱华，立国，国兴", etc.

During the "Cultural Revolution", people born at that time were usually named "革命，学军，立新，革新，志红，卫红，向红", etc.

2.4 First Month Confinement

first month confinement 坐月子

The post delivery period is one of the most challenging

for women. Known as the "cold phase" or "sit the month" period, new mothers during this time are advised with complete bed rest. Whatever the time of the year, they are properly wrapped in head covers, warm clothes, socks and blankets to keep the body warm. According to ancient wisdom, this keeps women from falling sick in their old age.

The confinement period, *zuoyuezi*, lasts for a period of 30 days. The mother is confined to the bed and she can not do any heavy work, including housework. Her job is to feed the baby. The mother is kept warm at all times with her head, hands and feet being covered. She is encouraged to eat strength-building foods like **pig trotters**, and ginger soaked in vinegar, or protein-rich soup (considered "hot"), which would increase breast milk and balance the "coldness" of the **postpartum** period. Bathing and washing hair are completely ruled out. The intention of following this practice for 30 days is to expel air and **lochia** from the womb and help the mother to recover after child delivery. In the old days, people believed that *zuoyuezi* could protect the mother and child from evil spirits. Nowadays these customs are slightly relaxed to accommodate the new beliefs. Most women who still follow *zuoyuezi* strongly believe that though it is very uncomfortable, it promises good health when they turn older.

pig trotter 猪蹄

postpartum 产后的

lochia 恶露，瘀血

2.5 First Month Celebration

The baby's first birthday is celebrated 30 days after birth. ***Manyue*** or "full moon" celebration marks the child's entry into the community. The baby is now formally introduced to the family. The mother is allowed to take her

manyue 满月

first bath and wash her hair now (old custom), while the ritual of hair shaving is also performed on the baby on this day. The baby will be dressed up in new clothes, particularly in red, decorated with gold accessories for the celebration.

For some families, **incense** is burned and food offerings are made to inform the ancestors of the new family member and pray to the deities for child protection.

incense(常用于宗教仪式中的)香

Celebrations are in the form of presenting red-colored eggs to the relatives which are a symbol of good luck and prosperity. The relatives are supposed to give gifts to the newborn baby in return, such as gold bangles, chains and usually money in red envelopes.

Modern *manyue* celebrations are always organized in restaurants in the form of a dinner. Families, relatives and friends are invited to have a feast together, celebrating the first month of the baby.

2.6 First Birthday Celebration

A child's first birthday is a grand event which can be celebrated on either the lunar calendar or the solar calendar. Usually the parents will hold a big banquet for family and friends.

There is a game played on this occasion—***zhuazhou***—an ancient method for predicting an infant's future career. It has been delicately preserved as a traditional custom. Many Chinese parents still hold the event on their child's first birthday. *Zhua*, meaning "to pick", and *zhou*, meaning "first anniversary", is a ceremony at which parents place a variety of objects on a plate and then have the child pick one.

zhuazhou 抓周

Each object is symbolic of a future career path, so what the child selects is supposed to reveal their future career as well as certain personality traits and interests.

The tradition which is said to have started during the Three Kingdoms Period arose following the death of Sun He, the prince of the Eastern Wu Kingdom. His father, the emperor Sun Quan, grew worried about which of his grandsons would ascend the throne, so a Wu citizen named Jing Yang suggested that he place a few items on a plate and ask each of his grandsons to pick. Sun Hao grabbed a **bamboo slip**—an ancient form of Chinese paper — in one hand, and an **imperial belt**— symbolizing royal power — in another. Both seemed to suggest that he was destined to be the new emperor. This prediction was self-fulfilling. By a curious twist of fate, Sun Hao finally ascended the throne.

bamboo slip 简册

imperial belt 绶带

Traditionally, the items laid out for boys and girls are different. In ancient China, items like a ruler, makeup, needles and thread were placed on a girl's plate, as women were expected to stay at home, take care of the family and do the needle work. For boys, parents would select swords, pens and books to see if they would become a hero, scholar or poet. It was also common to have shallots and celery for both boys and girls as additional choices, because Chinese characters for both of these vegetables are **homonyms** for virtuous temperaments: If a child picked celery, it meant the child would be diligent. If he chose shallots, it meant he would be intelligent. Nowadays, Chinese people have replaced some old-fashioned objects like the thread and needle with the new ones that correlate with more fashionable

homonym 同音异义词

career paths, such as cell phones, a computer mouse and ipad indicating the computer-related professions.

The meanings behind some items are pretty straightforward and clear while others require some knowledge of Chinese language or culture to understand:

Measuring Tape — Designer / Architect

Sword — General/ Soldier

Stethoscope— Doctor

Abacus/ Calculator — Businessperson

Yuanbao (money used in ancient China) — A life of fortune

Book — Scholar

Calligraphy Pen — Writer

Peanuts — Long Life

stethoscope 听诊器

abacus 算盘

Yuanbao 元宝

2.7 Other Birthday Celebrations

Traditionally, Chinese view a few birthdays as important, namely 1st, 10th, 60th, 70th, 80th birthday. The reason why the seniors and the babies celebrate the birthdays is that in Chinese culture, the elderly are respected and children mean the extension of the bloodline and the clan.

For the elderly, the gifts are usually items that symbolize longevity, including old miniature trees, wine, packages of long noodles, homemade peaches (steamed wheat shaped like peaches) and money in red envelopes. They are often given in even numbers. Never present a clock as a gift to the elderly.

Part II Western Birth Customs

1. Throw a Baby Shower

1.1 Baby Shower

baby shower 迎婴聚会

A **baby shower** is a way to celebrate the expected or delivered birth of a child by presenting gifts to the mother at a party, whereas other cultures host a baby shower to celebrate the transformation of a woman into a mother.

Traditionally, baby showers are given only for the family's first child, and only women are invited, though this has changed in recent years. Activities at baby showers include gift-giving and playing games such as bingo, and sometimes being pregnancy-themed, such as "guess the mother's measurements" or "guess the sex of the baby". Baby showers help strengthen the bonds between the close friends attending the shower and the expectant mother, and give the new family an opportunity to express gratitude ahead of time.

Because the party centers on gift-giving, the baby shower is typically arranged and hosted by a close friend rather than a member of the family, since it is considered rude for families to ask for gifts on behalf of their members. However, this custom varies in different cultures and in some it is customary for a close female family member to host the baby shower, often the baby's maternal grandmother.

When a baby shower is held after the birth of a baby, an invitation to attend the shower may be issued together with a baby announcement. In the US, if a baby shower doesn't happen before the arrival of the baby, a **sip-and-see party** or other similar event can be organized after the birth.

A sip and see party is a welcoming party for a new baby, while light refreshments are served. 迎婴派对(提供小食)

Guests bring small gifts for the expectant mother. Typical gifts related to babies include diapers, blankets, baby bottles, clothes and toys. It is customary to open the gifts during the party; sometimes the host will play a game of opening gifts to make it entertaining such as baby-gift bingo.

The baby shower is a family's first opportunity to gather people together to help play a part in their child's life and share their joy upon the coming of the new baby.

1.2 History of the Baby Shower

The term "baby shower" is relatively new, but the celebrations and rituals associated with pregnancy and childbirth are both age-old and enduring.

1.2.1 Ancient Greece

The ancient Greeks also celebrated child birth, with a shout (*oloyge*) after the labor had ended, to declare that "peace had arrived". Five to seven days after the child birth, there was a ceremony called *Amphidromia* to introduce the baby into the household. In wealthy families, the public *dekate* ceremony, after ten days, was a naming ceremony for the child. It also signalled the mother's return to society. (The ten-day period is still observed in modern-day Iran.)

1.2.2 Medieval Europe

Given that a mother might die in childbirth, the child delivery was recognized as having a great risk of spiritual danger in addition to the physical danger. Priests would often visit women during labor so they could confess their sins. After the birth, usually on the same day, a baptism ceremony would be held for the baby. In this ceremony, the **godparents** would give gifts to the child, including a pair of silver spoons.

godparent 教父母

1.2.3 Renaissance Europe

Pregnancies at this time were celebrated with many different kinds of birth gifts like wooden trays and bowls, paintings, sculptures and food, etc. Childbirth was seen as almost mystical, and expectant mothers were often surrounded with references to the **Annunciation** as a means of encouragement and celebration.

Annunciation 圣母领报，天使报喜

1.2.4 Victorian Britain and North America

Victorian women would keep their pregnancies secret, but after the baby was born, other women would often hold tea parties for the new mother. Gifts were usually handmade, but the grandmother would give silver.

1.2.5 Modern North America

In the 1950s and 1960s, the modern baby shower started during the baby boom era for the purpose of providing the expectant mother and her home with material benefits. This started the tradition of "showering" the mother with gifts, and brought about a more relaxed atmosphere with regards to the pregnancy.

While continuing the traditions from the 1950s, modern

technology has changed the form a baby shower takes: games can include identifying baby parts on a **sonogram**, and while traditional baby showers were female-exclusive, mixed-sex showers have gained increasing popularity in modern times.

sonogram 超声波图

2. The Infant Baptism Ceremony

2.1 Ceremony

Infant baptism is the practice of baptising infants or young children.

The exact details of the baptismal ceremony vary among Christian **denominations**. Many follow a rite or **liturgy**. In a typical ceremony, parents or godparents bring their child to their **congregation**'s priest or minister. The rite would be the same as that denomination's rite for adults, i.e., by pouring holy water (affusion) or by sprinkling water (aspersion).

denomination 教派，宗派

liturgy 礼拜仪式

congregation 教堂会众

Eastern Orthodox and Eastern Catholic traditions practise total immersion and baptise babies in a **font**, and this practice is also the first method listed in the baptismal ritual of the Roman Catholic, although pouring is the standard practice within the Latin branch of Catholicism. At the moment of baptism, the minister utters the words "I baptise you (or, 'The servant of God (name) is baptised') in the name of the Father, and of the Son, and of the Holy Spirit" (see *Matthew* 28:19).

font 圣洗池

By convention, many parents and godparents choose to dress the baby in a white christening gown for the baptism ceremony. Christening gowns often become treasured **keepsakes** that are used by many other children in the family and passed down from generation to generation. Traditionally, this gown is white or slightly off white and decorated with much lace, trim and delicate designs. In the past, a gown was used for both boys and girls; in the present day it has become universal to dress children in a baptismal outfit. It's also normally made of white fabric, consisting of a **romper** with a vest or other accessories. These clothes are often kept as a **memento** after the ceremony.

keepsake 纪念品

romper(幼儿的)连衫裤

memento 纪念品

2.2 Origin

In theological discussions, the practice of baptising infants or young children is sometimes referred to as **paedobaptism**, or pedobaptism.

Based on their understanding of *New Testament* passages such as *Colossians* 2:11-12, paedobaptists believe that infant baptism is the *New Testament* counterpart to **circumcision**. In the *Old Testament*, all male converts to **Judaism**, male infants born to Jewish parents and male servants were circumcised as a ceremony of introducing them into the Jewish community. Paedobaptists believe that baptism has substituted for *Old Testament* circumcision and is the religious ceremony of initiation into the Christian community.

During the medieval and Reformation eras, infant baptism was seen as a way to integrate newborn babies into the **secular** community as well as inducting them into the Christian faith.

paedobaptism 幼儿洗礼

circumcision 割礼

Judaism 犹太教

secular 世俗的，非宗教的

Different Christian denominations who practice infant baptism attach different meanings to the **sacrament** and explain its efficacy in different ways.

The **Roman Catholic Church** considers baptism so important that "parents are obliged to see that their infants are baptised within the first few weeks" and, "if the infant is in danger of death, it is to be baptised without any delay". Born with original sin, children also have the need of the new birth in baptism to be freed from the power of darkness and brought into the realm of the freedom of the children of God, to which all men are called. The Church and the parents would deny a child the priceless grace of becoming a child of God if they were not to be baptised shortly after birth.

The **Eastern Orthodox Church** and the **Assyrian Church** of the East also insist on the need to have infants baptised as soon as possible. Similar to the Roman Catholic Church, they teach that baptism is not merely a symbol but actually conveys grace. Baptism is a sacrament because it is an "instrument" instituted by Jesus Christ to impart grace to its recipients. Infants are traditionally baptised on the eighth day, corresponding to the biblical **injunction** to circumcise on the eighth day. However, this is not mandatory. In many of these churches, the Sacred Mystery of **Chrismation** (**Confirmation** in the Roman Catholic Church) is administered by the priest immediately after baptism. **Holy Communion**, in the form of **consecrated wine and bread**, is also given to infants after they are baptised.

sacrament (基督教)圣事,圣礼

Roman Catholic Church 罗马天主教会

Eastern Orthodox Church 东正教会

Assyrian Church 亚述教堂

injunction 命令,禁令

Chrismation 抹圣油

Confirmation 坚振礼,坚信礼(从而正式成为基督教会的成员)

Holy Communion 圣餐

consecrated wine and bread 圣酒,圣饼

Lutheran 路德宗信徒

regeneration 重生

For **Lutherans** baptism is a "means of grace" through which God creates and strengthens "saving faith" as the "washing of **regeneration**" in which people are reborn: "baptismal regeneration". Lutherans believe that babies are born sinful and therefore need to be born again to enter the kingdom of heaven. Through baptism the Holy Spirit works rebirth, creates faith in them and saves them.

3. Naming Ceremony

3.1 Christianity

Naming a child is usually through the baptism ceremony in Christianity. A Christian name, sometimes referred to as a baptismal name, is a religious personal name historically given on the occasion of a Christian baptism, though now most are often given by parents at birth. In English-speaking cultures, a person's Christian name is commonly their first name and is typically the name by which they are primarily known.

In more modern times, a Christian name has been used interchangeably with given name, first name and forename in traditionally Christian countries, and is still common in day-to-day use.

3.2 Civil Naming Ceremony

A civil naming ceremony is non-religious ceremony welcoming the arrival of a baby and symbolizing the entry of a newborn into society. It is performed at the local registry office and contrasts with the religious baptism performed by the church. Civil naming ceremonies have no legal status. Instead they confer moral obligations to the parents and godparents. The occasion provides the opportunity for parents to make public commitments to nurture and raise the child to adulthood. In Continental Europe, the equivalent concept is a civil baptism at the municipal town hall. (Birth registration is a legal requirement).

3.3　Naming Conventions in the West

In Western culture, nearly all individuals possess at least one given name (also known as a first name, forename or Christian name), together with a surname (also known as a last name or family name). Take Steve Jobs for example, Steve is the given name, while Jobs is the family name, indicating that the individual belongs to a family, a tribe or a clan. Where there are two or more given names, typically only one (in English-speaking cultures usually the first) is used in normal speech.

Middle names are actually (to mention several types of common cases)

part of a two-word given name (e.g. Mary Anne, about Mary Anne Clarke):

a **maiden name**

a **patronymic**

a **baptismal name**

a **maternal surname**

In the United States, such names are specifically referred to as middle names; in some other countries, they would simply be regarded as second, third, etc. given names. In the US, the "middle name" is often abbreviated

maiden name (女子的)婚前姓

patronymic 从父名衍生出来的姓或名字

baptismal name 教名

maternal surname 母姓

to the middle initial (e.g. *Michelle Lee Robinson* becomes *Michelle L. Robinson*, which is usually standard for signatures) or omitted entirely in everyday use (e. g. just *Michelle Robinson*). An individual may have more than one middle name, or none. In the United Kingdom, for comparison, she would usually be referred to as either *Michelle Robinson*, *M. L. Robinson* or *Michelle Lee Robinson*, or she may choose *Lee Robinson*, and informally there may be familiar shortenings.

3.4 Adopting Namesakes

Babies who were born in Elizabethan England (1558-1603) may have been named by their parents just a few days after birth at their baptism. Like many other newborns of the time, they were named after one of their godparents, carefully chosen for their higher socioeconomic status. The pool of names considered acceptable during this time was significantly smaller compared with what we are using today. Elizabeth, Anne, Joan, Margaret, Alice, Mary and Agnes accounted for approximately sixty-five percent of all girls' names. Likewise, John, Thomas, William, Richard and Robert comprised approximately sixty percent of male names. Naming options broadened during the classical revival period when French and Italian words were brought in, giving greater diversity and choice in names.

Today, throughout predominately Christian Europe, you find various customs in adopting **namesakes**—that is, who your child will be named after. **Orthodox** Greeks have customarily named their babies after the fathers' parents. The

namesake 同名的人

orthodox 传统的，正统派的

French often use a child's middle name to pay homage to a set of grandparents, using both grandmothers' first names for a girl and both grandfathers' names for a boy. The Spanish, known for their traditionalism, have rigid rules even for today: the first-born daughter is named after the father's mother, whereas the first son is named after the father's father, and so on. Many other European countries also have customs of naming after the parents. In the common, patronymic style, the "Jr." wears his father's **moniker**. For example, the former US President George Bush is named after his father, so "Jr." is attached as the name suffix. Likewise, but much less common, a girl may become her own mother's namesake.

moniker 名

4. Western Birthday Traditions

4.1 Birthday Parties

In Western cultures, particularly in the United States and Australia, birthday parties are often accompanied by colorful decorations, such as balloons and **streamers**. A birthday cake is often served with candles on it. While the birthday cake is being brought to the table, the song *Happy Birthday to You* is sung by the guests. Candles are to be blown out after a "birthday wish" has been made. For wealthy people and celebrities as well as many others, they would like to hire an event management agency or a party service to organize a birthday party.

streamer 装饰彩纸条

A child's birthday party may be held at home or in a

savoury 咸味的，美味的

public place. Soft drinks and both sweet and **savoury** foods are typically served to the guests. Birthday parties for children often feature entertainment, costumes, party games, and a theme. Adults' birthday parties in Western countries are often held in bars or nightclubs, though some are held at a restaurant or even at home.

4.2 Birthday Presents

In addition to parties, it is common for people to receive gifts on their birthday. Popular gifts include toys, books, jewelry, clothes, flowers, technical devices, gift cards, checks, cash, etc. Usually they are not expensive. Items such as underwear and socks are generally not appreciated by younger children.

4.3 Birthday Greetings

In most English-speaking countries it is traditional to sing the song *Happy Birthday to You* to the honored person celebrating a birthday. This song is prevalent worldwide; similar songs exist in other languages. This song is a common greeting used on birthdays, coupled with birthday cards and verbal greetings with messages such as "I wish you a Happy Birthday" or "Happy Birthday".

punch 拳打

4.4 Punches, Bumps and Other Birthday Torments

"The bumps", or "the dumps" in Scotland is a birthday torment common in countries such as the UK, Ireland, Canada and India. The friends and family of the honored person celebrating a birthday take him or her by the arms and legs, and "bump" him/her up into the air and down onto the floor. The number of "bumps" given equals the age of the person in years plus one "for luck". Usually "the bumps" are administered only to children, partly because grow-ups are so heavy for the process.

In French-speaking Canada, the US and Australia, "birthday punches" are given in a similar fashion, with the person whose birthday it is being punched a number of times equal to his/her age, often with one additional punch "for luck". In some places, instead of a punch "for luck", the person is **pinched** "to grow an inch". In Brazil, Hungary, Argentina, Italy and other countries, the person has his/her **earlobes** pulled. The Hungarian tradition also involves pulling the earlobes, wishing the person a happy birthday or reciting a rhyme whose English translation is "God bless you, live so long so your ears reach your ankles".

pinch 捏，掐

earlobe 耳垂

Similar to birthday punches are birthday **spankings**. While they are usually administered to children under the age of 16, the practice is somewhat common, even in areas and communities or among families where **corporal** punishment is otherwise frowned upon. The spankings are mostly given in such a mild way that they do not hurt the recipient at all, or if they do, it is usually only a small "sting". With this tradition the birthday recipient, as a general rule, gets spanked on his or her buttocks the same number of times as his or her age plus a final, extra spank for "one to grow on".

spanking 打屁股

corporal 肉体的

Birthday punches are administered throughout the day, but if the birthday recipient hides from the punches, one final punch is allowed to be given.

Part III Comparison and Contrast

1. Views on Life and Death in China VS in the West

Chinese society is fundamentally influenced by Confucianism and Buddhism, while Western society is predominantly a Christian one, as a result, Chinese and Westerners differ greatly in their views on life and death. On the whole, nearly all the religions believe in afterlife, **reincarnation**, heaven and hell, or soul. But on the other hand, the concept of life and death in different religions or philosophies differs a lot.

Confucianism

Confucius states that the afterlife is beyond human comprehension. Humans should live a righteous life so as to promote ideal social relations and harmony in society, rather than to act based on the expectations of rewards or punishments after death. "Ren", a core concept of Confucian doctrine, can be embodied in the love of people; a meaningful life is to develop their moral potential to the fullest while fulfilling all of their social obligations. Although Confucius does not typically believe the individual **salvation** or **damnation** of persons beyond this life, ancestor worship is an important part of Confucian faith and practice. It's commended as a means of cultivating the virtue of **filial piety** as well as achieving harmony in society.

Buddhism

According to Buddhism, our life does not begin only at the moment of birth; and death does not imply the end of everything. Actually, we existed before we were born, and we will have another life after death. The cycle of life and death will continue endlessly, which is determined by our **karma**. (The energy that is left behind by our actions or thoughts, be it good or evil, is referred to as "karma".) The good and evil karma of this life and past lives will also affect our future lives. If we improve ourselves and become a better person in this life, we will create good prospects for our future. If not, we may lose our human status in the next life. Thus, the Buddha Dharma says, "We reap what we sow".

reincarnation 转世，再生	salvation 救赎，超度	damnation 罚入地狱
filial piety 孝道，孝心	karma（印度教和佛教的）业，因果报应	
purgatory 炼狱		

Christianity

Death is one of the most important events in the Christian religion, as it is the end of a person's earthly life and the beginning of eternal life in heaven, in the presence of God. According to Christianity, each person's soul leaves his or her body at death and goes to an afterlife in heaven or hell. Catholics also believe in the existence of a middle state between heaven and hell called **purgatory**. Heaven is believed to be a gift from God to those who believe in God and have lived a righteous life. There are several religious practices (such as last rites) that take place before and after the death of a Christian to prepare the soul for the afterlife and honor the deceased's religious life.

2. Chinese Child Birth VS Western Child Birth

Traditionally families have been the **cornerstone** of Chinese society. Chinese take blood ties and **lineage** as the essence. They forge strong family bonds and build the extended family network based on the blood relations. In

order to have thriving families, Chinese have advocated the productivity and fertility of women. Women in the ancient China were encouraged to bear as many children as possible. If a wife was **infertile**, according to the law, the husband was allowed to divorce his wife and send her away. This could be explained by the fact that Chinese society was, and in many ways still is, a Confucian one. Confucianism claimed that: "There are three things which are **unfilial**, the worst is to have no offspring." So producing offspring (mainly male children) was the uppermost duty of marriages in the past. And in a **patriarchal** society, fathers ruled the family with absolute authority, and children should be obedient to their fathers and take care of them when they got old due to Confucian filial obligation. So many Chinese people were willing to produce more offspring partly because they wanted children to secure their old life. Although today people are more and more casual about it, most people still prefer to have children in their lives.

cornerstone 基石	lineage 宗系，血统	infertile 不能生育的
unfilial 不孝的	patriarchal 父权制的	

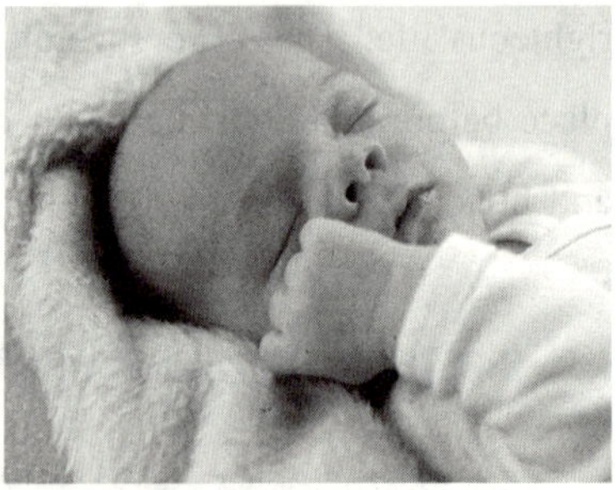

However, Westerners assert individuality and hold a strong sense of equality and independence. Under the influence of Christianity, they believe all the people are equal, including parents and children. Parents have their freedom in deciding whether to have children and how many children to have. The new life is also considered as an independent entity. In the process of their growth, they are entitled to the human rights to live as an individual and to make their own decisions regardless of young age. When they reach adulthood at the age of 18, they must work to support themselves. Westerners take self-reliance as their core value, and family ties are not as close as that of the Chinese people. They tend to view family relationships as more temporary and unstable.

3. Longevity Noodles VS Birthday Cakes

Longevity noodles are indispensable food for birthdays in China. Typically, the dish is only made with wheat noodles, because rice noodles are too delicate and break easily. Noodles are a symbol of longevity in Chinese culture. It is considered very unlucky to cut a **strand** of noodles, which means a shortened lifespan. In some areas, it is also considered a taboo to fill up noodles to the **brim** of bowl, as this would indicate a full lifespan. It's said that the idea of longevity noodles became popular during the Tang Dynasty. In a poem, Tang Dynasty poet Liu Yuxi once wrote, "Holding up noodles with chopsticks while citing verses to wish a bright future," recording the tradition of eating noodles to celebrate a birthday. Another story is about Emperor Xuan Zong and his wife who experienced a hard time during his reign in the Tang Dynasty. When living resources were scarce, the empress had to exchange a purple **shawl** for a bowl of longevity noodles to give to the emperor for his birthday. The story is an illustration of the custom of eating longevity noodles on birthdays. This tradition has been well preserved until today.

longevity 长寿	strand 股，缕	brim（杯、碗的）口，边沿
shawl 披巾，披肩	tart 甜果馅饼	icing 糖霜（用以装饰糕饼等）
fondant 软糖料	Artemis 阿尔忒弥斯（月神与狩猎女神）	

A birthday cake with lit candles in many countries is as much a part of birthday celebration as longevity noodles in China. Variations of the typical birthday cake include birthday cupcakes, cake pops, pastries and **tarts**. They are baked in a variety of shapes and decorated with **icing** or **fondant**, often in multiple colors. It's said that cakes and candles originated in Ancient Greece. Ancient Greeks baked moon-shaped cakes to offer to **Artemis**, goddess of the moon, as a tribute. They lit candles on the cake to make it glow like the moon. Modern birthday parties stemmed from the 18th century German celebration "Kinderfeste". On the morning of a child's birthday, he or she would receive a cake with lit candles equal to the kid's age, plus one. This extra candle was called the "light of life", representing the hope of another full year lived.

Part IV Reflection and Presentation

1. Introduce some peculiar birth customs in your hometown or in some other places and analyze the underlying reasons.

2. How do the young people in China and America celebrate their birthdays? Please compare and give a report on the similarities and differences.

3. What are the English names Chinese usually choose for themselves? What names are popular with Americans or English people? Conduct a survey and analyze the connotation and appropriateness of these names.

Part V Mini-pedia

1. Baby's 100-Day Birth Celebration

Baby's 100th day celebration is a grand event in China, especially in the old days. Because of fragility of the newborn baby and poor medical conditions at that time, many babies couldn't survive for 100 days. Thus, a baby's 100 days became a milestone for both the child and parents. Usually the parents hold a big banquet for family and friends on that day. Guests present gifts to the baby and offer their blessings. The custom of celebrating a baby's 100-day birth to wish for long life is documented in Meng Yuanlao's *Dong Jing Meng Hua Lu* in Song Dynasty. Until today, in many regions of China, people still follow the practice of holding a feast or taking photos for the baby on that day.

2. Baby Shower Game

Baby shower games also abound through both the Internet and traditional methods. Many test practical child-rearing skills—name that baby food, identify that baby item in the brown paper bag, and name that messy diaper. The messy diaper is created by melting chunks of broken chocolate bars onto the diaper in a microwave. It is passed around the group, and each guest gets a chance to smell the diaper and identify the original candy. The winner does not get to eat the diaper.

References

1. 何其亮，张晔. 英释中国传统文化[M]. 杭州:浙江大学出版社，2015.
2. 束定芳. 中国文化英语教程[M]. 上海:上海外语教育出版社，2016.
3. 徐行言. 中西文化比较[M]. 北京:北京大学出版社，2015.
4. 叶胜年. 中西文化比较教程 [M]. 上海:上海外语教育出版社，2016.
5. 钟敬文. 民俗学概论 [M]. 上海:上海文艺出版社，2009.
6. https://en.wikipedia.org/wiki/Baby_shower.
7. https://en.wikipedia.org/wiki/Birthday.
8. https://en.wikipedia.org/wiki/Christian_name.
9. https://en.wikipedia.org/wiki/Infant_baptism.
10. https://gbtimes.com/traditional-chinese-beliefs-about-pregnancy-and-childbirth.
11. https://image.so.com/view? q=新生儿图片.
12. https://www.pastemagazine.com/articles/2016/07/happy-birthday-longevity-noodles.html.
13. https://www.rd.com/culture/origin-of-birthday-cake/.

Unit 6

Chinese and Western Marriage Customs

Traditional Chinese Wedding

White Wedding

Learning Objectives

- To be familiar with the evolution of marriage forms in China as well as in the Western countries
- To get a better understanding of the different marriage customs in China and Western countries
- To compare the similarities and differences in traditional beliefs about marriage in China and in Western countries and analyze reasons

Lead-in Questions

- What do you know about the marriage customs at home and abroad?
- Do you know any peculiar marriage customs in your hometown or in a Western country?
- What are the differences in marriage philosophy between Chinese people and Westerners?

Part I Chinese Marriage Customs

1. Evolution of Marriage Forms

matrimonial 与婚姻有关的

promiscuous 淫乱的，滥交的

incest 乱伦

consanguine marriage 血缘婚

The traditional Chinese **matrimonial** customs involve complex protocols, forms, rituals and conceptions developed through the long history of China. Over one million years ago, people were in an uncivilized and barbaric state. They had **promiscuous** sexual intercourse regardless of their blood relations. Intercourse between father and daughter or between mother and son was common at that time. As the society developed, some restrictions were imposed on their sexual relationships, which are called "**incest** taboos" by folklorists. These taboos became the origin of marriage, one of which was the restrictions on sexual relationship between mother and son. Later this incest taboo was extended to all women of the mother generation and thus the first marriage form—**consanguine marriage** came into being.

1.1 Consanguine Marriage or Sibling Marriage

the Middle Paleolithic Age 旧石器时代中期

Consanguine marriage is estimated to come into existence in **the Middle Paleolithic Age**. It was a form of group marriage in the same generation of a family clan. In the same family clan, only the marriage of the linear relatives was excluded, like the marriage between an ancestor and his or her offspring, or a parent and his or her child. Brothers and sisters with the same parents and cousins were allowed to get married and became all husbands and wives of one another.

The legend of Fuxi and Nüwa proves the history of consanguineous marriages in ancient times. In some traditional literary works and folk songs, people prefer to use "brother" and "sister" to address their lover, which is a clear reflection of the ancient custom of consanguine marriage.

1.2 Punaluan Marriage

Punaluan marriage 族外婚

"Punalua" is a Hawaiian word for multiple sexual relationships, that is, an **exogamous** marriage that excluded the sexual relations between brothers and sisters from the same mother and from the collateral family as well. Instead, it allowed the group marriage of different families. A group of brothers were married to a group of sisters, or in the group marriage the husbands were of the same kinship group and the wives were members of another kinship group. It was **polygamous** outside the family clan. The wife could have two or more husbands, the same was true of the husband in such a group marriage.

exogamous 族外婚的

polygamous 多配偶(制)的

The practice of punaluan marriage is documented in many historical books and folklores. ***The History of the Late Han Dynasty*** recorded a story like this:

The History of the Late Han Dynasty 《后汉书》

Long time ago, there was a girl named Shayi in the Lao Mountain of southwestern China. One day when she was fishing in a river, she was suddenly knocked by a piece of wood in the stomach. Shortly afterwards, she found herself pregnant and then she gave birth to ten sons. They grew into a clan with the youngest son named Jiulong selected as their chieftain. At the root of Lao Mountain, there lived another family with ten daughters. Then the ten sons and ten daughters got married and gave birth to many children. Till the first century A D, they developed into a big clan—the Ailaoyi clan with a population of approximately ten thousand.

The Discourse of the States《国语》

The Discourse of the States also recorded the intermarriage among two or more clans. Huang Di and Yan Di were offspring of punaluan marriage between the young men of the Shaodian clan and the young women of the Youjiao clan. Later they developed into two big clans. The Ji clan of Huang Di and Jiang clan of Yan Di became an intermarriage group and practiced intermarriage for many generations.

matrilineal 母系的

the Big Dipper 北斗七星

Another interesting phenomenon in Chinese legends and mythology is that almost no saint in the primitive **matrilineal** society had a father. It could be explained by the custom and feature of the punaluan marriage. Since it was a group marriage outside the family clan, it was difficult to identify the father of a child. People had to explain the pregnancy as a result of the unusual confrontation with some supernatural or transcendental force. For example, Huang Di was conceived when his mother saw a lighting flashing around the **Big Dipper**; Yan Di was conceived when his mother met a dragon soaring to the sky; Jiandi was pregnant and give birth to Qi after eating the swallow's egg by accident.

1.3 Pairing Marriage

Pairing marriage 对偶婚

It was basically characterized by the cohabitation of a man and a woman from different clans for a period of time, with the exclusion of the opening sharing of husbands and wives as in the primitive group marriage. It came into being in the transition period from the matrilineal society to the **patrilineal** society. In the early stage of pairing marriage, a husband moved in and lived with his wife's family, and their children adopted their mother's family name. Hereafter, they could continue to stay together or look for another wife or husband, so it was quite common for a man to have a chief wife among his many wives, and for a woman to have a chief husband among others. In the latter pattern of paring marriages, the man lived mainly with his wife's family, which developed into the "**uxorilocal marriage**".

patrilineal 父系的

uxorilocal marriage 入赘婚

According to ***The Records of Emperors***, Emperor Ku had four wives, among which Jiang Yuan was the chief wife and had stable cohabitation with Ku.

The Records of Emperors《帝王世纪》

1.4 Individual Marriage

Individual Marriage 个体婚，亦称单偶婚

Around 4000-5000 years ago, the Chinese society was finally transformed from the matrilineal one to the patrilineal one. With the emergence of private property and the establishment of **patriarchy**, men had the supreme power in family life and social life. The pairing marriage developed into the individual **monogamous** marriage (monogamy was for the women only, but not for the men). Through the stable monogamous private family, the men could ensure the

patriarchy 父权制，家长制

monogamous 单配偶

bequeath 遗赠

purity of his children's bloodline and **bequeath** their property to their own descendants.

Individual monogamous marriage is a big advance in the marriage history of humankind. During its development, many patterns of the individual marriage came forth successively, such as the marriage by service, the marriage by capture, the marriage by purchase and the arranged marriage.

marriage by service 服役婚

1.4.1 Marriage by Service

The marriage by service, also called the "Test Marriage", was formed in the transformation of the family organization. In the patrilineal society, the husband-to-be was required to work for the wife's family for a certain period of time without being paid before taking the wife back to his clan for the individual marriage. For example, according to ***Records of the Grand Historian***, Emperor Shun wanted to marry E'huang, Emperor Yao's daughter. First, he went to Emperor Yao's home to work for him, cultivating, fishing, making pottery and doing some other chores. His performance was observed and evaluated by Emperor Yao and his daughter. After Shun had fulfilled his service, Emperor Yao approved of their marriage, and beyond that, he gave Nvying, E'huang's younger sister, to him as the "secondary wife".

Records of the Grand Historian《史记》

marriage by capture 掠夺婚

1.4.2 Marriage by Capture

The Book of Changes recorded this marriage custom as "A bandit-like man, on the back of a pinto horse, came to a woman's home with weapons in hand, seized the crying woman from her families and forced her to go with him." The "bandit-like" man was not a real **bandit**, but the husband-

The Book of Changes《易经》

bandit 土匪，强盗

to-be. He led his men to take his wife-to-be back home.

Marriage by capture was the transitional marriage pattern from pairing marriage to individual marriage. As women had been used to living in their mothers' family and were reluctant to go to their husbands' homes, men had to force their wives to leave for their homes by **plundering**.

plunder 掠夺，抢劫

Marriage by capture is still common among some ethnic minority groups in China such as the Yao, Miao, Yi and Dai people. But as time goes by, it becomes an entertaining game between two families to create the happy atmosphere at the wedding.

1.4.3 Marriage by Purchase

marriage by purchase 买卖婚

Marriage by purchase was a product of the patrilineal system and the presence of private property. In a patriarchal society, women were taken as personal belongings. The individual marriage required the wife to live with the husband, which means the husband claimed the ownership of this private property. To compensate economically for the loss of the woman's family, the husband had to offer free service to them. With the increased productivity, people had surplus products and began to substitute grain or livestock for free service. Later it was developed into the **betrothal** gifts. Marriage by purchase was considered as a substitute for the marriage by service and marriage by capture, since it was a more peaceful way to trade material objects for the brides instead of plundering.

betrothal 婚约，订婚

1.4.4 The Arranged Marriage

arranged marriage 聘娶婚

The arranged marriage was also called "**etiquette marriage**", in which the union of a man and a woman was

etiquette marriage 礼俗婚

based on certain rites or etiquette during the whole process from the proposal to the wedding. Most of the rites had been preserved as part of the traditional customs, with the Confucian doctrine as the fundamental concept. The arranged marriage was acknowledged by the society as the dominant pattern since the establishment of the individual marriage.

six rituals 六礼

The Book of Rites 《礼记》

Ji Dan 周公姬旦

The relatively mature arranged marriage took shape in the Zhou Dynasty with "**six rituals**" recorded in ***The Book of Rites***. The "six rituals" were invented or compiled on the wisdom and experiences of the predecessors by Duke Zhou (**Ji Dan**), a famous political figure in the early Zhou Dynasty. The arranged marriage was first popularized in the ruling class and among the nobility, later it was spread to the civilians in **the Spring and Autumn Period**. According to ***The Etiquette*** and *The Book of Rites*, the so-called "six rituals" of marriage referred to the six procedures and relative rites in the whole process of a marriage:

the Spring and Autumn Period 春秋时期

The Etiquette《仪礼》

—Proposing a marriage 纳采

—Asking birthdates 问名

—Matching birthdates 纳吉

—Presenting betrothal gifts 纳征

—Selecting an auspicious wedding date 请期

—Holding a wedding ceremony 亲迎

2. Rituals and Customs of the Arranged Marriage

2.1 Parents' Authority

The Chinese people considered marriage as sacred in

ancient times, for they believed any couple's marriage was authorized by heaven's will, which was also referred to as "the marriage **preordained** in one's life". Therefore, the idea that marriage came by destiny became the underlying principle to guide the procedures and customs.

preordain 注定

However, "heaven's will" or "destiny" is something abstract. In a patrilineal society, the prospective couples' parents (especially fathers) became the spokespeople for the will of heaven. The parents' authority could not be challenged and they made the final decision in their children's marriage. Children were not only viewed as private property, but also as a means to safeguard and promote the interests of the clan or the family by marriage. Parents' authority and dominating role in the children's marriage was a typical feature of the arranged marriage, and the so-called "destiny" becomes a synonym of "parents' sanction".

2.2 Marriage Considerations

Prospective couple should be of marriageable age. According to ***The Rites of Zhou*** and *The Book of Rites*, a man's marriageable age usually ranged from 20 to 30, and for a woman, it was from 15 to 20 before Qin Dynasty. After **the Warring States Period**, girls were expected to marry at an earlier age owing to the labor shortage caused by frequent wars. The Northern Song Dynasty saw a gradual rise in marriageable age. In Qing Dynasty a man generally married at around 20, a girl at 17 or 18. The age gap between men and women also needed to be appropriate, with a maximum gap of 10 to 12 years.

The Rites of Zhou 《周礼》

the Warring States Period 战国时期

The groom's family and bride's family should have well-matched social status. This idea could date back to Zhou Dynasty that spouse selection should take into account the two families' social ranks and background. Marriage alliances among the families of the same social class were quite common, especially among the nobility. The notion of strict hierarchy in marriage was **ingrained** in Chinese culture.

ingrained 根深蒂固的

The prospective couple's talents and appearances were important factors accounting for a harmonious marriage. When choosing a spouse, a man attached importance to the appearance and disposition of a woman, while a woman placed value on a man's virtues and talents.

Wealth was an important standard to judge whether they were a good match in marriage. The bridegroom's family expected a large **dowry**, while the bride's family expected abundant **betrothal gifts**. The amount of money from both families was an important factor to consider when giving consent to the marriage.

dowry 嫁妆

betrothal gifts 聘礼，彩礼

2.3 Matchmaker's Words to Guarantee Marriage

Matchmaker's words to guarantee marriage 媒妁之言

The matchmaker played an important role in authorizing marriage in the **feudal society** of ancient China. Official matchmakers had the function similar to the marriage registration office today. They provided legal testimony of a marriage. From Tang Dynasty onwards, the matchmakers' importance was written into the legal regulations. ***The Tang Code*** prescribed, "Marriage should be conducted under the guidance of the matchmakers... If a marriage is conducted illegally, the matchmaker will be punished."

feudal society 封建社会

The Tang Code《唐律疏议》

2.4 Rituals of the Arranged Marriage

In ancient China, the pre-wedding discussion (carried out in private) began with a proposal from the groom's side, delivered by the matchmaker, together with gifts as a token of sincerity. In the pre-Qin period, people offered wild geese as **betrothal gifts**. After the Qin and Han Dynasties, the type of gifts changed greatly, but they were never costly. If the gift was accepted by the woman, the man's family would ask the matchmaker to take another gift to the woman's family for exchanging more detailed information (name, birth time, the birth place, the names and relevant information of three parental generations, etc). The exact time of birth was referred to as **eight Chinese characters** to describe the year, month, day and hour that one was born in, and it should be written on the red paper. Then the two families would study the information and ask the fortune-teller to judge whether the marriage was suitable.

betrothal gifts 纳采礼

eight Chinese characters 八字

Generally speaking, if the bride's parents gave their consent, the groom's family **offered** them some **minor betrothal gifts** to formally confirm their **matrimonial** relationship. In ancient marriages, the acceptance of the betrothal gifts was a symbol of engagement. The gifts mainly included the jewelry (necklaces, earrings, bangles and rings), tea, meat, wine or others. The ceremony of offering the betrothal gifts was also called "the tea ceremony" and the acceptance of the gifts by the woman was called "**taking the tea**".

offer minor betrothal gifts 纳征，下聘礼，放小定

matrimonial 婚姻的

taking the tea 吃茶订婚

In ***A Dream of Red Mansions***, Wang Xifeng said

A Dream of Red Mansions《红楼梦》

jokingly to Daiyu, "Since you have taken our tea, why not marry brother Baoyu?" Her words were actually a pun generated from this custom.

send major betrothal gifts 放大定

Along with the feast and the celebration, the match-maker and the relatives from bridegroom's family **sent major betrothal gifts** to the bride's family in the morning. The amount of the gifts should correspond to the economic and social status of the groom's family (The gifts generally included jewelry, cloth for the bride, wine, money, food, tea. They should be in even numbers). The gifts were shown in the courtyard to the neighbors, thus raising the bride's status at her husband's home. In return, the bride's family also sent some gifts back to the groom's family. Then it came to the exchange of marriage certificates. There were two kinds: official and private. The former was issued by local government and the latter was signed by the match-maker and parents of both families. The latter certificate was usually recognized by the local government and the law.

auspicious day 良辰吉日

the Five Elements 五行(金、木、水、火、土)

augury 占卜

Next, it was time to fix the day of the wedding by both families, or rather the bridegroom's family. The choice of the wedding date must be cautious and it must be an "**auspicious day**". People would turn to **the Five Elements** for guidance, or ask the fortune-teller to choose the date by **augury**.

trousseau 嫁妆

Once both sides had agreed on the wedding date, wedding preparations began. While the family of the bridegroom prepared the bridal chamber and furniture, the bride's family engaged in the preparation of the **trousseau**. After receiving the betrothal gifts from the bridegroom, the bride's family would start to send the dowry. Before the dowry arrived at the groom's residence, people would beat drums and blow pipes or set off fireworks to welcome its arrival.

On the night before the wedding, the bride usually expressed her sorrow, fear, or even anger at her departure by crying and singing sad songs. She **improvised** on the lyrics to express her gratefulness towards her parents, condemn the **paternalism** and the arranged marriage, and curse the matchmaker. As time went by, this behavior became a universal ritual before the wedding.

improvise 即兴创作
paternalism 家长作风，专制

On the wedding day, the first part of the wedding ceremony was to escort the bride from her home to the bridegroom's residence where the wedding ceremony would be held. In the southern part of China, usually two **sedan chairs** were prepared, a beautifully decorated one for the bride and a wooden one for the bridegroom. While in the north, only one sedan chair was prepared and the bridegroom would be riding a horse in front of the sedan chair, with a big red flower on his chest.

sedan chairs 轿子

When the groom arrived at the bride's home, the bride's family would close the door to stop the bridal carriage from going in. It was called "**stopping the marriage**". Originally it signified their reluctance to part with the bride. Gradually it developed into a custom to ask the groom for some treat or money. Amidst the happy music, the bride would dress up and make up. She would change her hairstyle and wear traditional wedding dress. The dress included a red coat and a skirt **embroidered** with a variety of auspicious

stopping the marriage 拦门
embroider 刺绣

phoenix coronet 凤冠

designs, and a **phoenix coronet** decorated with pearls and jade. The bride would cover her face by draping a piece of red cloth sent by the bridegroom's family over her head. Then the bride should be carried into the sedan chair by her father, brother or uncle, and sent to the groom's home.

The formal wedding ceremony followed. People would set up an altar called "Heaven and Earth Table" in the wedding hall. When the auspicious time came, incense and candles would be lit, music would be played, and fireworks would be set off. As the music stopped, the master of ceremony would declare the beginning of the ceremony. The bridegroom and the bride would stand side by side, with the bride on the right and the groom on the left. The new couple would "first bow to the Heaven and Earth, second to their ancestors, third to their parents and fourth to each other (or 3 bows)".

holding a red ribbon 牵巾，绾同心结

steelyard 杆秤

sitting on the bed 坐帐

sitting on happiness 坐福

nuptial cup 合卺酒，交杯酒

Sending the couple to the bridal chamber was another ritual. It was called "**holding a red ribbon**". The groom "pulled" the bride into their chamber. Next the groom would lift his bride's red veil using the arm of a Chinese **steelyard**. The couple was supposed to sit on the bed side by side. It was called "**sitting on the bed**" or "**sitting on happiness**". Some people would throw sweets, peanuts and multicolored coins on the bed and in the chamber. The most important ceremony in the bridal chamber was called "a happy reunion", or "**nuptial cup**". The couple drank from the nuptial cup in return, or drank half of the wine in one cup, then exchanged the cups and drank the other half of the wine. The climax of the wedding was not the banquet, but teasing in the bridal chamber. "**Teasing the bride**" or "**teasing the bridegroom**" referred to the celebration in the bridal chamber. Relatives and friends would play jokes or tricks on the couple to have fun.

teasing the bride/ bridegroom 闹洞房

On the following day after wedding, in the company of the husband, the bride had to meet the groom's parents, uncles and brothers. Another post-wedding ceremony was the ritual of "**worshiping the Kitchen God**" or "cooking for the bride's parents-in-law".

worshiping the Kitchen God 祭灶礼

The newly weds would **visit the bride's family** one month after the wedding, that is, after the honeymoon. (Some paid the visit on the fourth day, or the ninth day). On that day, the bride's family would invite some relatives and host a bouquet for the newly weds.

visit the bride's family 回门

3. Marriage Customs of Chinese Ethnic Minority Groups

3.1 Mosuo's Walking Marriage

walking marriage 走婚

Mosuo people near Lugu Lake of Ninglang County, Yunnan Province still keep the tradition of walking marriage. Their society has remained matrilineal. They call their partners in walking marriages ***xiaobo*** (love companion). The man visits the woman's home upon invitation, stays in a "flower room" over the night, and returns to his own home at daybreak. Hereafter, they can continue to stay together or look for another *xiaobo*.

xiaobo 肖波

3.2 Yao, Yi, Dai's "Marriage by Capture"

The bridegroom, in the company of his friends, takes a

capture the bride “抢新娘”

broadsword to “**capture the bride**” from her parents' family. The groom has to chase the bride for three times in public, or it can be conducted in secrecy. The groom captures the bride by surprise while she is away from her parents' home. However, no matter how the “capture” takes place, the groom has to obtain consent from the bride's parents in advance.

In the Yi and Dai ethnic groups, the bride and groom's families invite relatives to join in the capture and defense. The bride pretends to cry for help and relatives pretend to rescue her. However, the final winner must be the groom. Today, the custom of “marriage by capture” becomes a fun game for the wedding.

3.3 Zhuang's Spouse Selection by Singing

Young men and women in the Zhuang ethnic group can't get married without singing. They hold regular song fairs to express their love in public. During the process of singing, those who have an attachment for another can leave the group and begin dating privately. If they get along well with each other, they can ask their respective parents to prepare for the wedding. For example, Liu Sanjie married her beloved man through songs.

3.4 The Tujia's Crying at a Bride's Departure

The night before the wedding, the bride's friends will visit her and say goodbye. As it is hard to part with her friends, the bride can't help crying and singing in a **woeful** tone. The “lyrics” are so moving that the family and friends will shed tears and sing sorrowful songs. This collective

woeful 悲惨的，忧伤的

activity will continue till late at night.

Part II Western Marriage Customs

1. White Wedding

1.1 Origin

A white wedding is a traditional formal or semi-formal wedding originating in Great Britain. It is derived from the white color of the wedding dress, which first became popular with upper class people after Queen Victoria wore a white lace dress at her wedding. Now the term also refers to the entire Western wedding routine, especially in the Christian religious tradition, which generally includes a ceremony and a reception.

1.2 Preparations

The full white wedding today typically requires the family to arrange for printed or engraved wedding invitations, musicians, decorations such as flowers or candles, clothes and flowers for **bridesmaids**, **groomsmen**, a flower girl and a ring bearer. They may also add optional features, such as a guest book or commemorative wedding leaflets.

bridesmaid 伴娘

groomsmen 伴郎

1.3 Ceremony

When the guests arrive for a wedding, the **ushers**, if

usher 男傧相,引座员

any, help the guests to their seats. In a typical white wedding ceremony, the bride and groom will stand side by side (the bride standing to the left of the groom) at the front of the church or other venue throughout most or all the ceremony. Usually some guests prefer to sit on the side closer to the person they know best. Typically, the bride's family is seated on the left facing the altar and the groom's family on the right. The first few rows are generally reserved for close family members or friends.

escort 陪同

According to different customs, age, situation and personal preferences, the bride may walk alone or be **escorted** by her father, both of her parents, one or more relatives she wishes to honor, or the groom. In Swedish white weddings, the bride and groom usually go down the aisle together. Likewise, some couples choose to have the groom escorted to the altar by his family.

page boys 男花童

Whether the bride is the first or the last of the wedding party to enter the church varies in different countries. In the US, the bride is typically the last, coming after the rest of the wedding party. In the UK, she leads the procession, followed by bridesmaids, flower girls and **page boys**. Sometimes the groom is already present in the church; at other times, he and any groomsmen form part of the procession. The music called "a wedding march" is played during this procession, no matter what songs are played.

If the wedding is part of a religious service, then conventionally the service begins after the arrival of the participants, commonly with a prayer, blessing, or ritual greeting. During the ceremony, the couple makes marriage vows to each other in front of the marriage **officiant**. The ceremony might include the singing of **hymns** or performance of a popular song, a *Bible* reading, or a poem.

officiant 主祭
hymn 赞美诗，圣歌

After the wedding ceremony ends, the bride, groom, officiant and two witnesses generally go off to a side room to sign the wedding register in the United Kingdom or the state-issued marriage license in the United States. Without the signing of the register or the marriage license, the marriage is not legally acknowledged.

Afterward, guests may cheer the departure of the couple from the church by throwing flower petals, confetti, birdseed, or rice over them. Or they may blow bubbles at the couple instead of throwing the previously mentioned items.

1.4 Reception

After that, a reception is held at which the newly married couple greets the guests in a receiving line. Although it's now commonly called a reception regardless of the style of party, wedding celebrations range from simple receptions, dinner parties to grand wedding balls.

Food and drinks are served, particularly including a wedding cake. Wedding cakes are often **multi-tiered** and elaborately decorated with white icing. Cutting the wedding cake often becomes a ritual, complete with sharing a symbolic bite of the cake. During the reception, some short speeches or toasts may be given in honor of the couple.

multi-tiered 多层的

If there is dancing, the bride and groom, as the guests of honor, are expected to be the first people to begin dancing. This is usually termed the bridal waltz, even if the contrive 设计，策划

couple has arranged for a different style of music. Some families **contrive** a series of arranged dances between the newlyweds and their parents, or other members of the wedding party, and guests are expected to watch the performances. Wedding dance creates the happy atmosphere and makes a fun experience.

As the guests of honor, the newlywed couple is the first to leave the party. Ancient Romans would shower the newly-weds with wheat as they departed, which symbolized fertility. By the Middle Ages, wheat was replaced with rice, which was also considered to be a symbol of fruitfulness. However, the tradition of throwing rice is not practiced by all couples today.

In Western cultures, guests might tie tin cans or a sign saying "Just Married" to the bumper of the couple's car, if they depart in their own car rather than a hired one.

2. British Wedding Customs

banns of marriage (教堂的)结婚预告

impending 即将发生的

parish(有独立教堂和牧师的)教区

(1) Invitations are extended to the guests to the wedding or the reception. For church weddings, "**banns of marriage**" (or simply known as the banns or bans) are read or published three Sundays before the ceremony, which are the public announcement of an **impending** marriage in a Christian **parish** church or in the town council.

(2) Traditionally the bride stands to the right of her Father (one who symbolically "gives away" the bride. If her father is deceased or otherwise unavailable, another male relative, often an uncle or brother, will give the bride away)

at the wedding ceremony. They lead the procession, followed by the bridesmaids, flower girls and pageboys.

(3) A typical order of service will run as follows: Entrance of the bride, welcome and introduction by the **celebrant**, hymn, readings, **sermon**, exchange of marriage vows, prayers/hymn, the signing of the register, the final blessing and exit.

celebrant 宗教礼仪主持人

sermon 布道，讲道

(4) A wedding is often followed or accompanied by a wedding reception, which in some areas may be known as the "Wedding Breakfast", which is a feast given to the newlyweds and guests after the wedding. Nowadays the wedding breakfast is not normally a morning meal, but it's referred to as "breakfast" as the newlywed couple is starting a new day together from the moment of their marriage. The wedding feast is their first meal as newlyweds. Another reason is that traditionally couples used to **fast** from the night before their wedding, only breaking the fast after their vows. The modern Wedding Breakfast includes the service of food to guests ranging from traditional roasts, buffets, to regional treats.

fast 禁食，斋戒

(5) Wedding etiquette dictates that the top table should be from the left: Chief bridesmaid, groom's father, bride's mother, groom, bride (the new couple in the middle), bride's father, groom's mother, **best man**. Today people are more casual about it. They may try a non-traditional plan with two or three top tables. Parents can host their own tables, leaving the bride and groom to sit with friends.

best man 首席男傧相，(主)伴郎

(6) The first wedding speech is given by the father,

ending with a toast to the bride and groom. Then the groom thanks the bride's parents and guests before making a toast to the bridesmaids. Finally it's the best man.

(7) The newlyweds have the first dance. Etiquette dictates the groom should also dance with both mothers. The bride should dance with both fathers, the mother of the bride with the father of the groom and vice versa. The best man also dances with the chief bridesmaid.

grandiose 浮夸的

white-frosted 覆有白色糖霜的

(8) Cutting the cake is an important part of the reception. Traditionally, a wedding cake is a **grandiose**, tiered, **white-frosted** fruitcake, often with a couple of little figures on top of the cake, but today anything is acceptable.

bouquet 花束，新娘捧花

garter 袜带

(9) A bride may throw her **bouquet** to the assembled group of all unmarried women in attendance. It's believed that the person who catches it will be the next to wed. A fairly recent equivalent is the groom throwing the bride's **garter** to the assembled unmarried men; the man who catches it is supposedly the next to wed.

stag party 单身汉派对

hen party 准新娘聚会

(10) The groom's male friends will hold a "**stag party**"(also known as a stag night or weekend, or stag do) for the groom shortly before his wedding, while the bride holds a "**hen party**" the night before.

(11) Another Victorian tradition is for brides to wear or carry "something old, something new, something borrowed, something blue" during the service. It is considered good luck to do so. Often the bride attempts to have one item that meets all of these needs, such as a borrowed blue handkerchief which is "new to her" but lent by her

grandmother (thus making it old). Another peculiar custom is to put six pence or a coin in the bride's shoe to bring prosperity.

3. American Wedding Customs

Most weddings in the United States follow a similar pattern to an English wedding. It traditionally follows the white wedding type.

(1) The host sends invitations to the wedding guests, usually one to two months before the wedding. Invitations may most formally be addressed by hand to show the importance of the occasion. Large numbers of invitations may be printed or engraved. Receiving an invitation does not impose any obligation on the invitee other than promptly accepting or declining the invitation, and offering congratulations to the couple.

(2) It's customary that invited guests who attend the wedding choose to give gift to the newlywed couple. Wrapped gifts can be brought to the wedding ceremony or reception, but it's considered thoughtful to have them delivered to the address on the wedding invitation or to the address given with the couple's **bridal registry**. Typical gifts are useful household items, such as dishes, silverware, kitchen utensils and appliances, or towels. Guests are not obligated to use the couple's registry information.

bridal registry (为避免重复赠送结婚礼物而编制的)购物单

A bridal registry or wedding registry, is a service provided by a website or retail store that assists engaged couples in the communication of gift preferences to wedding guests. Selecting items from store stock, the couple lists desired items and files this list with the chosen merchant. The list is then made available to wedding guests, either by the couple's family or by the merchant. Upon the purchase of a listed item, the merchant updates the gift registry accordingly. In addition to providing valuable information for the buyer, the system helps prevent the receipt of duplicate or unwanted gifts, potentially saving time for both the giver and the recipient.

(3) The groom's friends throw a party for the groom, called a "bachelor party". It usually involves alcohol and **racy** entertainment, as this is supposedly the groom's last chance to engage in **debauchery** before marriage. It has become increasingly popular for the bride's friends to organize similar "**bachelorette**" parties.

racy (风格)活泼的，不雅的
debauchery 放纵
bachelorette 未婚女子

(4) The wedding shower is very popular in America. It has a long tradition and typically it's attended only by women. The bride may wear a hat or carry a bouquet fashioned from the ribbons and bows that decorated the gift packages. It is once an occasion for gift giving, the wedding shower today becomes generally more casual and fun.

(5) The bridal shower is a pre-wedding celebration in honor of the bride. The bridal shower is usually hosted by the bridesmaids, the bride or groom's mother, or other close female relatives. Traditionally it is an opportunity for guests to shower the bride with gifts to help set up her new home. While the types of gifts and bridal shower games or themes

have become much more varied in recent years, fundamentally it's still a daytime women-only event in celebration of the bride's upcoming marriage.

(6) American brides usually wear a white, off-white, silver, or other very light-colored dress, particularly at their first marriage. Brides may choose any color, although black is strongly discouraged by some as it is the color of mourning in the West.

(7) After the wedding, the bride and groom traditionally leave for their honeymoon which could last for a few days or even several weeks. This period is significant for the **consummation** of the marriage.

consummation 圆满

(8) Another tradition is unmarried young women collected a **trousseau** in a "Hope Chest" in anticipation of married life. A "Hope Chest", also called dowry chest, **cedar** chest or glory box, is a piece of furniture traditionally used to collect items such as clothing and household linen, **cutlery**, etc. Girls used it to plan and save for their future marriage. The collection of a trousseau was a common **coming-of-age** rite until approximately the 1950s. (In the United Kingdom, the term is "bottom drawer").

trousseau 嫁妆

cedar 雪松木

cutlery 餐具

coming-of-age 成年

Some customs are not peculiar to America or Britain. Due to cultural transmission, it's not unusual to find some customs in one culture are integrated into some other cultures.

Part III Comparison and Contrast

1. Confucian Marriage VS Christian Marriage

Hierarchical Marriage

The feudal society in China was characterized by rigid **hierarchy**. Under the influence of Confucianism, the core value of the traditional marriage was patriarchy, that is, it prescribed a strict male-dominant hierarchical system. This view made the husband the "ruler" over "his" wife and "his" household. They considered the husband-father to be "**sovereign**" over the family. They were the family leader, protector and decision-maker. They called for a wife to show complete obedience to them. In modern times, these ideas are rejected and a sense of equality between men and women has been fully developed in China.

hierarchy 等级制度	sovereign 最高统治者	egalitarianism 平等主义
proponent 支持者	Gentile 非犹太人	

Christian Marriage

In Christian marriage, the union between a man and a woman is instituted and ordained by God as the lifelong relationship between husband and wife. Conservative Christians consider marriage as the most intimate human relationship, a gift from God, and a sacred institution. Christian **egalitarianism** interprets the *New Testament* as teaching complete equality of authority and responsibility between the man and woman in marriage. Christian egalitarians believe in an equal partnership of the wife and husband with neither being designated as the leader in the marriage or family. Its **proponents** teach "the fundamental biblical principle of the equality of all human beings before God". "There is neither Jew nor **Gentile**, neither slave nor free, nor is there male and female, for you are all one in Christ Jesus."

2. Chinese Marriage Philosophy VS Western Marriage Philosophy

Chinese Marriage Philosophy

(1) Marriage involves personal commitment and responsibility. Once two people get married, they are supposed to commit themselves to this **marital** relationship for life. Although sometimes they feel uncomfortable or unhappy living with each other, they would still choose to **compromise** and maintain the marital relationship for the sake of children or "face".

(2) Chinese people are always cautious and prudent to choose their **spouse**. Even though they love each other, they would take his or her characters, education, family background, income, health and career into account, because it is a decision that will determine his or her future life.

(3) Marriage means devotion and sacrifice in the eyes of Chinese women. After getting married, many Chinese women give up their own lifestyle, hobbies, etc., and put their whole heart into family life and children.

(4) Marriage is not personal, and it involves two families, their parents-in-law and other relatives, who will interfere in their family life. In China, there are many stories about conflicts between the mother and daughter-in-law, which may lead to the **disintegration** of the marriage.

marital 婚姻的　compromise 妥协，互让　spouse 配偶
disintegration 瓦解　subordinate 隶属的，次要的

Western Marriage

(1) Marriage is a private matter and no one can intervene without permission.

(2) They have the freedom and right to love and to be loved. Once they find that their marriage is a mistake, they will make the second choice, because it is inhuman to force two people who don't love each other to live together.

(3) Marriage or love seems relatively "simple" to Westerners. If they love someone, they are brave to express or accept love without hesitation.

(4) Marriage has become primarily a personal contract between two equals seeking love, stability and happiness. No one is **subordinate** to the other. After getting married, they share the housework or the responsibility of raising children, etc. But they still assert their individuality and have their own space in the marital relationship.

(5) Marriage is personal and it's built on mutual affection. They expect their spouse to be their soul mate.

3. Scattering Nuts on Bed VS Throwing Rice on the Couple

In the Han Dynasty, Emperor Wu accepted Li Yannian's younger sister as an imperial **concubine**. On the wedding day, Li Yannian (a famous musician) asked the emperor and his sister to sit on the bed. Amidst the festive music, he held a plateful of **red dates**, chestnuts, peanuts and **longans**, and scattered them around while dancing and singing. The maids standing by the two sides shouted together: "Dates and chestnuts, have a baby as soon as possible!"

In China, this custom originated in Han Dynasty and became prevalent in the Tang Dynasty. When the couple were "sitting on the bed"(坐帐), people would throw sweets and multicolored coins on the bed and in the **bridal chamber** to wish for **fertility**. When scattering the articles, people would sing a song(撒帐歌). Even today in some regions or countryside, people still have carried on the tradition or custom.

concubine 妃子	red dates 红枣	longan 桂圆	bridal chamber 婚房
fertility 生育	tribute 致敬	confetti 五彩纸屑	

Similarly, in the West, people have the tradition of throwing rice on the newly-wed couple when they leave the church. The tradition could trace back to Ancient Rome. Ancient Romans would shower a newly-wed couple with wheat, which symbolized fertility. By the Middle Ages, wheat was replaced by rice. Showering a new couple with rice was believed to help them have children and keep evil spirits away from the bride and groom. Today the tradition of throwing rice is not practiced by all couples. There are dozens of alternatives to throwing rice that still pay **tribute** to this ancient tradition. Some couples use birdseed, although this can be just as unpleasant as being hit with rice. Guests may choose to throw rose petals or **confetti**, fly paper airplanes or blow bubbles to make for a beautiful photo opportunity.

Part IV Reflection and Presentation

1. Give an introduction to modern marriage customs in China, with elaboration on the evolution of customs. (Some customs are developed from the old ones.)

2. Conduct research on the marriage customs in some foreign countries and introduce some peculiar ones to your classmates. Explore different marriage philosophies in these countries.

Part V Mini-pedia

1. Choosing a Husband by Casting an Embroidered Ball

Compared with the arranged marriage, choosing a husband by casting an embroidered ball was more democratic and progressive. The girl could pick her husband by casting a ball at him. If her choice was acceptable to her parents, they would consent to their marriage. The folklorist Gu Jiegang collected a large amount of evidence to show this custom was very popular among the ethnic minority groups in southwest China. Sometimes it was man who cast his ball to his favorite girl. If the girl brought a cup of tea to the man after accepting the ball, it meant she agreed!

2. Wedding Veil

In America, it is customary for the bride to wear a veil as part of her wedding ensemble. Traditionally the groom is not supposed to see the bride during the day of the wedding until she walks down the aisle. It's considered bad luck to do otherwise. In much older times, the veil was a requirement so that the groom did not see the bride's face before the ceremony was complete. In this way he would not have the opportunity to change his mind about marrying her if he did not like the way she looked.

References

1. 李翠英,等. 婚嫁趣谈[M]. 上海:上海外语教育出版社, 2010.
2. 钟文,等. 中国婚俗文化[M]. 北京:外文出版社, 2010.
3. Wanyan, Shaoyuan. *The Marriage Customs in China*[M]. Shanghai: Shanghai Chinese Classics Publishing House, 2010.
4. https://en.wikipedia.org/wiki/Bridal_registry.
5. https://en.wikipedia.org/wiki/Wedding_customs_by_country.
6. https://en.wikipedia.org/wiki/White_wedding.
7. https://www.brides.com/story/bridal-shower-etiquette.
8. https://www.weddingforward.com/american-wedding-traditions/.
9. https://www.weddingideasmag.com/a-z-of-british-wedding-traditions-and-wedding-etiquette/.

Unit 7
Chinese and Western Holidays and Festivals

The Jade Hare

Easter Bunny

Learning Objectives

- To be familiar with the customs of different holidays and festivals
- To get a better understanding of the cultural connotations of holidays
- To compare and contrast similarities and differences among certain Chinese and Western holidays (such as Easter, Qingming Festival, Halloween) and analyze related customs

Lead-in Questions

- Why were there holidays and festivals? Can you tell the origin of a specific holiday?
- Compare Halloween with Chinese Hungry Ghost Festival. Which one are you familiar with? Discuss with your classmates.
- List customs of the Spring Festival and Christmas and make a comparison between them.

Holidays are an essential part of a country's traditions and culture. Some say the word "holiday" was derived from the word "holyday" which was intended to allow individuals to celebrate or commemorate an event or tradition of cultural or religious significance. Many of the early holidays are associated with harvests or worships. When people cultivated their land, planted crops, celebrated the harvest and enjoyed their fruit, they hold a ceremony and the ceremony gradually became the holidays and festivals.

The word "holiday" has different connotations in different regions. In the United States the word is used exclusively to refer to the nationally, religiously or culturally observed day(s) of rest or celebration, or the events themselves, whereas in the United Kingdom and other Commonwealth nations, the word may refer to the period of time where leave from one's duties has been agreed, and is used as a synonym to the US preferred "vacation". This time is usually set aside for rest, travel, or the participation in recreational activities. In this chapter, "holiday" refers to the widely-accepted rest days with particular customs.

Part I Traditional Chinese Holidays and Festivals

Chinese holidays vary from region to region, from ethnic group to ethnic group. Even at the same area, people may have quite different customs. Traditional holidays are generally celebrated in Chinese speaking regions. However, only the Spring Festival, the Qingming Festival, the Dragon Boat Festival and the Mid-Autumn Festival are statutory public holidays. Some Chinese observe Buddha's Birthday and Chongyang Festival. Most traditional holidays are scheduled according to the Chinese lunar calendar, so the dates of the traditional holidays vary from year to year on the Gregorian calendar.

1. The Spring Festival

Spring Festival, the major festival of the Chinese year, with a 7-day long holiday, is a period of renewal and family reunion, the final days of the old year are given over to intense preparation, as houses are cleaned in the belief that disappointments and mistakes are swept away along with the dirt and dust of the past, these days are also the time to settle debts, **resolve arguments** or **return favors**, to avoid carrying any misfortune into the coming year.

resolve argument 解决纠纷
return favor 感恩

The first day of Spring Festival usually begins on the new moon that appears between 21 January and 20 February. As the most brilliant annual event, the traditional holiday celebration lasts longer. Observances traditionally take place from the evening preceding the first day of the year to the Lantern Festival, up to two weeks, and the climax arrives around the Lunar New Year's Eve.

deity 神明
ancestor 先人

The festival was traditionally a time to honor **deities** as well as **ancestors**. Within China, regional customs and traditions concerning the celebration of the New Year vary widely, but decoration of windows and doors with red **paper-cuts** and **couplets** are almost everywhere. Popular themes among these paper-cuts and couplets include that of good fortune or happiness, wealth and longevity. Other activities include lighting firecrackers and giving money in red paper envelopes. For the northern regions of China, dumplings are featured prominently in meals celebrating the festival. People may put candies or coins into the dumplings,

paper-cut 剪纸
couplet 对联

and the one who gets the special dumpling is believed to have good luck in the coming year. People in the south usually eat rice dumplings with sweet fillings.

China during this period is dominated by **iconic** red lanterns, loud fireworks, massive banquets and parades, and the festival even triggers **exuberant** celebrations all around the world.

iconic 标志性的

exuberant 生机勃勃的

In old times, because all stores closed during the Spring Festival, people started the preparation long before the lunar new year. There is a traditional folk song which sings "**sticking the mouth of Kitchen God with Glutinous candy on Dec 23, sweeping the house on Dec 24, making *tofu* on Dec 25, stewing lamb on Dec 26, killing the cock on Dec 27, brewing the dough on Dec 28, steaming *mantou* on Dec 29 and stay up all night on Dec 30**". This folk song sets a system of routine works for Spring Festival preparation.

歌谣意思如下:
二十三糖瓜粘
二十四扫房子
二十五磨豆腐
二十六炖羊肉
二十七杀只鸡
二十八把面发
二十九蒸馒头
三十晚上熬一宿

On 23rd December of the lunar calendar, paper images of the **Kitchen God** are taken down and ceremoniously burned to release his spirit. It is believed that the kitchen God has been guarding the family, observing their goodness and evilness, and now it is time for him to report to the **Jade Emperor** in heaven. Before burning the Kitchen God, incense and candies are offered to him to make sure his lips are smeared with sweet food so that his report on the family will be sweet. The Kitchen God returns to the family on December 30th, when new images are hung on the walls and he begins his watch once again.

Kitchen God 灶王爷

Jade Emperor 玉皇大帝

On the first day of lunar new year, sweeping the floor is

viewed as cleaning away all the good fortune as well. Therefore, Chinese families clean houses before the Spring Festival. Another custom is avoiding throwing away your trash on the first day of the new year. It is said your luckiness may be thrown away, too. On the second day, married couples visit the wives' parents. Husbands bring special gifts to their parents-in-law. On the third day, people go to temples, offering fruit to their ancestors and keep visiting their relatives. On the fourth day, people stay home to get rich. According to the legend, **the God of Wealth** is going to come down and people stay at home to welcome him. So, it's not an appropriate day to visit others. In some areas of China, people stay at home on the third day or fifth day of the new year. On the fifth day, people set off firecrackers to drive away the "**five poor things**": poor in wisdom, poor in learning, poor in words, poor in life, and poor in networking. People get up early on this day to clean the house. Firecrackers are set off as people walk through the door from inside to outside, symbolizing the pushing away of all unlucky things. On the sixth day, stores and restaurants open for shopping and dining. Business owners set off firecrackers as a symbol of good luck and fortune in the new year. Families also empty their homes of rubbish from the day before, as a symbol of throwing away anything unlucky.

the God of Wealth 财神

five poor things 五种穷，分别是智穷、学穷、文穷、命穷、交穷

2. The Qingming Festival (Tomb Sweeping Day)

The Qingming Festival falls on the first day of the fifth solar term of the traditional Chinese calendar. This makes it the 15th day after the **Spring Equinox**, either 4 or 5 April in a given year. During the Qingming Festival, Chinese families visit the tombs of their ancestors to clean the grave sites, pray to their ancestors, and make ritual offerings. Offerings would typically include traditional food dishes, and the burning of incense and **joss paper**. The holiday recognizes the traditional reverence of one's ancestors in Chinese culture.

Spring Equinox 春分

joss paper 烧纸

Many people observe the customs of the **Cold Food Day** on Qingming and don't cook.They can only eat the cold food which is prepared before. The festival originated from the **commemoration** of Jie Zitui, a nobleman of the state of Jin (modern Shanxi) during the Spring and Autumn Period. He followed his master Prince Chong'er to **exile** around China. In their exile, he once even cut meat from his own **thigh** to provide his lord with meat soup. After Chong'er was **enthroned** as duke, he was generous in rewarding those who had helped him. But Jie Zitui refused and retired to his hometown with his elderly mother. Chong'er ordered his men to set fire to the forest in order to force Jie Zitui out. When Jie Zitui and his mother were killed instead, the people of Shanxi **revered** Jie Zitui as an **immortal** and avoided lighting fires the day he died.

Cold Food Day 寒食节(寒食和清明本来是两个节日，但是从唐朝以来，习俗逐渐融合。)

commemoration 纪念

exile 流亡

thigh 大腿

enthrone 使……登基

revere 崇敬

immortal 永生不灭者，神

This is also a day for most people to go hiking or flying kites. The traditional food of the Qingming Festival includes *qingtuan* (green dumplings made of **glutinous rice** and Chinese **mugwort** or barley grass), *sanzi*, *aiba* and *zituimo*.

glutinous rice 糯米

mugwort 艾蒿

The Qingming Festival has been observed by the

ostentatious 卖弄的，讲究排场的

Chinese for over 2, 500 years. It became a public holiday in Chinese mainland in 2008. The present importance of the holiday is credited to Emperor Xuanzong of Tang. To stop the **ostentatious** ceremonies by wealthy citizens, Xuanzong declared that such respects could be formally paid only once a year, on Qingming.

elaborate 复杂的
ancestral 祖先的
posthumous 死后的
filial piety 孝顺

The Qingming Festival commemorates the life of the departed in an **elaborate** set of rituals often mistranslated in the West as **ancestral** worship. Actually, it is a Confucian form of **posthumous** respect and **filial piety** offered to a Chinese person's ancestors, departed relatives, or parents. Not all Chinese persons pray directly to their ancestors in ancestral spirit but almost all observe the Qingming rituals.

3. The Dragon Boat Festival

summer solstice 夏至

The Dragon Boat Festival occurs near the **summer solstice**. The festival now falls on May 5th of the lunar calendar, which is the source of the festival's alternative name, the Double Fifth Festival.

calamus 白菖蒲

The fifth lunar month was considered an unlucky month in ancient times. People believed that natural disasters and illness were common in the fifth month. To get rid of the misfortune, people would put **calamus**, mugwort above the doors in the fifth of May. Since the shape of calamus leaf is like a sword and with the strong smell of the herbal plants, it is believed that the evil spirits will be removed.

centipede 蜈蚣
scorpion 蝎子

In old times, people believed that poisonous animals like snakes, **centipedes** and **scorpions** became active and people might get sick easily because of the environment after this day. Therefore, during the Dragon Boat Festival, people spare no effort in avoiding the bad luck. For example, they paste pictures of the five poisonous creatures on the wall and stick needles in them. People also make a special belly bond with the patterns of five creatures and wrapped them around the abdomen of their children. Big ceremonies and performances develop from these practices in many areas, making the Dragon Boat Festival a day for getting rid of diseases and bad luck.

The best-known story in modern China connects the festival with Qu Yuan. He was the poet and minister of the ancient state of Chu during the Warring States Period. However, Qu Yuan's opposition to allying with the increasingly powerful state of Qin annoyed the king. He was banished and even accused of treason. Twenty-eight years later, Qin captured **Ying**. In despair, Qu Yuan committed suicide by drowning himself in the Miluo River. It is said that the local people, who admired him, raced out in their boats to save him, or at least retrieve his body. When his body could not be found, they dropped balls of glutinous rice into the river so that the fish would eat them instead of Qu Yuan's body. *Zongzi* making and dragon boat racing originated from this story.

Ying 郢，楚国都城

Three of the most widespread activities conducted during the Dragon Boat Festival are racing dragon boats, making and eating *zongzi* and drinking **realgar wine**.

realgar wine 雄黄酒

Dragon boat racing and *Zongzi* have a rich history of ancient ceremonial and ritualistic traditions, which originated in southern central China more than 2, 500 years ago.

Each year, people in the south will hold a dragon boat racing competition. The dragon-shape boat is long and narrow with dragon head, tail and scale. A dragon boat team consists of 20 paddlers sitting two **abreast**, a **cox** who steers the dragon boat and a drummer who sits at the front and boost the morale of the team. Zigui, which is said to be the hometown of Qu Yuan, usually hold a ceremony to commemorate Qu Yuan before the competition. The dragon boat racing is not only popular in China, but in foreign cities with a large population of Chinese immigrants. The International Dragon Boat Festival in Vancouver is well-known all around the world. Each year, different nations send their teams to Vancouver to attend the competition. The festival last three days on the False Creek.

abreast 并列，并肩

cox 舵手

People traditionally wrap *zongzi* in leaves of reed, lotus or banana, forming particular shapes, such as pillow, pyramid and horn. The leaves also give a special aroma and flavor to the glutinous rice and fillings. Choices of fillings vary depending on regions. Northern regions in China prefer sweet *zongzi*, with **bean paste**, **dates** and nuts as fillings. Southern regions in China prefer salty *zongzi*, with a variety of fillings like **marinated** pork, sausage and salted duck eggs. Young people prefer crystal *zongzi* made from **sago**.

bean paste 豆沙

date 枣

marinate 腌

sago 西米

Realgar wine or *xionghuangjiu* is a Chinese alcoholic drink that is made from Chinese yellow wine dosed with powdered realgar, a yellow-orange mineral. Regularly, it is often used as a pesticide against mosquitoes and other biting insects during the hot summers.

In some regions of China, parents braid silk threads of 5 colors and wear them on their children's wrists. People believe this can help keep **apparition** and disease away.

apparition 鬼

Other common activities include taking long walks and wearing herbal medicine bags. Some prefer a game of making an egg stand at noon. If someone succeeds in making the egg stand at exactly 12:00 noon, that person will be lucky for the next year. All these activities, together with the drinking of realgar wine and hanging mugwort and calamus, were regarded by ancient Chinese as effective approaches in preventing disease or evil of the evil month, while promoting health and well-being.

4. Mid-Autumn Festival

The Mid-Autumn Festival is a harvest festival celebrated on the August 15th of the lunar calendar with full moon at night. The term "Mid-autumn" first appeared in ***Rites of Zhou***, a written collection of rituals of the Western Zhou Dynasty. The celebration as a festival only started to gain popularity during the Tang Dynasty. Emperor Xuanzong started to hold formal celebrations in his palace after exploring the Moon Palace.

Rites of Zhou《周礼》

To modern Chinese, the Mid-Autumn Festival is a time for family reunion. The whole family sit together, enjoy the moon and share mooncakes. In Chinese folk culture, a round shape symbolizes completeness and reunion. Thus, sharing and eating round mooncakes become one of the unique traditions of this festival.

Tubo 吐蕃
Hu cake 胡饼
concubine 妃子
Mongol 蒙古人

After Emperor Taizong's victory against Xiongnu, some **Tubo** business people offered him **Hu cakes**. The emperor took a round cake, pointed to the bright moon in the sky with a smile and said, "I'd like to invite the toad to enjoy the cake", and then shared the cakes with his generals and soldiers. The custom of eating Hu cakes spread throughout the country. When Emperor Xuanzong ate Hu cakes with his favourite **concubine** Yang Yuhuan, Yang Yuhuan named the cake "mooncake". Although the legends explain the beginning of mooncake, its popularity and ties to the festival began during the Song Dynasty.

Another popular legend concerns the Han people's uprising against the **Mongols** at the end of the Yuan Dynasty. The Han people concealed the message that they were to rebel on Mid-Autumn Day in mooncakes and delivered them to other rebels. On the appointed day, they revolted and defeated the Yuan Army.

In cities like Yangzhou, people hold a moon-worship ceremony. This custom originated from imperial palace and spread throughout China gradually. People set up an altar, usually a desk in the courtyard and offer food to deities. Food offerings include mooncakes, *tuanyuanbing*, lotus root, fruit and clear water. Incense is burned when people bow.

Nowadays, seasonal fruits with a round shape are shared on the Mid-Autumn Festival, too. After dinner, people may go to the countryside or a park to enjoy the bright moon. What is interesting is that the moon may not be the roundest on August 15th, the roundest moon may appear on August 16th or 17th.

Part II Western Holidays and Festivals

1. Shared Holidays

Many of the Western holidays are associated with Christianity. Whether they are Christians or not, many of the Westerners observe these holidays. Christmas is associated with the birth of Jesus Christ, Easter is associated with the resurrection of Jesus and even Thanksgiving is viewed as a time to show their thanks to the God.

1.1 Christmas

Since the early 20th century, Christmas has gradually become a holiday for family reunion, observed by Christians and non-Christians alike. The Christian elements are not emphasized and the holiday is marked by an increasingly elaborate exchange of gifts.

To Christians, Christmas starts from **Advent** which means "coming" or "arrival". The emphasis is on preparedness for the arrival of Jesus, whom Christians believe to be God in human form. Mary's pregnancy and the preparations she made for the birth of her son are remembered.

Advent 降临节、待降节，是为了庆祝耶稣诞生的准备期与等待期，亦可算是教会的新年

Traditionally, it is believed Mary laid the baby in a manger.Some shepherds out at night looking after their sheep saw an angel who told them the joyful news. A whole chorus of angels then sang praises to God, and the shepherds decided to go and see the baby. They told people what they had heard from the angel and returned to their sheep, rejoicing and praising God. People argued about the birthday of Jesus and there was a time in Britain that people didn't celebrate Christmas for this.

Many churches hold a service beginning before midnight on December 24 because midnight marks the beginning of Christmas Day, when the first act of the worshipers is to receive **Holy Communion**. Around the world the services held on Christmas Day vary enormously in length and style, as do public and private celebrations. This is the first of the twelve days of Christmas.

Holy Communion 圣餐

The end of the twelve-day Christmas season is marked by the feast of **Epiphany**. Depending on the tradition, this is held on January 6 or on the first Sunday after Christmas. Epiphany celebrates the arrival of the wise men, the first people from outside the Jewish world to see and believe in the infant Christ. Many churches also celebrate the "showing forth" of Jesus as an adult when he was identified at his baptism as God's son.

Epiphany 主显节，正教称为洗礼节，新教称为显现日，是基督教的一个重要庆日

The food eaten at Christmas varies from country to country, often depending on what is locally available for a feast. In the United Kingdom, turkey has replaced the goose or **boar** of earlier centuries. In France, **a carp**, a large fish, is a traditional Christmas dinner. Mince pies, which are pastry shells filled with dried fruit, were originally **oval** in shape to represent the infant Jesus lying in the manger. Italians eat a special cake called panettone. Norwegians bake bread known as Julecake, filled with raisins, spice and

boar 野猪
carp 鲤鱼
oval 椭圆的

candied peel.

Stollen is a traditional German bread eaten during the Christmas season. It is a bread of nuts, spices and dried or candied fruit, **coated** with powdered sugar or icing sugar. People bake it one month before Christmas, then the bread is stored to get a particular flavor and sliced to eat on Christmas day.

coat 给……涂层

The custom of Christmas trees started in Germany, around the sixteenth century, when families would either bring in a tree or make a small pyramid of wood, and decorate it with ornaments. A story tells that it began with Martin Luther: the founder of **Protestantism**. Apparently, walking home one Christmas Eve he saw stars shining. He thought them so lovely that he tried to recapture that beauty by tying candles to the branches of a **fir** tree. Germans and Ukrainians often decorate their trees with mock spider webs; Swedes often make decorations from straw. Christmas plants include **mistletoe**, holly and ivy. Some believed the custom of having Christmas tree at home was brought to Britain by Albert, the husband of Queen Victory I, who was born in Germany.

Protestantism 新教

fir 冷杉树

mistletoe 槲寄生

1.2 Easter

Nearly three months of the Christian year are devoted to celebrating the events that surrounded the end of Jesus' life on earth: his death by **crucifixion** and his rising to life again and ascending to heaven. The period begins on **Shrove Tuesday** and continues through Holy Week and Easter to **Ascension Day**. The dates of these festivals are fixed in relation to each other but Easter varies from year to year

crucifixion 钉死在十字架上

Shrove Tuesday 忏悔星期二

Ascension Day 耶稣升天节

between late March and late April.

The name "Easter" probably comes from a Germanic pre-Christian goddess Eostre, who had a festival around this time. In many languages the festival is called by some variation of "**Pesach**", the **Jewish Passover Festival** when these events first took place.

Pesach/Jewish Passover Festival (犹太人)逾越节

Bread and yeast cookery are powerful symbols of Easter, since the dough rises again after being "punched down". People in many countries bake a traditional Easter bread or yeast bun. It is usually rich in eggs, milk and sugar—all of which have been given up in **Lent**. Hot-cross buns are the British and American equivalent. In eastern Europe, loaves are brought to church to be blessed early on Easter morning, and then taken back home for a festive breakfast.

Lent 大斋期

Lent is a time of preparation, both mental and physical, for the events of Good Friday and Easter Day. It also recalls the forty days that Jesus spent in the desert without food or water, as a preparation for his public teaching and healing activities. For Christians it is a time of self-discipline and solemn reflection: some refrain from eating meat and other animal products, such as cheese and eggs; other do not get married at this time; while yet others give up some favorite items such as candy or alcoholic beverages.

On **Ash Wednesday**, the first day of Lent, church services are held in which Christians receive a mark of ashes seared on their forehead in the shape of cross, as a sign of **repentance**.

Ash Wednesday 圣灰星期三

repentance 悔恨

On Easter Saturday evening, many churches begin a

vigil which lasts until the early morning of Easter Day. After midnight, the church is **decked** with light and color again. People exchange the traditional Easter greeting: "Christ is Risen!"— "He is risen indeed—Alleluia!" Easter morning services are joyful and full of music.

vigil (基督教)节日前夕的守夜

deck 装饰,打扮

Some congregations or families build an Easter Garden — a small model of Jesus' tomb, made of earth and stones which is placed either in the church or garden. Sometimes it includes three crosses on a hill representing Jesus and the two criminals who were executed with him. On Easter Sunday, the stone barring the tomb is rolled away, showing the empty grave.

Since the fourth century, the egg with its potent connotations of new life and rebirth, has been associated with Easter. In the West, the custom is generally to give chocolate eggs which are a twentieth-century invention. In **Orthodox** countries, such as Russia, Greece and parts of eastern Europe, the custom is to hollow out eggshells and paint them in bright colors. Children often crack their eggs against each other's, like chestnuts, seeing whose will break first.

Orthodox 正统的;东正教的

1.3 Halloween

Halloween is a celebration observed in European and American countries on 31 October, the eve of All Hallows' Day. It is widely believed that many Halloween traditions originated from ancient Celtic harvest festivals, particularly the **Gaelic** festival **Samhain**.

Gaelic 盖尔人(的)

Samhain 萨温节,夏末节

Halloween activities include trick-or-treat, attending

divination game 占卜游戏
prank 恶作剧

Halloween costume parties, carving pumpkins into jack-o'-lanterns, lighting bonfires, apple bobbing, **divination games**, playing **pranks**, visiting haunted attractions, telling scary stories, as well as watching horror films.

Trick-or-treat is a customary celebration for children on Halloween. Children dress in costumes, go from house to house, knock at the doors and ask for treats such as candy or sometimes money by shouting "Trick or treat?" The word "trick" implies a "threat" to perform mischief on the homeowners or their property if no treat is given.

vampire 吸血鬼
celebrity 名人
archetype (一种人或物的)典型
ninja 忍者

Halloween costumes are traditionally modeled after supernatural figures such as **vampires**, monsters, ghosts, skeletons, witches and devils. Over time, popular characters from movies, **celebrities**, and generic **archetypes** such as **ninjas** and princesses are new choices.

stingy 小气的
drunkard 酒鬼
rind 外皮

A jack-o'-lantern is a carved pumpkin, turnip, or other root vegetable lantern associated with Halloween. The name is tied to the Irish legend of **stingy** Jack, a **drunkard** who bargained with Satan and was doomed to wander through the earth with only a hollowed turnip to light his way. When carving a jack-o'-lantern, the top of the pumpkin or turnip is cut off, the inside flesh is scooped out, and a scary or funny face is carved out of the **rind**. To create the lantern effect, a candle or tea light is placed within the vegetable. Nowadays, there are artificial jack-o'-lanterns with electric lights. It is common to see jack-o'-lanterns used as decorations everywhere prior to and on Halloween.

Apple bobbing, also known as bobbing for apples, is a game often played on Halloween. The game is played by filling a **tub** or a large basin with water and putting apples in the water. Players try to catch the floating apples with their mouths and teeth. Hands are tied behind the back to prevent cheating.

tub 盆,桶

Christmas, Easter and Halloween are widely celebrated around the world now, especially by children and youths. For Chinese children, Christmas means a big meal and gifts, Easter means Easter eggs and Easter bunny, and Halloween means costume parties.

2. British Holidays

2.1 Traditional National Days

Feast days such as St. Patrick's Day, St. Andrew's Day, St. George's Day and St. David's Day are traditional national days of different parts of UK. St. Patrick's Day is the national day of Northern Ireland; St. George's Day is the national day of England; St. Andrew's Day is the national day of Scotland; St. David's Day is the national day of Welsh.

feast(一年一度的)宗教盛典,乡村节日;(圣人)纪念日,节日

St. Patrick's Day is a cultural and religious celebration held on 17 March, the traditional death date of Saint Patrick, the **foremost patron** saint of Ireland. St. Patrick's Day was made an official Christian feast day in the early 17th century. The day commemorates Saint Patrick and the arrival of Christianity in Ireland, and celebrates the heritage and culture of the Irish in general. Celebrations generally involve public parades, Irish traditional music sessions, and the

foremost 最重要的

patron 赞助者,资助人

shamrock 三叶草
liturgical(与)礼拜仪式(有关)的
Lenten(与)大斋期(有关)的
propagate 传播，宣传
canonization 封为圣者
wane 衰落，减少
festoon 用花彩装饰
garland 花环

wearing of green attire or **shamrocks**. Christians who belong to **liturgical** denominations also attend church services and historically the **Lenten** restrictions on eating and drinking alcohol were lifted for the day, which has encouraged and **propagated** the holiday's tradition of alcohol consumption.

St. David's Day is the feast day of Saint David, the patron saint of Wales, and falls on 1 March, the date of Saint David's death in 589 AD. The feast has been regularly celebrated since the **canonization** of David in the 12th century, though it is not a national holiday in the UK. Traditional festivities include wearing daffodils and leeks, recognized symbols of Wales and Saint David respectively, eating traditional Welsh food including cawl and Welsh rarebit, and women wearing traditional Welsh dress. An increasing number of cities and towns across Wales including Cardiff, Swansea and Aberystwyth also put on parades throughout the day.

St. George's Day was a major feast and national holiday in England from the early 15th century. The tradition of celebrating St. George's day had **waned** by the end of the 18th century after the union of England and Scotland. A traditional custom on St. George's day is to fly or adorn the St. George's Cross flag in some way: pubs in particular can be seen on 23 April **festooned** with **garlands** of St. George's crosses. It is customary for the hymn "Jerusalem" to be sung in cathedrals, churches and chapels on St. George's Day, or on the Sunday closest to it. Traditional English food and drink may be consumed.

St. Andrew's Day is the feast day of Saint Andrew. It is

celebrated on 30 November. Saint Andrew's Day is Scotland's official national day. The celebration of Saint Andrew as a national festival is thought to originate from the reign of Malcolm III. It was thought that ritual slaughter of animals associated with Samhain was moved to this date, so as to assure enough animals were kept alive for winter. But it is only in more recent times that 30 November has been given national holiday status. In Scotland, and many countries with Scottish connections, St. Andrew's Day is marked with a celebration of Scottish culture with traditional Scottish food and music. In Scotland the day is also seen as the start of a season of Scottish winter festivals encompassing St. Andrew's Day, **Hogmanay** and Burns Night. There are week-long celebrations in the town of St. Andrews and in some other Scottish cities.

Hogmanay（苏格兰）除夕

2.2 Pancake Day

Pancake Day, or Shrove Tuesday, is the traditional feast day before the start of Lent on Ash Wednesday. Shrove Tuesday always falls 47 days before Easter Sunday, so the date varies from year to year and falls between February 3 and March 9. Shrove Tuesday was the last opportunity to use up eggs and fats before embarking on the Lenten **fast** and pancakes are the perfect way of using up these ingredients.

fast 斋戒

A pancake is a thin, flat cake, made of **batter** and fried in a frying pan. A traditional English pancake is very thin and is served with Golden syrup or lemon juice and caster sugar. The pancake has a very long history and was featured in cookery books as far back as 1439. Part of the fun of

batter 面糊

cooking pancakes is in the tossing. The tradition of tossing or flipping them is centuries-old. To toss a pancake successfully takes a combination of the perfect pancake and good technique. It's quite possible to end up with half the pancake being stuck to the pan while the other half flying away. An important part of the Shrove Tuesday celebrations in the UK is pancake races. Large numbers of people in fancy dress race down streets tossing pancakes. People rush to the finishing line, carrying a frying pan with a cooked pancake in it and flipping the pancake as they run. The most famous pancake race takes place at **Olney** in Buckinghamshire. According to tradition, in 1445 a woman of Olney heard the shriving bell while she was making pancakes and ran to the church in her apron, still clutching her frying pan. The Olney pancake race is now world-famous. Competitors are local housewives who wear an apron and a hat or scarf.

Olney 奥尔尼

2.3 Bonfire Night (Guy Fawkes Night)

"Remember, remember, the fifth of November/The Gunpowder Treason and plot/ I see no reason why Gunpowder Treason/Should ever be forgot," — this slightly haunting rhyme introduces Bonfire Night, also known as Guy Fawkes Night, one of the most unique holidays in the UK. Guy Fawkes Night is not a holiday shared by all four countries in the UK, it is a holiday for England, Scotland and Wales. Instead of celebrating something that happened, Bonfire Night celebrates something that didn't happen: the 1605 Gunpowder **Plot**. Fawkes and other passionate Roman Catholics were involved in a **conspiracy** to blow up

plot 密谋
conspiracy 阴谋

parliament and **assassinate** King James I. With much of London made from wood at the time and the entire royal **elite** present, it would have spelled disaster. A **renegade** informed the plan to the government and Fawkes was killed.

assassinate 刺杀

elite 精英

renegade 叛变者

To celebrate the collapse of the terrorist plot, **Brits** mark 5 November by making bonfires, setting off fireworks, and burning **effigies** of Guy Fawkes. Today, the popularity of Guy Fawkes Night has somewhat decreased due to dwindling interest and increased safety regulations. The holiday is not celebrated in Northern Ireland at all, and some argue that the celebrations are immoral as Fawkes also represented the persecuted Catholic minority and suffered a violent death.

Brit 英国人

effigy 模拟像

3. American Holidays

After arriving in the American continent, European immigrants developed their own unique holidays. Among them, Thanksgiving is the most popular one.

3.1 Thanksgiving

Americans view Thanksgiving as a time for family and friends to give thanks for the good things in their lives. Thanksgiving commemorates a meal shared between **pilgrims** and native Americans in the seventeenth century.

pilgrim 清教徒前辈移民

To escape religious discrimination in England, on August 5, 1620, the pilgrims went aboard the Mayflower and Speedwell, but were forced to abandon the Speedwell and continue to America on the Mayflower alone.

In September 1620 the pilgrims landed at Cape Cod. During their first harsh winter, more than half of them died of hunger and disease. The small group that survived did so with the help of Native Americans, who showed them how to grow crops such as corn and sweet potatoes. The pilgrims celebrated their survival and harvest with their native friends in 1621. This is viewed as the first Thanksgiving. These first settlers have become known as the Pilgrim Fathers.

Many of the pilgrims were seeking peace and religious freedom, but later colonists often forgot these ideas. Some religious groups in America now see Thanksgiving as an occasion for mourning the subsequent exploitation and killing of Native Americans by European colonizers.

American thanksgiving and Canadian thanksgiving are not at the same time. Canadian Thanksgiving holiday falls on the second Monday of October and American thanksgiving is on the fourth Thursday of November. Canadians may gather for their Thanksgiving feast on any day during the long weekend and Sunday is considered the most common. Foods traditionally served at Thanksgiving include roasted turkey, mashed potatoes with **gravy**, sweet potatoes, cranberry sauce, sweet corn, various autumn vegetables (mainly various kinds of squashes but also **Brussels sprouts**), and pumpkin pie. Baked ham and apple pie are also fairly common, and various regional dishes and desserts may also be served, including salmon, **butter tarts** and **Nanaimo bars**.

gravy 肉汁

Brussels sprouts 孢子甘蓝

butter tarts 黄油挞

Nanaimo bars 一种加拿大甜点

3.2 Washington's Birthday

Washington's Birthday is a United States federal holiday

celebrated on the third Monday of February in honor of George Washington, the first president of the United States, who was born on February 22, 1732. Since the *Uniform Federal Holidays Act* of 1971, its observance can occur from February 15 to 21, inclusive.

Actually, the day is now widely known as Presidents' Day and an occasion to honor all who have served as president, not just George Washington. The day is a state holiday in most states. Depending on the specific law, the state holiday might officially celebrate Washington alone, Washington and Abraham Lincoln, or some other combination of US presidents.

Part III Comparison and Contrast

1. Qixi Festival VS Valentine's Day

Chinese celebrate the holiday on July 7th. The festival originated from the romantic legend of the weaver girl and the herd boy. The name herd boy and weaver girl first appeared in *Book of Songs* and the complete legend first appeared in ***The Collection of Anecdotes***. The weaver girl was busy weaving everyday, the emperor of heaven pitied her and married her to the herd boy. The weaver girl forgot to weave rosy clouds after her marriage, so they were separated and could only met once a year.

Girls go to the local temple to pray to the weaver girl for wisdom. Paper items are usually burned as offerings. Girls may pray for **dexterity** in **needlework**, which in ancient China symbolizes the talents of a good spouse. Divination could take place to determine possible dexterity in needlework. Girls make wishes for marrying someone who would be a considerate and loving husband. During the festival, girls make a display of their domestic skills. Traditionally, there would be contests amongst those who attempted to be the best in threading needles under low-light conditions like the glow of an ember or a half moon.

The Collection of Anecdotes《述异记》 dexterity 灵巧 needlework 女红
martyr 殉道者 Geoffrey Chaucer 杰弗里·乔叟
confectionery(总称)糖果和巧克力

Valentine's Day is celebrated annually on February 14. It is recognized as a significant cultural, religious and commercial celebration of romance and romantic love in many nations around the world. There are numerous legends associated with Valentine's Day. One of the most famous legends is about a priest named Valentine who secretly married many couples while the emperor forbade them to marry because he wanted them to join the army. Valentine was put into prison and the blind daughter of his judge fell in love with him. He wrote her a letter signed "Your Valentine" as a farewell before his execution.

Actually, the holiday was established by Pope Gelasius I in honor of the Christian **martyr**, Saint Valentine of Rome. The day first became associated with romantic love because of a poem written by **Geoffrey Chaucer** in the 14th century, when the tradition of courtly love flourished. In the poem, he wrote, "For this was on Saint Valentine's day, When every fowl comes there his mate to take." In 18th-century England, it grew into an occasion in which couples expressed their love to each other by presenting flowers, offering **confectionery** and sending greeting cards (known as "valentines"). Heartshape, doves and winged Cupid are all symbols of Valentine's Day.

2. *Caishen* VS Santa Claus

Caishen (the Chinese God of Wealth) is the mythological figure worshiped in the Chinese folk religion and Taoism. He has been identified with many historical figures, among them there are Zhao Gongming, Fan Li, Guan Yu and Bi Gan. *Caishen*'s name is often invoked during the Chinese New Year celebrations. He is often **depicted** riding a black tiger and holding a golden rod. He may also be depicted with an iron tool capable of turning stone and iron into gold.

Several versions of *Caishen*'s **incarnations** and way of **deification** are circulated. One of them is generally known as ***Caibo Xingjun***. **Li Guizu** was born in the Zichuan District in Shandong Province and held position as a country **magistrate**. Li Guizu contributed significantly to the district, whilst people built a temple to worship Li Guizu after his death. Li Guizu was then conferred the title *Caibo Xingjun* by the Emperor Wude of Tang Dynasty.

Guan Yu is regarded as military *Caishen*. People who worship him set off fireworks and burn paper money on the January 5th of the lunar calendar. *Caishen* sometimes appears as a door god in Taoist temples, usually in partnership with the Burning-lamp Taoist.

depict 描绘	incarnation 化身	deification 神化
Caibo Xingjun 财帛星君	Li Guizu 李诡祖	magistrate 执法官
portly 肥胖的	elf 精灵	reindeer 驯鹿

Santa Claus is a legendary figure who brings gifts to the homes of well-behaved children on the night of Christmas Eve and the early morning of Christmas Day. Before they go to bed, children hang a stocking and they will get the gifts next morning. The modern Santa Claus grew out of traditions surrounding the historical Saint Nicholas (a 4th-century Greek bishop and gift-giver of Myra).

Santa Claus is generally depicted as a **portly**, joyful, white-bearded man. He prefers to wear a red coat with white fur collar, white-fur-cuffed red trousers, a red hat with white fur and black leather belt and boots and carries a bag full of gifts for children.

It is said Santa Claus makes lists of children throughout the world, categorizing them according to their behavior, and delivers presents to all of the well-behaved children in the world, and coal to all the misbehaving children, on the night of Christmas Eve. This task is accomplished with the aid of his **elves**, who make the toys in his workshop at the North Pole, and his flying **reindeers**, who pull his sleigh. Commonly portrayed as a fat and gentle old man who lives at the North Pole, he is famous for his laughs in a way that sounds like "ho ho ho".

3. The Jade Hare VS Easter Bunny

The Jade Hare or Moon Hare is a figure in Asian folklore who lives on the moon. This image often occurred on the food of Mid-Autumn Festival. The folklore originated in China and then spread to other Asian cultures. The hare is seen as pounding with **a mortar and pestle**, but the contents in the mortar differ among Chinese, Japanese and Korean folklore. In Chinese folklore, the hare is portrayed as a companion to the Moon Goddess Chang'e, constantly pounding the **elixir** of life for her. In some Chinese versions, the rabbit pounds medicine for the mortals.

An early Chinese anthology called *Chu Ci*, from the Warring States Period, noted that there was a hare on the moon. This notion is supported by later texts, including the *Taiping Imperial Encyclopaedia*. The story of hare's pounding the medicine probably appeared in *The Musical Bureau* for the first time. As rabbits were not yet introduced to China during the Western Han Dynasty, the original image was not a rabbit but a hare.

Han Dynasty poets called the hare on the moon the "Jade Rabbit" or the "Gold Rabbit", and these phrases were used often to take the place of the word for the moon. The sun is called "Gold Crow" in China . A famous poet of the Tang Dynasty, Li Bai, related how "The rabbit in the moon pounds the medicine in vain" in his poem.

a mortar and pestle 研钵和杵　　elixir 仙丹，灵丹妙药

hermaphrodite 雌雄同体

The Easter Bunny (also called the Easter Rabbit or Easter Hare) is a folkloric figure and symbol of Easter, depicted as a clothed rabbit bringing Easter eggs. Originating among German Lutherans, the Easter Bunny initially played the role of a judge. He evaluated whether children were good or disobedient in behavior at the start of the season of Easter. The Easter Bunny is sometimes depicted with clothes. According to the stories, the creature carries colored eggs, candy and sometimes even toys in his basket, to the homes of children. The image shows similarities to Santa Claus, as they both bring gifts to children on the night before their respective holidays.

In medieval church art, the hare was a popular motif. In ancient times, it was widely believed the hare was a **hermaphrodite** and it could reproduce without loss of virginity. The idea led to an association with the Virgin Mary, with hares sometimes occurring in illuminated manuscripts and Northern European paintings of the Virgin and Christ Child. It may also have been associated with the Holy Trinity, as in the three hares' motif.

Part IV Reflection and Presentation

1. Many Western holidays are popular among Chinese now. For example, urban people celebrate Christmas, Valentine, Easter, Halloween, etc. What do you think of this phenomenon?

2. Besides the existing official public holidays, which traditional holiday in China should be set as a public holiday?

3. Find some holidays which are celebrated exclusively in UK, US, Australia and Canada.

4. Find holidays celebrated on November 11th all over the world and make a comparison.

Part V Mini-pedia

1. No Haircut in the First Lunar Month

No haircut can be done in the first lunar month. There is an old rumor among Chinese that if someone has a haircut in the first lunar month, then his uncle on his mother's side will die for this. Some old people believe it and they urge the youth to observe this custom too. Another version about the custom is from an ancient Chinese medical book. It is said that it will benefit a lot if people don't cut the hair and let it grow freely in spring.

2. April Fool's Day

April Fool's Day, sometimes called All Fools' Day, is one of the most light-hearted days of the year. People play jokes on others and the recipients are called "April fools". Its origins are uncertain. Some see it as a celebration related to the turn of the seasons, while others believe it stems from the adoption of a new calendar. Ancient cultures celebrated New Year's Day on or around April 1. In medieval times, much of Europe celebrated March 25, the Feast of Annunciation, as the beginning of the new year. In 1582, Pope Gregory XIII ordered a new calendar (the Gregorian Calendar) to replace the old Julian Calendar. The new calendar called for New Year's Day to be celebrated on Jan. 1. That year, France adopted the reformed calendar and shifted New Year's Day to Jan.1. Many people either refused to accept the new date, or knew nothing about it, and continued to celebrate New Year's Day on April 1. Other people began to make fun of these traditionalists, sending them on "fool's errands" or trying to trick them into believing something false. Eventually, the practice spread throughout Europe.

References

1. 桂胜, 张友云. 荆楚民间风俗[M]. 武汉:武汉出版社, 2014.
2. 刘春芳,等. 中西文化对比教程[M]. 北京:中国人民大学出版社, 2017.
3. 束定芳. 中国文化英语教程[M]. 上海:上海外语教育出版社, 2016.
4. 王焱,等. 中西文化比较[M]. 北京:清华大学出版社, 2017.
5. 乌丙安. 民俗学原理[M]. 长春:长春出版社, 2014.
6. 钟敬文. 民俗学概论[M]. 北京:高等教育出版社, 2010.
7. Elizabeth Breuilly, Joanne O'brien, Martin Palmer. Consultant Editor: Professor Martin E. Marty. *Festivals of the World—The Illustrated Guide to Celebrations, Customs, Events and Holidays*[M]. New York: Checkmark Books, 2002.
8. https://en.wikipedia.org/wiki/Easter.
9. https://en.wikipedia.org/wiki/halloween.
10. https://en.wikipedia.org/wiki/Holiday.
11. https://en.wikipedia.org/wiki/moon rabbit.
12. https://en.wikipedia.org/wiki/thankgiving.
13. http://www.china.org.cn/travel/2010-12/15/content_21550089.htm.

Unit 8
Chinese and Western Folk Art

Suona

Bagpipe

Learning Objectives

- To understand the origin of some forms of Chinese and Western folk art
- To be acquainted with different Chinese and Western folk artifacts
- To compare and contrast the features of Chinese and Western traditional art forms in the context of folk culture

Lead-in Questions

- What do you know about different forms of folk art? Can you name a few?
- What local art forms do you know about in your hometown? Introduce one to the class and try to explain its cultural indication.
- How would you interpret the messages conveyed by Scottish bagpipe and Chinese *Suona*, both traditional musical instruments?

Folk art covers all forms of functional or utilitarian artistic production in the context of folk culture. Predominantly being useful rather than purely aesthetic, folk art is a creative expression of the human struggle towards civilization and reflective of the cultural life of a community. Historically folk art includes tangible objects that are crafted and transmitted in traditional environment. Intangible performance art defines folk art in a broader sense, such as folk music, dance, or narrative structure.

Traditional folk art forms represent and reflect diverse community groups: ethnic, religious, occupational, geographical, age-based and gender-based. In the broadest sense, folk art refers to the art of "people", as distinguished from the elite or professional products that constitute the mainstream of art in highly-developed societies. Therefore, the focus of this unit should fall into the category of usual sense of folk art, separating from classic or fine art.

Part I Chinese Folk Art

Chinese folk art is an important part of the country's extremely rich cultural and art heritage from a regional or ethnic scene in China. It has won recognition and praise from experts both at home and abroad for its great variety, rich flavor of life, distinctive local style and its artistic approaches of romanticism. Individual folk arts have a long history, and many traditions are still practiced today. In artistic representation and expression, works of folk art are straightforward, natural, flexible, vivid and intimate. Some of these ancient art forms include jade carvings, performance art such as music and their respective instruments, textile art such as paper cuts and clothing.

1. Folk Arts and Crafts

Crafts, the largest category of folk art, perfectly combine the material and spiritual life of the people because they have both utilitarian and aesthetic value.

1.1 Chinese Knotting

Chinese knotting 中国结

The art of tying knots dates back to prehistoric times. Due to the delicate nature of the medium, few examples of prehistoric **Chinese knotting** exist today. Some of the earliest evidence of knotting have been preserved on bronze vessels of the Warring States Period (475 BC-221 BC). Other evidences have been found in Buddhist carvings, on silk paintings and in literature.

knotted strings 结绳(记事)

In ancient times, people used **knotted strings** to record events. The size of the knot indicated the significance of the event. When people started drawing and later writing to take record, knot-tying lost its initial function. However, the art of knot-tying never dies in China because of the messages being conveyed with cultural implications. Historically knots could symbolize love, marriage or reunion in Chinese culture. In more recent years a knot is often exchanged as a gift or a pray for good luck or to warn off evil spirits.

Chinese knots are usually lanyard type arrangements where two cords enter from the top of the knot and two cords leave from the bottom. The knots are usually double-layered and symmetrical. There are many different shapes of knots, the most common being butterflies, flowers, birds, dragons, fish and even shoes. Nowadays Chinese knots are usually in red for decoration, hanging up on walls, doors of home and are in shops to create and enhance festivity.

1.2 Needlework and Embroidery

needlework 针线活/女红
agrarian society 农业社会
dexterity 灵巧

There has been an age-long tradition in China for female to be good at **needlework**. As a historically **agrarian society**, **dexterity** and skills of needlework indicate a potential competent and industrious wife. This really counts in Chinese history since male and female are not supposed to look for their spouses themselves and match-making is a major means towards marriage.

embroidery 刺绣

Naturally young girls will be tutored by senior females of the family to practice their needlework. It's said that the needlework to make clothes stronger and more enduring later evolves to **embroidery**. The rich colors and delicate patterns of embroidery make it obviously ornamental rather than functional.

Qixi Festival 七夕节,乞巧节,女儿节

Young girls dream to have the expertise to find a good husband. There is even a festival for this dream. In every Chinese lunar year, the seventh day of the seventh month is called **Qixi Festival**. On this special day girls will have certain rites to worship the moon and they compete with each other to see who is the best at threading needles under low-light conditions like the glow of an ember or a half moon. They make wishes for marrying someone who would be a good and loving husband. This is why this day is also known as "Girls' Day".

1.3 Lacquer Ware

Lacquer used to be a very popular form of decoration and protective covering in ancient China. It was used to color and beautify screens, furniture, bowls, cups, sculpture, musical instruments and coffins, where it could be carved, incised and inlaid to show off scenes from nature, mythology and literature.

lacquer 生漆；大漆

China has a long history of lacquer work, dating back to the Neolithic Period. The earliest known lacquer object, a red wooden bowl, was unearthed at a **Hemudu Culture** site (c. 5th millennium BC) in Zhejiang Province. The ancient Chinese artists used the sap of the tree which was native to eastern and southern China and was sometimes referred to as the "Lacquer Tree". Lacquer existed in many colors by adding certain chemicals, for example, black was made by adding carbon, yellow by adding **ochre**, and a brilliant red was achieved by mixing in **cinnabar**. These were the three most popular colors in ancient Chinese lacquer painting.

Hemudu Culture 河姆渡文化

ochre 赭石

cinnabar 朱砂

The resulting lacquer, when dried slowly in humid conditions, is remarkably resistant to heat, damp and chemicals. For this reason, lacquer was often used to **coat** and protect goods of more perishable material which might be easily damaged such as bamboo, silk and wood. As the lacquer is very thin when applied it requires many layers of coats to provide an even finish, but an advantage is that the lacquer can be used to cover almost any type of surface, uneven or otherwise. The preceding coat must be absolutely dry and be highly polished before applying the next one,

coat 涂层，形成保护层

lacquerware 漆器

with some objects having as many as 100 such layers, illustrating why producing **lacquerware** was a time-consuming and expensive business.

1.4 *Nianhua* / New Year Picture

Nianhua /New Year Picture 年画

woodblock print 木版画

Nianhua, or the New Year Picture is a form of Chinese colored **woodblock print** for decoration during the Chinese New Year holiday. Customarily, as each Chinese New Year arrives, every family replaces its new year picture in order to "say goodbye to the past and welcome the future" (辞旧迎新).

hand-colored 手工上色

iconography 视觉艺术

Nianhua was one of the most ubiquitous forms of Chinese traditional popular culture. Primarily the peasantry throughout China purchased and sometimes produced them. These woodblock prints, occasionally **hand-colored**, were sold in millions all across China. Some *nianhua* have changed very little over generations; their images are thought to collectively constitute the major representation of Chinese **iconography**.

Door Guardian 门神

illiterate 文盲

Nianhua could be dated back to the image of **Door Guardian** of the Tang Dynasty, but it was not until the late Ming Dynasty(1368-1644) and especially the Qing Dynasty (1616-1911) did it begin to appear everywhere in China. Its popularity in China lies largely in the fact that the colorful, readily available and inexpensive *nianhua* appealed to the vast peasant population, many of which were estimated **illiterate**. Even the poorest peasant family could beautify their home with woodblock prints of gods, heroes, auspicious symbols and popular narratives.

Other than being new year household ornaments, *nianhua* could be found in homes all year long which speaks of and suggests good things. Prosperity, fertility, longevity and protection are the core subjects of *nianhua*. Animals and deities, chubby babies and distinguished officials, folk tales and moral lessons, were all depicted in vivid, colorful, dynamic compositions.

Nianhua provided a visual delight for the illiterate, and could cross barriers of speech and dialect, nonetheless language plays a significant role in them. Not only are written characters often included in the compositions for identification and explanation, but visual-verbal **puns** and **allusions** are part of the language of *nianhua*. Bats are auspicious by virtue of their name, "fu", which is also the reading of the Chinese character for "good luck". Not only does Buddhism lend an auspicious aura to the lotus, but the reading of its name, "lian", is also that of the character for "in succession", hence an allusion to a wish for many sons. Shared understandings of words and images formed a coherent discourse from one end of China to the other, encouraging cultural integration of the vast country.

pun 双关语

allusion 典故

2. Chinese Folk Music

2.1 Folk Songs

Folk songs are composed of lyrics (literature) and tunes (music) and have obvious ethnic and regional features. Karl Marx (1818-1883) labeled folk songs as the "**chronicles**" of

chronicles 编年史

each nationalities.

work songs 劳动号子

2.1.1 **Work Songs**

Work songs have a history as old as the music record itself. Anthropological evidence suggests that most agrarian societies tend to have them. Most agricultural work songs were rhythmic **a cappella** songs. They serve both purposes of synchronizing physical movements in work groups and reducing the feeling of boredom. Nowadays commentators on work songs tend to include both songs sung while work and about work in the category, since they are viewed as interconnected.

a cappella 无伴奏合唱,也可称作"阿卡贝拉"

Common types of work songs are domestic, agricultural work songs, **sea shanties**, African-American work songs, etc.

sea shanty 船工号子

ditty 小调，小曲

2.1.2 **Ditty**

The song *Jasmine Flower* is a ditty, or a short tune of Han people with many regional variations. It has gained popularity both in China and abroad. It has been used during grand events such as the Transfer Ceremony in Hong Kong 1997, 2004 and 2008 Summer Olympics, 2010 Shanghai Expo Opening Ceremony. The song echoes the features of folk customs in Southern China, mild and sweet. The song became one of the first Chinese folk songs to become widely known outside China. The melody has become well-known among Western listeners as it was used by **Giacomo Puccini** in his opera ***Turandot***.

Giacomo Puccini 意大利歌剧作曲家贾科莫·普契尼

Turandot《图兰朵》

2.1.3 Urtiin duu: Mongolian Folk Long Song

Urtiin duu 乌日图道(蒙古语发音)

The **Urtiin duu** or "Long Song" is one of the two major forms of Mongolian songs, the other being the "short song" (bogino duu). Urtiin duu or the "**Long Song**" dates back to the 7th century AD when the Mongolians were shifting from a hunting life to a nomadic one on the western Mongolia Grasslands.

(Mongolia) Long Song(蒙古)长调

As a ritual form of expression associated with important celebrations and festivities, Urtiin duu plays a distinct and honored role in Mongolian society. It's performed at weddings, the birth of a child, the branding of foals and other social events celebrated by Mongolia's nomadic communities. The Urtiin duu can also be heard at the **Naadam**, a festivity featuring wrestling, archery and horse-racing competitions.

Naadam 那达慕(蒙古族传统的体育竞技和娱乐节日，以举行"男儿三艺"比赛——摔跤、射箭、赛马为主)

This Mongolian folk music is called "Long Song" not only because the songs are long, but also because each syllable of the lyrics lasts for a long duration. Mongolian Long Song sounds bright and broad, just like the vast prairie and the brave, strong nomadic people on the horseback. It is now an Oral and Intangible Heritage of Humanity.

2.2 Folk Musical Instruments

2.2.1 The Legend of **Ling Lun**

Ling Lun 伶伦(传说为黄帝的乐官，十二音律的创作人，笛子的发明者)

Ling Lun is the legendary founder of music in ancient China. It's said that the Yellow Emporer ordered him to find a way to denote and play music instead of just making separate sounds. He had trouble making any melody even with all his expertise and efforts. Fortunately he was able to have created bamboo flutes by imitating the sounds of many birds, especially that of the mythical phoenix. In this way, he invented the five notes of the ancient Chinese **pentatonic**

pentatonic scale 五声音阶

scale and the eight sounds made by eight musical instruments.

This is of course a legend that has never been documented in history. But there are hard evidences to prove Chinese traditional music. In 1986 more than 20 bone flutes were excavated from an early Neolithic tomb in Jiahu, Wuyang County, Henan Province. These bone flutes are made from the wings of cranes. They are open-ended and vary in the number of their finger holes. Thus they can produce sounds either in traditional Chinese pentatonic scale or the Western **heptatonic scale**. The bone flutes dated back to 7, 800 to 9, 000 years ago which for the first time support the theory that Chinese traditional instruments could be applied to heptatonic scale.

heptatonic scale 七声音阶

2.2.2 Eight Sounds

There was an important ancient system in Chinese traditional musical organization. The system called the **eight sounds** (*bayin*) was used to classify the many kinds of instruments. It was based on the material used in the construction of instruments, the eight being metal, stone, clay, hide/skin, silk, wood, gourd and bamboo.

eight sounds/ *bayin* 八音

Eight Sounds	Means of Performance	Musical Instruments
Metal 金	Percussion Instruments 打击乐器	Chime Bells / *Bianzhong* 编钟 Gong 锣
Stone 石	Percussion Instruments	Stone Tablet / *Bianqing* 编磬
Clay 土	Wind Instrument 吹奏乐器	Clay Ocarina / *Xun* 埙 *Taodi* / Clay Flute 陶笛

Continued

Eight Sounds	Means of Performance	Musical Instruments
Hide/Skin 革	Percussion Instruments	*Yaogu* 腰鼓 *Bolanggu* / Pellet Drum 拨浪鼓
Silk 丝	String Instrument 弦乐乐器	*Guqin* 古琴 *Se*/Stringed Zither 瑟
Wood 木	Percussion Instruments	*Zhu* 柷; *Yu* 敔; *Bangzi* 梆子
Gourd 匏	Wind Instrument	*Sheng* 笙 *Yu* 竽
Bamboo 竹	Wind Instrument	Bamboo Flute End-blown Flute / *Xiao* 箫

3. Chinese Folk Dances

3.1　The Origin of Chinese Folk Dances

Folk dances usually reflect people's life of a certain country or region. In this sense all folk dances are ethnic dances, but not all ethnic dances are folk dances. Early Chinese folk dances were essentially ritual enactments of folk beliefs performed in the hope of a good harvest, or—in the case of the earliest Chinese folk dances—in the hope of a good hunt, since the earliest Chinese folk dances were performed by hunter-gathering folk.

No written records have been correspondingly documented, but archaeologists have found **pottery shards** in China dating from the 4th millennium BC (about 6,000 years ago) which depict dancers brandishing spears and other weapons that were used for hunting. This was done in the

pottery shards 陶瓷碎片

belief that by performing these rituals, the hunter thus gained power over the hunted.

Later during the Han Dynasty, when most of the hunting folks had long become primarily farmers who supplemented their annual harvest with the gathering of freely growing fruits and nuts as well as with fishes caught from rivers, lakes or the ocean and of course some hunting, especially with the aid of traps, was practiced. Therefore the folk dances that were developed during this period reflected a belief that in making ritual sacrifices to the gods in appreciation of the "harvest" one could persuade the gods to provide another bountiful harvest in the following year. A good case in point is the popular folk dance in northern China called ***Niuyangge***. "Niu" refers to your body movement to twist a little from left to right or reverse it, matching with your dancing steps in a cross pattern. The origin of this dance step was probably the labor work in the crop field, when farmers tried to avoid stepping on the rice sprouts while planting them. That's how the dance was named—it literally means "**rice sprouts song**" in Chinese.

Niuyangge 扭秧歌

rice sprouts song 秧歌

3.2 Dragon Dance

The **dragon dance** has been indispensable to Chinese festivals since ancient times. It has become a symbol of Chinese culture as Chinese people, who claim to be the "**descendants of dragon**", spread and bring the tradition to every corner of the world. Chinese dragons symbolize wisdom, power and wealth, and they are believed to bring fortune and auspiciousness to people.

dragon dance 舞龙/舞龙灯

descendants of dragon 龙的传人

The origin of the dragon dance can be dated back to the Han Dynasty (206 BC-220 AD). It was then used in a ceremony for worshiping ancestors and praying for rain, and it gradually developed into an entertainment activity. By the Tang Dynasty (618-907) and the Song Dynasty (960-1279), it had become a common ceremonial activity in festivals like Chinese New Year.

The costume used for a dragon dance is made of materials like grass, bamboo, paper and cloth. Odd numbers of the dragon's joints are regarded as auspicious, so people often make a 9, 11, or 13-jointed dragon, or even a 29-jointed dragon. Dragons made of more than 15 joints are too heavy to dance, and are mainly used for display, so this kind of dragon puts more weight on decoration and boasts a high degree of both craft and technology. Those mock dragons under 15 joints that actually dance require **acrobatic** leaps in order to suggest the swooping motions of such a large creature, though the dancers support the mock dragon on poles that can be raised, lowered and swung about as needed.

acrobatic 杂技般的

A person holding a rod with a big ball at the top leads the dragon during the dance. The ball is moved left and right, back and forth, up and down, and the dragon follows the ball. Its body, moving in waves, appears to be dancing.

The dragon is welcome everywhere it goes, and sometimes the team conducting the dragon dance can receive banquets up to five or six times, which are called "dragon exchanging wine".

A dragon dance can usually be seen at the Spring

Festival (Chinese New Year) and the Lantern Festival, but sometimes companies commission a dragon dance to bring good fortune to their business, especially if opening a new branch.

3.3 Ethnic Minority Folk Dance

choreography 编舞艺术
matrimonial bliss 婚姻的祝福
communal bond 族群纽带

China has 55 ethnic minority groups, whose dances reflect the peculiarities of each group's cultural and historical narrative. Their **choreography** and their colorful costumes naturally reflect this ethnic narrative. However, many of the dances of ethnic minority groups also share common themes such as rivalry, jealousy, love and forgiveness as well as **matrimonial bliss** and the **communal bond** which on festive occasion reinforce social cohesion among the group. The folk dance is one of the most cherished forms of artistic expression among the Chinese people. In a sense, it can be interpreted as the simplest and most immediately available form of informal theatre.

repertoire 全部剧目

While the heritage of the folk dance that was passed down the generations among ethnic groups as a whole was rich and varied, it was unevenly distributed from group to group, partly because whole chapters of the tradition had been lost for various reasons. With efforts of recovery and restoration, the richness of the original ethnic folk dance, both in terms of choreography and **repertoire** as well as in terms of the exact replication of the original costumes has slowly made a comeback, and today is recognized as a world cultural heritage worthy of preservation.

4. Chinese Folk Drama

4.1 Shadow Play/Shadow Puppetry

Chinese **shadow play** is an art form that is performed by moving flat articulated cut-out figures (shadow puppets) which are held between a source of light and a **translucent** screen or scrim. The shadow puppets are made of animal skins or cardboard. Various effects can be achieved by moving both the puppets and the **light source**. A talented puppeteer can make the figures appear to walk, dance, fight, nod and laugh.

shadow play (puppetry) 皮影戏

translucent 半透明的

light source 光源

Although the singing style and storyline of shadow puppetry seem similar to Chinese opera, there are no live actors or actresses in the performance. The art form has been transmitted through a master-apprentice style until recently. The most common troupe roster is one puppeteer, singer and musicians.

Shadow play has been an ancient art in Southeast Asia, and still a living folk tradition in China, India and Nepal. It is also known in Egypt, Turkey, Greece, Germany, France and the United States.

4.2 Traditional Chinese Opera/Drama

Traditional **Chinese opera**, or ***Xiqu***, together with Greek tragic-comedy and Indian Sanskrit Opera are the three oldest theatre art forms in the world. The early forms of Chinese drama are simple, but over time they incorporated

Chinese opera / *Xiqu* 戏曲

various art forms, such as music, song and dance, martial arts, acrobatics, costume and make-up art, as well as literary art forms to become traditional Chinese opera.

It's commonly believed that traditional opera originated partly from the witchcraft practiced by ancient witches, especially on occasions of worshiping and praying to gods, healing ill patients or exorcism. The reason why it can last for a thousand years while traditional Greek and Indian opera have died is because of the rich performance art forms. The performers use four main skills: **song, speech, dance acting** which includes pure dance, pantomime and all other types of dance and the last one **combat**, which includes both acrobatics and fighting with all manner of weaponry. All of these skills are expected to be performed effortlessly, in keeping with the spirit of the art forms.

song, speech, dance acting, combat 唱念做打

What appeals to foreigners most might be the different styles of facial make-up, which is one of the highlights and requires distinctive techniques of painting. This tradition allegedly originated from an ancient general "**Prince of Lanling**". He was said to have a very beautiful, even a little feminine face. In order not to be taken lightly he always wore a terrifying mask in the battlefield. This finally developed to the tradition of colorful **facial make-up** in Chinese opera. Exaggerated designs are painted on each performer's face to symbolize a character's personality, role, and fate, and illustrate the character's emotional state and general character.

Prince of Lanling 兰陵王

facial make-up 戏曲脸谱

Connotations of Colors Used in Facial Make-up

white	sinister, evil, crafty, treacherous and suspicious
green	impulsive behavior, violence, no self-restraint or self-control
black	valor, fierce, rough
red	brave; loyal
yellow	ambitious, fierce, or intelligent
pink	sophisticated, cool-headed
blue	steadfast, fearless, calculating

Part II Western Folk Art

The history of prehistoric visual art in Europe started as mobile rock and cave painting and was characteristic of the period between the Paleolithic and the Iron Age. Written histories of European art often begin with the art of the Ancient Middle East and the Ancient Aegean civilizations, dating from the 3rd millennium BC.

Parallel with these significant cultures, art of one form or another existed all over Europe, wherever there were people, leaving signs such as carvings, decorated artifacts and huge standing stones. And all these could be regarded as early forms of folk art. Besides, there are more forms of tribal arts, ethnic arts and indigenous arts throughout Europe and America.

1. European Folk Music

European folk music has some of the most important and pioneer type of folk music in the world, these genres are famous and listened all around the world, so maybe they are not counted as folk music for many people anymore. But the truth is they are still part of traditional music in their origin country. Some example would be: Flamenco from Spain, Gypsy music of east Europe, different genres of Balkan music, Irish and Scottish music, etc.

1.1 Scottish Folk Music: Bagpipe

bagpipe 风笛

There was a flourishing culture of popular music in Scotland during the late Middle Ages, but most of the music didn't survive to present days. The first clear reference to the use of the Highland **bagpipes** mentions their use at a battle.

Bagpipe didn't originate from Scotland. It was introduced to Scotland roughly around 15th century. Records of a battle indicated that "warpipes" were carried into the battle. This is probably the most concrete record of the origin in Scottish bagpipe which had an appearance in a military text. Why do people only recall Scottish bagpipe when it was actually popular internationally? It is because Scottish bagpipe is not only a musical instrument, but also a very important part of Scottish culture as well as a cultural icon.

Scottish bagpipe has also been adopted by many countries that were formerly part of the British Empire, despite their lack of a Scottish or Irish population.

1.2 American Folk Music

bluegrass 蓝草乐（乡村音乐的分支）

gospel music 福音音乐

American folk music is also known as roots music. Many American folk music have been sung in the same family or folk group for generations. Roots music is a broad category of music including **bluegrass**, **gospel**, old time music, **Appalachian folk**, blues, native American music. It is considered "roots music" because it served as the basis of music later developed in the United States, including rock and roll, rhythm and blues, jazz and soul.

Appalachian folk music 阿巴拉契亚民间音乐

Gospel music is a genre of Christian music which can be traced to the early 17th century, with roots in the black oral tradition. The black slaves prayed in the field for less pain and labor after they were converted to Christianity. Later the prayer developed to **musical improvisation**.

musical improvisation 即兴音乐表演

After the **abolishment** of slavery, black people had their own churches and this musical improvisation became one of their church activities. Most of the churches relied on hand clapping and foot stomping as rhythmic accompaniment.

abolishment 废除

2. Western Folk Artifacts

2.1 Russian Nesting Dolls

Russian nesting dolls, also known as in Russian name "Matryoshka dolls" are the set of wooden dolls of decreasing size placed one inside another, which separates at the middle, top from bottom, to reveal a smaller figure of the same sort inside, which has, in turn, another figure inside of it, and so on. The first Russian nesting doll set was carved in 1890 by wood turning craftsman and wood carver from a design by a folk crafts painter. Traditionally the outer layer is a woman, dressed in a **sarafan**, a long and shapeless traditional Russian peasant jumper dress. The figures inside may be of either gender; the smallest, innermost doll is

Russian nesting doll (俄罗斯)套娃

sarafan 俄罗斯传统服装

typically a baby turned from a single piece of wood. Much of the artistry is in the painting of each doll, which can be very elaborate. Matryoshka dolls are often designed to follow a particular theme; for instance, peasant girls in traditional dress. Themes could have a wide range. In the West, Matryoshka dolls are often referred to as babushka dolls, babushka meaning "grandmother" or "old woman".

fertility 生育

Matryoshka is often seen as a symbol of the feminine side of Russian culture, being closely associated with family and **fertility**. Matryoshka dolls are a traditional representation of the mother carrying a child within her and can be seen as a representation of a chain of mothers carrying on the family legacy through the child in their womb. Furthermore, Matryoshka dolls are used to illustrate the unity of body, soul, mind, heart and spirit. Sometimes people employ the term "Matryoshka principle" or its equivalent "onion principle" to refer to the "object-within-similar-object" design (for example, the design of tables, where a smaller table nests within a larger table, and a smaller one within that) or the description of shell companies and similar corporate structures that are used in the context of **tax-evasion** schemes in low-tax jurisdictions (for example, offshore tax havens).

tax-evasion 逃税

Scottish tartan 苏格兰格子花呢

criss-crossed 十字交叉的

2.2 Scottish Tartan

Tartan is a pattern consisting of **criss-crossed** horizontal and vertical bands in multiple colors. It's a traditional Scottish pattern of coloured squares and crossed lines, or cloth, especially wool cloth, with this pattern. Tartans originated in woven wool, but now they are made in many other materials. The earliest documented tartan in Britain dates from the 3rd century AD. It was uncovered at Falkirk in central Scotland. The fragment was stuffed into the mouth of an earthenware pot containing Roman coins.

Due to political struggles, the use and dress of tartan has been severely restricted. Although George III **lifted the ban**, it was not until George IV visited Edinburgh in 1822 that Scottish tartans revived. But what really made Scotland tartan popular is British Queen Victoria. The Queen designed Victoria Tartan, and her husband Prince Albert designed the Balmoral Tartan. Both were used as decorations for the Royal family's Summer Palace in Balmoral Castle, Scotland, together with other various tartan patterns as interior decoration of the palace.

lifted the ban 解禁

Today tartan is particularly associated with Scotland. Scottish kilts almost always have tartan patterns. Tartan is regarded as a cultural icon of Scotland.

2.3 Irish Metalworking

The history of Irish art starts around 3200 BC with **Neolithic** stone carvings at the Newgrange **megalithic** tomb. There was a widespread metalworking in early Bronze Age. Irish gold personal ornaments began to be produced within about 200 years either side of 2000 BC, especially in the thin crescent-shaped disks which was probably first made in Ireland. A range of thin decorated gold discs, bands and plaques, often with pin-holes, were probably attached to clothing, and objects that appear to be earrings have also

Neolithic 新石器时代的

megalithic 巨石造成的

been found.

Indigenous 本土的

2.4 Indigenous American Mask-making

Native Americans have a long history of mask-making. The meaning and significance vary among different tribes. Indian or Native American masks were made for ceremonies, decoration, war rituals, shaman rituals, rituals initiating young man into the tribe, in healing rituals, in entertainment, given as gifts and spiritual rituals.

There are 2 types of masks with different themes: spirit masks and portrait masks. Spirit masks resemble animals which are spirits representing nature. Portrait masks are made to narrate stories.

The masks can represent people's characteristics; the portrait can represent a certain person; it can also stand for someone's status and spirit. When a mask depicts an animal, it usually symbolizes clan descended from some animal. Masks could be made from a single piece of wood. It has moveable parts, like eyes could open and shut. Masks can be transformational when closed one mask it could reveal another. Different colors of the masks have distinctive implications. Here are some examples:

Red represents happiness and faith;

Yellow and orange represents intellect;

Green represents healing, harmony and nature;

Purple represents mystery and magic;

Black represents victory and success;

White represents light and purity;

Blue represents intuition and wisdom.

2.5 Inuit Sculpture

Inuit 因纽特人

People use local material for the creation of folk art. Since there are no trees in the Arctic region, wood would be impossible to be applied in Inuit sculpture and art. Therefore, stones turn out to be the best choice. And the Inuit artists, the carvers, prefer a primitive and unpolished appearance of the sculpture.

3. Western Folk Dance

3.1 Morris Dance of England

Morris dance 莫里斯舞

Morris dance is a form of English folk dance usually accompanied by music. It is based on rhythmic stepping and the execution of **choreographed** figures by a group of dancers, usually wearing bell pads on their shins. Implements such as sticks, swords and handkerchiefs may also be wielded by the dancers. In a small number of dances for one or two people, steps are near and across a pair of clay tobacco pipes laid one across the other on the floor. The earliest known and surviving English written mention of Morris dance could be dated back to 1448, recording the payment of seven shillings to Morris dancers by the Goldsmiths' Company in London. Later in 16th century the Morris dance became attached to village fetes, and the **May Day** revels; Shakespeare says "as fit as a Morris for May Day".

choreograph 编舞设计

May Day 五朔节

3.2 Traditional Country Dance

country dance 乡村舞(一种传统英国交际舞，特别是男女面对面排成长列而跳的舞蹈)

Country dance is a genre of social dance for several couples, and is the characteristic form of folk dance of the British Isles. In England after about 1550, the term "country dance" referred to a dance of the upper classes, but the similar dances, usually called traditional dance, existed contemporaneously among country people and persisted in popular tradition.

Country dances are performed in three characteristic formations: 1) circular, for an indefinite number of couples ("round" dances), 2) "longways" set, double-file line for an indefinite number of couples, men on one side, women on the other, and 3) geometric formations (e. g., squares, triangles) or sets, usually for two, three, or four couples. The dancers execute a succession of varied patterns of figures. In "progressive-longways" dances, continuous interchange brings a new leading couple to the head of the set with each repetition of the pattern of figures. Round and longways dances predominate in the folk tradition. Longways and geometric sets are more frequent among courtly dances.

Country dances from England were assimilated into the traditional dance of other countries—e. g., Portugal and Denmark. English colonists carried them to North America, where they began a new folk-dance tradition as the "contra", or longways dance (e. g., the Virginia reel), and, in modified form, as the American square dance.

Flamenco 弗拉明戈舞

3.3 Spanish Flamenco

Flamenco is a variety of Spanish musical styles

developed as early as the 19th century. The oldest record of flamenco dates to 1774. Flamenco is one of the most characteristic elements of Spanish culture, especially throughout the southern region of **Andalucía**. That's the place where Gypsies supposedly started this passionate dance as a result of the fusion of **Moorish**, Jewish and Gypsy elements. Flamenco is incorporated art form of song, dance and guitar. And Flamenco dance is known for its emotional intensity, proud carriage, expressive use of the arms and rhythmic stamping of the feet.

Andalucía 西班牙南部的安达卢西亚
Moorish 摩尔人的

Part III Comparison and Contrast

1. Paper Cutting in Chinese & Western Style

Chinese paper-cutting, as one of the typical traditional art forms, was connected to ancient activities of worshiping ancestors and gods. It originates from the 6th century, although some believe that its history could be traced as far back as the Warring States Period (475-221 BC), long before the paper was invented. At that time, people used other thin materials like leaves, **silver foil**, silk and even leather, to carve hollowed patterns. People realized paper was easy to cut, store or discard after it was invented. Then paper became the major material for this type of artwork.

Paper cutting was not only a kind of handcraft, but also a piece of artwork, as it could express people's ideas and perception of life. In the Ming and Qing

Dynasties, paper-cutting experienced its peak development, being used to decorate doors, windows and walls. Red is the most commonly used color as it is meant for celebration and happiness in Chinese culture. Chinese paper cuts are mostly done in folk people's common artistic sense and **freehand** with no pre-designing. They are often flat on the same surface. The basic cut-outs consisting of a single image usually forms a **symmetrical** design. Normally paper cuts are used on festivals like the Spring Festival, or weddings and childbirth. Chinese paper cuts are mainly designed for good intentions of health, prosperity and auspiciousness with decorative purposes. Although paper cutting is a global folk art form, Chinese paper cutting is the only one on the **UNESCO Intangible Cultural Heritage** Lists since 2009.

silver foil 银箔	freehand 徒手(剪)
symmetrical 对称	UNESCO 联合国教科文组织
Intangible Cultural Heritage 非物质文化遗产	silhouette 剪影

Compared to Chinese paper cutting, Western-style paper cutting applies different colors to achieve various visual experience which are highly expressive. The cut-outs are the demonstration of individual feelings. Unlike the Chinese paper cuts, Western paper cuts are usually multidimensional; the vivid presentation of images in different layers of paper cuts shows rich texture and sophistication. Chinese paper cut-outs are practical in private places for rituals or ornament, while Western paper cuts could be displayed in more public areas. One major difference in European countries like Britain, France or Germany is that **silhouette** is more popular which emphasizes the outline or the contrasting color of black and white. In America the paper cuts are more practical and many of which are full of creativity and imitation of children style.

2. Chinese Lion Dance VS English Long Sword Dance

Lion dance is a form of folk dance in Chinese culture and other Asian countries in which performers mimic a lion's movements in a lion costume to bring good luck and fortune. It is usually performed during the Chinese New Year and other Chinese traditional, cultural and religious festivals. It may also be performed at important occasions such as business opening, special celebrations or wedding ceremonies to bring prosperity as well as chase away evil spirits. Accompanied by the music of beating drums, clashing **cymbals** and **gongs**, lion dances imitate a lion's various movements or demonstrate **martial arts** agility, depending on the style: The southern style performance could be based on the study of a lion's behavior which is vivid and entertaining, even comical. And the northern lion dance has close relations to Chinese martial arts which is gymnastic, involving rolling, wrestling, leaping, jumping, climbing, or **kowtowing**. The lion symbolizes power, wisdom and superiority. Lion dance is an excellent example of Chinese folk culture spreading across the world.

cymbal 钹　　gong 锣　　martial arts 武术　　kowtowing 叩头
Plough Monday 显现节后第一个周一，旧时有些地区该日会有庆祝或纪念活动
blunt tip 钝尖　　edge 刀刃　　long sword sides 长剑舞队列

The long sword dance is a hilt-and-point sword dance recorded mainly in England. The dances are usually performed around Christmas time and were

believed to derive from a rite performed to enable a fruitful harvest. It's believed that the dances originated from a religious or magical ceremony that was performed around **Plough Monday** to promote fertile soil. Long sword dances vary in the way they are performed, with some being slow and militaristic; others have different features including variations of numbers of dancers and distinctive movements. In long sword dances "swords" are not actual swords, but implements specifically made for the dance. The dancers are usually linked one to another via the swords, with one end of each held by one dancer and the other end by another. The long sword is about 2.6 feet (0.8 meters) long, with a wooden handle at one end, a **blunt tip**, and no **edge**. Sometimes ribbons are threaded through a hole in the tip of the sword, and the dancers grab on to them during the course of the dance. **Long sword sides** usually consist of five to eight dancers. There is often a supernumerary "character", who dances around, outside and inside the set.

Part IV Reflection and Presentation

1. Many artists and scholars have pointed out that ultimately art depends on human nature. (Steven Pinker) How do you understand this quote? Can you relate your answer to the interpretation of the term "folk art"?

2. There must be varieties of local folk art forms in your hometown. Choose one of them that you are familiar with and introduce it to your classmates.

3. Folk art is usually made and being observed in the context of folk culture, which is largely in contrast with academic art (or high art as some will put it.) In many cases the lines between them are blurred. Can you name a few differences between folk art and academic art?

Part V Mini-pedia

1. Chinese *Guqin*

Guqin is a plucked seven-string Chinese musical instrument of the zither family with a history of more than 3, 000 years. The first Chinese character "Gu-" (meaning "ancient") was later added for clarification. *Guqin* has traditionally been favoured by scholars and literati as an instrument of great subtlety and refinement, as highlighted by the quote "A gentleman does not part with his *Qin* or *Se* without good reasons (士无故不撤琴瑟)".

In 1977, a recording of a piece of *Guqin* music "Flowing Water" was chosen to be included in the Voyager Golden Record sent into outer space by NASA spacecraft. The reason of being selected is because the tonal structure of the instrument—its musical scale—is derived from fundamental physical laws related to vibration and overtones, representing the intellectual capacity of human beings on this subject. In 2003, *Guqin* music was proclaimed as one of the Masterpieces of the Oral and Intangible Heritage of Humanity by UNESCO.

2. Ocarina

The ocarina is an ancient wind musical instrument, a type of vessel flute. It originates from the traditional Italian carnival whistles of earthenware meaning "little goose" in Italian. It's often bird-shaped and sounding only one or two notes. Variations exist, but a typical ocarina is an enclosed space with four to twelve finger holes and a mouthpiece that projects from the body. It is traditionally made from clay or ceramic, but other materials are also used—such as plastic, wood, glass, metal, or bone. The ocarina is a well-known European example of the globular flute, a form that occurs in many ancient and modern cultures. Similar musical instruments are *Xun* in China and globe flute in Africa.

References

1. 刘春芳,等. 中西文化对比教程[M]. 北京:中国人民大学出版社, 2017.
2. 束定芳. 中国文化英语教程[M]. 上海:上海外语教育出版社, 2016.
3. 王焱,等. 中西文化比较[M]. 北京:清华大学出版社, 2017.
4. 钟敬文. 民俗学概论(第二版)[M]. 北京:高等教育出版社, 2010.
5. Ching-Yi Wang. The Integration of Folk Art into the Art Curricula with Implications for Teacher Education. *The International Journal of Organizational Innovation*,2010,3(1):116-127.
6. Danial Lombardo. Painting European Folk Art. *Library Journal*, Mar 15, 2001: 126, 5; ProQuest Pg. 82.
7. Debra Kodish. Cultivating Folk Arts and Social Change. *Journal of American Folklore*, 126(502):434-454.
8. Martin Myrone. *Instituting English Folk Art*, *Visual Culture in Britain*, 2009, 10:1, 27-52, DOI: 10.1080/14714780802686480.
9. https://www.britannica.com/art/folk-art.
10. http://www.historyofmasks. net/famous-masks/indian-masks/.

Unit 9
Chinese and Western Folk Beliefs

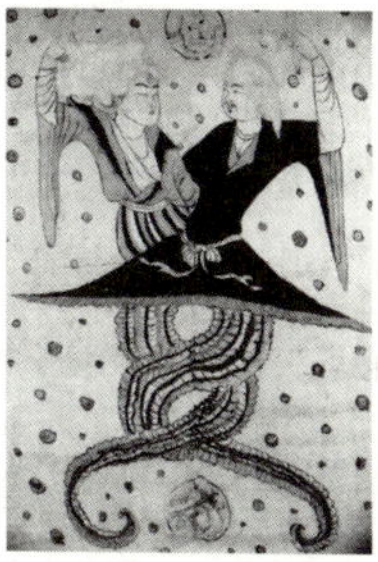
Fuxi and Nüwa

Cromlech in Scotland

Learning Objectives

- To be familiar with the different categories and features of Chinese and Western folk beliefs
- To get a better understanding of the different traditional beliefs of the Han people and ethnic minority groups
- To compare and contrast the similarities and differences about some typical folk images or items (such as dragon in Chinese culture VS in Western culture) and analyze reasons in terms of folklore

Lead-in Questions

- Do you find there are certain similarities in people's character with the same *shengxiao*, the Chinese zodiac, or the animal sign of your birth year? What about the star signs, the zodiac in Western culture?
- Why do people believe in seemingly "superstitious" ideas or theories such as *fengshui*, "karma", "fatalism"?

Part I Understanding Folk Beliefs

The term "folk belief" may refer to "folk religion; popular religion; communal religion" in different cultures. The term was first evidenced in use by British folklorist Laurence Gomme in 1892 and became widely-accepted in 1930s. Folk beliefs are spontaneous and symbolic behavior or rites to worship tangible objects in a certain community out of spiritual or psychological needs. Early as primitive time, our ancestors have sacrificial rites to worship holy spirits or their gods. This might be the primeval form of folk beliefs.

Without complete religious doctrines, disciplines and organizations, folk beliefs are fundamentally different from institutional religions like Christianity, Buddhism, or Islamism.

In Western folklore study the term "folk religion" is more commonly used than folk belief. This concept is flexible and not at all standardized. It is often used to describe popular religious practices of people in various world cultures, especially in the East. Eastern folk cultures tend to fuse together features of various religious traditions to create their own belief systems.

1. Origin and Sources of Folk Belief

collective consciousness 集体意识

(1) There are three major sources of the origin of folk belief: the concept of soul; supernatural power and **collective consciousness**. Folk belief is by nature a term relating to people's spiritual life. It originates from the idea that all things have souls. The concept of soul begins with the exploration into human's inner world. Men start to think about questions like: What cause people's death and stop

their breathing? Where do dreams come from? When people believe that natural phenomenon and materials, social phenomenon and dreams are all controlled and guided by souls, the **worship of the nature, ancestors, and objects** come into being.

worship of nature / ancestors /objects 自然崇拜/祖先崇拜/实物崇拜

(2) People long wonder what kind of power is behind mysterious natural phenomenon like the creation of steep cliff and the echo in the valley. Where does supernatural power come from, like Polynesian's belief of the existence of "mana", and the American Indian's "orenda"? And in China, people believe in the magic power of ***yin* and *yang* or *qi***.

yin and *yang* 阴阳

qi / *chi* 气

(3) Collective consciousness is the common beliefs and feelings shared by members of the same community. Primitive beliefs arise from **clan society** because of the lower productivity then. People have to gather up the strength of the collective group and share common beliefs for survival. The core of primitive belief is sacrificial rites. The purpose of rites is to help the communication between man and gods.

clan society 氏族社会

2. Objects of Worship

2.1 Worship of Soul

The first belief in **worshiping souls** starts with human itself. Ignorance and confusion of death and dreams lead to the idea that human being is made up of body and soul. Soul is attached to human body. It leaves the body temporarily when falling ill or having dreams. It leaves the body per-

worship souls 灵魂崇拜

manently when people die. Having the faith that all things have souls, ancient people even worship animals or household stuff.

2.2 Worship of Animals

animism 万物有灵论
Oroqen people 鄂伦春族

There has been a folk psychological belief in **animism**. Traditionally the **Oroqen people**, for example, have a special veneration for animals, especially the bear and the tiger, which they consider their blood brothers. Before they start hunting, there will be a launching ceremony, and should a bear has been hunted down, they will worship the bear by offering a ritual with sacred chanting. And the head of the bear will be put on the tree branches to have a burial by the nature (or more specifically, by the wind). People will worship the bear head to ask for forgiveness and for more preys in the future.

2.3 Worship of the God of Nature

God of Nature 自然神

God of Nature includes natural phenomena like the sky, the earth, the sun, the moon, stars, wind, lightning, etc. While there was no scientific explanation in ancient times, people in the past tend to believe these phenomena are the representation of holy gods. During the process it even develops to specific images. For example, the worship of mighty waterbody finally develop into the worship of "**He Bo, River Lord**", or "**Dragon King**".

He Bo /River Lord 河伯
Dragon King 龙王
totem 图腾(崇拜)

2.4 Worship of Totems

It's believed that the word "totem" comes from an

Indian dialect meaning "his kin". In clan society, every clan family has its own totem, be it a plant, an animal or something from the nature, it is something with a blood tie to the family. People regard this totem as their ancestors in the past and a present-day god of protection. For example, phoenix was the totem of Chu State (most of which is the present-day Hubei and Hunan Province) in Waring States Period of Chinese history.

2.5 Worship of Ancestors

The **ancestor veneration** is based on love and respect for the deceased. It is related to the beliefs that in some cultures ancestors are considered a part of the family whose spirits have the power to intervene in the affairs, even the fortune of the living.

ancestor veneration 敬祖

In different cultural background like European, Asian, Oceanian and African cultures, the goals of ancestor veneration differ from one another. For some it's a way to ask for special favors or assistance. For others there has been social or non-religious function of ancestor veneration to cultivate kinship values, such as **filial piety**, family loyalty, and continuity of the **family lineage**. Ancestor veneration occurs in societies with every degree of social, political and technological complexity.

filial piety (子女)孝顺

family lineage 家族谱系

2.6 Worship of Patron Saints by Occupation

A **patron saint by occupation** is the deity who is worshiped by the same trade and is usually referred to as ***Zu shiye*** in Chinese, meaning the founder and great master of

patron saints by occupation 行业神

Zushiye 祖师爷

that trade. In ancient times when both productivity and technology were underdeveloped, it was natural for people to praise and admire a famous person in history or legend as the patriarch of the trade. This person or god became the inventor and also the protector of the trade. This is clearly for the purpose of prosperous business. And the patron saint could play a very important part in bounding and connecting people of the same occupation or activity so that they could support and protect each other from suffering any business risk. That explains the popularity of patron saints of almost all trades. Here are some examples: **Lu Ban**, patron saint of carpenter; **Lu Yu**, patron saint of tea business; **Kitchen God**, patron saint of cook/chef; the list goes on with length.

Lu Ban 鲁班
Lu Yu 陆羽
Kitchen God 灶神

2.7 Worship of God of Auspiciousness

People pursue a happy life and avoid being attacked by disasters or diseases. This is why they worship the **God of Auspiciousness**. Ancient people summarize it as "**Five Auspiciousness**", namely, fortune, prosperity, longevity, wealth and happiness. The Chinese character "Fu" on a piece of red paper during the holiday season is exactly the symbol of God of Auspiciousness.

God of Auspiciousness 福神
Five Auspiciousness 五福

2.8 Heaven-Earth-Sovereign-Parent-Teacher

Heaven-earth-sovereign-parent-teacher system is a system of sacred images deriving from Confucianism. Confucianism does not believe in ghosts or spirits, so it develops a very unique system of worship for people to hold respect and awe; and to regulate people's behavior.

Heaven-Earth-Sovereign-Parent-Teacher 天地君亲师

2.9 Folklorization and Deification

When average people don't understand the profound meaning of doctrines of a certain religion, they tend to folklorize the deities of the religion. A great case in point is the localization of Guanyin from Buddhism. Also, ***Tian-guan-ci-fu*** from Taoism finally finds its place as the God of Wealth and Fortune.

Tian-guan-ci-fu 天官赐福

In addition, exceptional individuals may also become deified after death. Guan Yu is a well-known **tutelary**. While he is remembered for his loyalty towards Liu Bei, he is also known for repaying Cao Cao's kindness. People have been long honoring his heroic deeds and moral qualities. He became one of East Asia's most popular paradigms of loyalty and righteousness, being called the **Divus Guan** or **Lord Guan**. It's not uncommon that the achievements of those great figures are glorified to such an extent after their deaths that they were deified among the public.

tutelary 守护人

Divus Guan 关帝

Lord Guan 关公

3. Mediums and Rites

As for a certain folk belief, concepts and theories are the expression of people's beliefs and feelings, while rites are means to communicate with gods. People are convinced that the world is made up of the nature, human being and gods or ghosts. In order to communicate with gods and ghosts, people need a **medium**. Mediumship is the practice of mediating communication between spirits of the dead and living human beings. Practitioners are known as "mediums"

medium 媒介，灵媒

or "spirit mediums". Medium is usually someone with "**witchcraft**".

witchcraft 巫术，魔法

3.1 Classifications of Mediums

3.1.1 Witch and Wizard

In Chinese folk belief, the first spirit mediums are females called **witches**, and male practitioners are called **wizards** who came to practice later than witches. They both are capable of channeling with spirits. One way to communicate with a spirit is to invite the spirit to control the witch's body or voice so that the spirit could use it to send messages.

witch / wizard(女/男)巫师

3.1.2 **Oracle**

oracle 祭司

Oracles usually develop or grow from witches or wizards. They are the ones providing wise and insightful counsel or prophetic predictions of the future, inspired by the gods.

Oracles are mostly male. They might be able to communicate with the spirits at first, but their major task and expertise lie in conducting ancestor veneration and **sacrificial rites**. They are the first ones to acquire all kinds of knowledge, language and calendar. They are the king's supporters and consultants.

sacrificial rites 祭祀仪式

3.1.3 Witch Doctor; Fortune-teller; Geomancy

Other than those above, there are witch doctors, who use witchcraft and herbs to treat patients who get ill.

There are some sorcerers who practice **geomancy** to help people decide the location of temples, houses and even graves.

geomancy 地相术，风水

At last it comes to the fortune-teller, who are supposed

to predict whether your future life is miserable or prosperous.

3.2 Functions of Witchcraft

Both witches and wizards are able to communicate with the spirits. There are mostly 5 functions: First, working to predict whether your destiny is good and prosperous or not. Second, hosting the sacrificial rites to worship ancestors or the heaven. Third, practice witchcraft to ensure auspiciousness and keep away the diseases. Fourth, hosting ceremonies of a person's life, like birth celebration, wedding, or funeral. The fifth is to act as a judge or referee to settle down disputes.

4. Features of Folk Belief

4.1 Utilitarian

utilitarian 功利的

Folk beliefs are quite utilitarian since all activities related to them are for survival. Folk beliefs aim to ask for auspiciousnesss and prosperity; and they also help solve problems people meet in their real life. The prayer and the rites are all for realistic purposes. When there is a drought, people pray piously for the rain. Those who have fertility problems would pray desperately for a baby.

4.2 Mysterious

The rites are usually not open to the public during the process. All activities and skills of being a witch will only pass on generations through a father-to-son, or mother-to-daughter chain or through apprenticeship.

spontaneous 自发的

4.3 Spontaneous

Folk beliefs are spontaneous in the sense that they develop mainly through oral transmission, and arise from collective group. People of same regional or ethnic groups tend to create or recreate images based on local successful figures. **Mazu** in Fujian Province is the recreation of a kind and benevolent local female **Lin Moniang** combined with features of Guan Yin.

Mazu 妈祖

Lin Moniang 林默娘(也有称林默),妈祖的原型,据说经常救助和保护出海的渔民

inclusive 包容性

4.4 Inclusive

Folk beliefs are inclusive because they absorb elements and contents from other religions or folk beliefs in the process of establishment. A good case in point would be the spread of Buddhism in China.

Part II Chinese Folk Beliefs

1. Classification of Chinese Folk Beliefs

Classification	Branches	Examples
Communal Folk Beliefs	Local Deity Worship 地方神崇拜	* Earth God 土地神 * City God 城隍 * Mazu 妈祖 * Other deities that only locals know
	Ancestor Worship 祖先崇拜	

Continued

Classification	Branches	Examples
Individual Folk Beliefs	Fortune-telling Practices	* Palm and face reading 看手相，看面相 * Glyphomancy 测字；解读人名 * Numerology 命理学；测生辰八字 * Divination 占卜；卜卦
	Warding off Evil Spirits or Bad Luck	* Wearing a red waist belt in the zodiac year of birth 本命年系红腰带 * Selecting auspicious dates for conducting a wedding or opening a business 择吉日结婚或开业
	Geomancy 地相术；测风水	* Locating a good business site * Changing the location of doors and windows * Rearranging the household furniture * Locating the grave site for ancestors
Influence of "Three Teachings"	Confucianism Buddhism Taoism	* Benevolence and rites (Confucianism) * Karma and rebirth (Buddhism) * Life philosophy (Taoism)
Influence of Maritime Culture Among Han people	Mazuism (Worship of Mazu)	* A hybrid of local culture and Buddhist elements

2. Details of Chinese Folk Beliefs

2.1 Local Deity Worship

Communal folk beliefs refer to beliefs and ritual activities based on some local communities, mostly in rural areas. When people feel like worshiping **local deities**, the village temples are the places to go. Communal rites will be

local deity 地方神

practiced on important annual ceremonies such as the Chinese New Year and Lantern Festival, or on the birthdays of the gods. Whenever an individual wants to worship, he can go any time bowing and praying, proclaiming vows, making offerings of food or drink, **burning incense** and **spirit money**. These acts are usually followed by divination of the god's response by **dropping divine blocks** or **consulting divine poetry**.

burn incense 烧香
spirit money 纸钱
dropping divine block 抽签
consulting divine poetry 解签

2.2 Ancestor Worship

Chinese villages have been commonly comprised of one or several **clans**. The **clan temples** are often village-based and serve as one of the gathering places for the clansmen in the village and surrounding villages. Ancestor worship and local deity worship are intermingled. Functionally, ancestor worship and local deity worship are similarly contributing to collective solidarity and group cohesion, which are very much territory-based.

clan 宗族/氏族
clan temples 宗祠；祠堂

2.3 Individual Folk Beliefs

Individual folk beliefs refer to supernatural beliefs and practices that are independent of any collectivity. This includes: various fortune-telling practices that reveal and change an individual's fortune; practices to ward off evil spirits or bad fortune; the worship of the god of wealth and practices of *fengshui* in this type.

Fortune-telling is a good case in point. Fortune tellers claim to be able to predict your fortune or fate by carefully **reading palms** and faces. Another trick is called

reading palm/ face 看手相/面相

glyphomancy which means dissecting Chinese characters in the names. There are some other means including **numerology** and **divination**.

glyphomancy 测字/解读人名

numerology 命理学;测生辰八字

divination 占卜，卜卦

Wearing a red waist belt in the zodiac year of birth is a common practice. The idea is to ward off evil spirits and bad luck. Similar activity would be to select auspicious dates for conducting a wedding or opening a business. This elaborate choice of dates is supposed to keep troubles and problems away so that the business will be a very prosperous one.

Other than just keeping away from bad luck or events, people also want to take active actions to improve their situations or alter their fate. So **geomancy** is rather popular. It is the art of arranging buildings and areas in a good or lucky position. The master of geomancy can help locating a good business site or changing the location of doors and windows, rearranging the household furniture to enhance the physical and spiritual health of the individuals living in the home; and also locating the grave site for ancestors to maximize the worldly benefits of living individuals. No matter what has been done, it all symbolizes people's strong faith in their beliefs.

geomancy 地相术;测风水

2.4 Influence of "Three Teachings"

Early interests in Chinese folk religion were from Western missionaries and missionary-turned scholars. Later the interests developed into the perception that it was a complex combination of the "**Three Teachings**" of Confucianism, Buddhism and Taoism for the elites. For the commoners, ritual practices and the supernatural beliefs were

Three Teachings "三教"，指中国传统文化中的儒、释、道

all dismissed as superstitions. But when viewing commoners' religious life in an anthropological and scientific way, one could find folk beliefs instead of superstitions. Chinese folk beliefs include elements partly traceable to aspects of Confucianism, Buddhism and Taoism.

Confucianism 孔子学说，儒学

2.4.1 Influence of **Confucianism**

Confucianism is described as a tradition, a philosophy, a humanistic or rationalistic religion, a way of governing, or simply a way of life. Confucianism was developed from the teachings of the Chinese philosopher and educator Confucius during a period which was named "**Hundred Schools of Thoughts**". Confucius advocates *Ren* (benevolence), *Li* (rites), particularly stresses the respect for social hierarchy. He also stresses on the concept of **filial piety** and associated practices. Being famous for instructing students based on their intellectual inclinations, his teachings were later recorded by his students which was entitled ***The Analects***.

Hundred Schools of Thoughts 诸子百家

filial piety 孝顺

The Analects《论语》

2.4.2 Influence of Taoism

Taoism is a religious or philosophical tradition of Chinese origin which emphasizes living in harmony with the "Tao". The Chinese character literally means "way" or "path". Taoism differs from Confucianism by not emphasizing rigid rituals and social order. Taoist ethics in general tend to emphasize *wuwei*, which means action without intention, naturalness, simplicity and spontaneity. The most influential Taoist text is ***The Scripture of Ethics***, which was supposedly written by Lao-tzu (or Lao-zi). Its earliest texts have been excavated (written on bamboo slips) dating back to the late 4th century BC. In the system of

The Scripture of Ethics《道德经》

Chinese folk belief, numerous gods are organized into a hierarchy headed by the **Jade Emperor**, which was an image borrowed from Taoism.

Jade Emperor 玉皇大帝

2.4.3 Influence of Buddhism

Buddhism, as a foreign religion coming into Chinese culture, survived only because of its adaptation to the Chinese environment. This adaptation has largely been the compromise to and fusion of folk belief in China.

Chinese folk belief arises much earlier than the entering of Buddhism into China. So the only way for Buddhism to find a stand in Chinese culture would be its fusion with the folk belief. Many religious figures have proved this, including the image of Guanyin, Wenshu and Dizang. That's the most obvious and strong argument for the localization of Buddhism. The expression "Han Buddhism" shows that Buddhism in China is totally different from its original form.

2.5 Influence of Maritime Culture in the Han People

Mazu, or spelt as Matsu, is a Chinese sea goddess. She is the deified form of the historical Lin Mo or Lin Moniang, a Fujianese whose life span is believed to be dated from 960 to 987. Revered after her death as a **tutelary deity** of fishermen and sailors, her worship spread throughout China's coastal regions and overseas Chinese communities across Southeast Asia.

tutelary deity 守护神

Mazu represents the best of Chinese virtue. She is kind, generous, always ready to help fishermen and sailors in trouble at the sea. That's why she was worshiped so much and so widely.

In the late 10th century Mazu (then still called Lin Moniang) lived in Fujian. There are various sources and versions of the legend of Mazu, most of them indicating the connection with Guanyin (known to the West as **Goddess of Mercy**). In that era the coastal area of Fujian was greatly **sinicized** by influxes of refugees fleeing invasions of northern China. So **Mazuism** may represent a **hybrid** of Buddhist elements and local culture.

Guanyin / Goddess of Mercy 观音菩萨
sinicized 中国化
Mazuism 妈祖崇拜
hybrid 混合物

3. Folk Beliefs of Ethnic Minority Groups in China

Mongols 蒙古族
Shamanism 萨满教

3.1 Mongols: Tengri Worship

Shamanism is quite popular in Manchu, Evenki, Hezhe, Oroqen and some ethnic groups in present-day Russia. These are all Manchu-Tungusic speaking ethnic branches. The term "shaman" refers to witch in the language.

The dominant belief of Mongolian Shamanism is the worship of the heaven, that is **Tengri worship**. The core being of Tengri worship is the **Heavenly-father**, **Earth-mother** and **Animism**.

Tengri worship 长生天崇拜
Heavenly-father 天父
Earth mother 地母
Animism 万物有灵论

3.2 Tibetans

3.2.1 Worship of Mountain Deity

Worship of the nature is characteristic of almost every ethnic community. Tibetans are always in awe of the nature (more specifically the natural wonders such as high mountains). So they will burn cypress branches(煨桑) on Tibetan New Year. Crawling along the mountains clockwise(转山)

and offering sacrifices are also parts of the ritual.

3.2.2 Worship of Yaks

Yaks play an indispensable role in nomadic lives in Tibet. It seems natural to worship yaks since they are named "boat of the plateau". In **Tibetan Buddhism**, the yak head symbolizes **Dorje**. Tibetans intermingle the worship of mountain deity with the yaks. In their beliefs, the avatars of the famous mountain deities are all white yaks.

Tibetan Buddhism 藏传佛教

Dorje 多吉/金刚

3.2.3 Worship of Rocks

Rocks are just like mountains that are so mighty and need to be worshiped. The highest respect has been shown when Tibetans worship the **Mani Cairns**. These are stones engraved with the **6-syllabled mantra** from **Sanskrit**. Mani stones are intentionally placed together to form cairns or along the roads or rivers as an offering to spirits of the place.

Mani Cairns 玛尼堆

6-syllabled mantra 六字真言

Sanskrit 梵语

3.3 Hui People

3.3.1 Worship of Nature

Hui people believe in Animism, so they show respect and awe to animals, plants and natural phenomenon like rainbows and lightning.

3.3.2 Worship of Souls and Spirits

There are both good kind spirits and evil ghosts to Hui people. So for those who die a natural course and dead babies, Hui people hold burial rites and sacrificial rites for them. But some other spirits are personified and thought to be evil. People believe this evil spirits can drive people to do bad or immoral things. So these evil spirits become a reminder to behave themselves.

3.3.3 A Case Study

Why do the Hui people never kill spiders? And why can they only kill a pigeon with a gold knife?

cobweb 蜘蛛网

It's said that Saint Mohammed had once been fighting with enemies for 81 days. He finally retreated into a cave. Just when he was worried about being found, something miraculous happened: a perfect **cobweb** appeared and covered the entrance of the cave with a spider on it. When enemies were about to enter the cave, two pigeons flew out. So enemies left and went to search somewhere else. They assumed no one could be in the cave without frightening the pigeon or ruining the cobweb. After that, Saint Mohammed granted prosperity for spiders and pigeons. That's why Hui people will only sweep spiders out of their houses and they can only use a gold knife to kill pigeons for no one but serious patients.

Part III Western Folk Beliefs

1. Nature Worship

1.1 Worship of Huge Stones / Rocks

Stonehenge 巨石阵

Stonehenge is a prehistoric monument consisting of a ring of standing stones. These stones are believed to be constructed from 3000 BC to 2000 BC. The huge stone constructions are assumed to be monuments for ritual purposes but there are still no definitive answers. It could be related to burial ceremony and ancestor veneration. Because the construction has an obvious connection with sunlight-catching purpose, archaeologists assume it might be a gathering place for primitive people at annual **summer and winter solstice**. There's even a new theory suggesting that it could be a place of healing because some human bones found there appear to have deformities.

summer/winter solstice 夏至/冬至

The Stonehenge in **Salisbury Plain** becomes the British cultural icon. But there are some other stone constructions elsewhere:

Salisbury Plain 索尔兹伯里平原

Menhir is a tall upright stone erected in prehistoric times in western Europe.

Menhir 巨石柱/独石

Dolmen (Britain and France) is a large flat stone laid on upright ones.

Dolmen 石碑/牌坊(形状)

Cromlech is large flat stones laid on upright ones mainly found in Wales.

Cromlech 环状列石

With or without the muti-functions or shapes, these stones are a living proof of nature worship.

1.2 Worship of Sacred Mountains

History shows that mountains were commonly part of a complex system of mountain worship and ancestor worship. Ancient tribespeople etched special meaning into the mountain and mound terrain. The history of ancestors could be told by simply pointing at specific mountains and remembering the stories that were passed down throughout the generations. The worship of ancestors and the mountains were largely inseparable.

Various cultures around the world maintain the importance of mountain worship and sacredness. One example is New Zealand. Taranaki Tribe centers their whole life around Mount Taranaki, the sacred mountain. Tribespeople created a love story in which Taranaki Mountain found love with a neighboring volcano. This narrative plays out in the lives of the tribespeople where the mountain is their love and their life force.

The most symbolic aspect of a mountain is the peak because it's believed that it is closest to heaven or other religious world. Many religions have traditions centered on sacred mountains, such as Mount Olympus in Greek mythology. It's the highest mountain peak in Greece. It was once regarded as the "home of the Greek Gods/The Twelve Olympians of the **Hellenistic** World".

Hellenistic 早期希腊文化的

2. Ancestor Veneration

2.1 North America

The original inhabitants there honored the dead with various traditional ceremonies, including food offerings and prayers. In America and Canada, flowers, wreaths, grave decorations and sometimes candles or even small pebbles are put on graves year-round as a way to honor the dead.

2.2 Europe

Traditionally, in Celtic and Germanic Europe, the feast of **Samhain** was specially associated with the deceased, and

Samhain 死神节

in these countries, it was still customary to set a place for them at table on this day until relatively recent times. Today in most Catholic countries in Europe, November 1 (All Saints' Day, also known as Day of the Dead) has become the day when families go to the cemeteries and light candles for their dead relatives. In a British context, the autumn ancestor festival corresponds to Halloween, which derives from the Celtic Samhain.

2.3 Mayan Religion

The **Mayans** were big believers of the **afterlife**; believing that the soul never died but instead continued on a dangerous journey in the after world. They believed in heaven, but thought that it was reserved only for those who died at childbirth and the men and woman who were used as sacrifices to the Gods. They believed in **human sacrifices** because they felt that it was the only means of contact with the Gods. Sacrificing life was their way of feeding the Gods and receiving their blessings, and they feared that if they did not sacrifice humans, they would be severely punished. At the ceremonies the person being sacrificed had his or her own heart ripped out and burned as a way of showing the Gods the ultimate respect.

Mayan 玛雅人

afterlife 来生，来世

human sacrifice(活人)殉葬

3. Patron Saint

A **patron / patroness saint**, or "heavenly protector" is a saint who is regarded as the heavenly advocate of a nation, place, craft, activity, class, clan, family or person. The

patron/patroness saint 保护神

choice is often made on the basis of some real or presumed relationship with the persons or places involved. St. Patrick, for example, is the patron saint of Ireland because he is credited with bringing Christianity to the Irish people.

3.1 St. George of England

The Golden Legend 《黄金传说》

Crusade 十字军东征

chivalry 骑士精神

St. George as a early figure of martyr was probably a soldier. He is credited with enduring astounding tortures and performing equally astounding miracles, but it was the tale of his combat against a dragon to save a princess's life which really ensured his popularity. This first appeared in the *Legenda Aurea* (***The Golden Legend***) in the 13th century. His importance in Western Europe increased after a reported vision of him during the siege of Antioch in the First **Crusade** was taken as a sign of victory. A military and aristocratic cult rapidly developed. By the close of the Middle Ages he was regarded as the patron saint of England and a model of **chivalry**.

3.2 Saint Joan of Arc

Joan of Arc (圣女) 贞德

Hundred Years' War (英法) 百年战争

Joan of Arc is considered a heroine of France for her role during the **Hundred Years' War**. She was sent to the Siege of Orléans as part of a relief army. She gained prominence after the siege was lifted only nine days later. Several additional swift victories boosted French morale and paved the way for the final French victory. Unfortunately she was captured in May 1430 and burned to death at about nineteen years of age. In about 30 years after her death she was declared innocent by the Pope and in 19th century she became the national symbol of France. She remained the patron saint among French people despite the later recognition from the church and the emperor. She has also been a popular figure in literature, painting, sculpture and other cultural works since the time of her death, and many famous writers, playwrights, filmmakers, artists and composers have created, and continue to create cultural depictions of her.

Part IV Comparison and Contrast

1. Chinese Iconic Dragon VS. Western Evil Dragon

The mighty and mythical dragon appears in many legends and fairy tales around the world. But beliefs about dragon vary distinctively in different cultures. Dragons in Chinese culture are often depicted as wingless, four-legged, **serpentine** creatures with above-average intelligence. It is an **auspicious** creature that can cause weather changes and **summon** rain. Since Chinese society was founded on agriculture that thrived during the wet season, Chinese dragons were seen as **deities** and were worshiped. Eventually it became the symbol of **imperial power**. Even today, as a magical creature beloved by the people, it still represents wealth, wisdom, success, power and good fortune. Chinese people proudly claim to be the **descendants** of the dragon. The dragon also appears in the publications of Western media as the symbol of China.

There is one connotation that Western folklore lacks but wide-accepted in Chinese folk culture. Chinese dragons are part of the harmonious forces *yin* and *yang*, which play a large part in Chinese philosophy. Dragons are classified as *yang*, and considered bright, masculine and solar. The phoenix is *yin*, which is soft, feminine and lunar. At Chinese weddings, these two creatures appear together as symbols of harmony and a happy marriage.

serpentine 蛇形的	auspicious 吉利的，有助于成功的	summon 召唤，传召
deity 神	imperial power 皇权	descendant 后裔
Saint George Slaying the Dragon "圣乔治屠龙"		ravenous 饿极了的

Dragons in Western culture have often been depicted as winged, horned, four-legged, and capable of breathing fire. They are usually portrayed as monsters to be tamed or overcome, and other typical dragons protect caverns or castles filled with gold and treasure. An evil dragon is often associated with a great hero who tries to slay it, as in the popular legend of ***Saint George Slaying the Dragon***. A good one is said to give support or wise advice. Dragons usually have **ravenous** appetite, and their blood is said to have magical properties. These dragons appear frequently in Western fantasy literature, including *The Hobbit* by J. R. R. Tolkien, the *Harry Potter* series by J. K. Rowling, and *A Song of Ice and Fire* by George R. R. Martin.

2. Chinese "Fire-Inventor" VS Western "Fire-Stealer"

Suirenshi is a famous Chinese culture hero who was credited with inventing the technique of **making fire by drilling on wood**. As the legend goes, he spotted many **woodpeckers** pecking away at a big tree and the sparks would fly as the woodpeckers' beaks drilled into the trunk, lighting up the tree. He was inspired by the scene and decided to break off two branches and jabbed one stick against the other in quick succession. Eventually, he got the sticks to spark. That was how he built a fire. Suirenshi brought the technique home and taught his people how to start a fire to keep warm. Also at that time, people were eating raw meat and vegetables and getting sick. With fire, they learned to cook food before eating, greatly reducing illness from eating raw food. And cooked food was more delicious. In addition, fire could scare wild beasts away. The people were very appreciative of Suirenshi's invention of how to make fire and worshiped him as a great hero. Fire is not just a means leading to higher living standard, but an access to civilization from barbaric lifestyle. Chinese ancestors **apotheosize** Suirenshi and his story represents their attempts to make sense of the origin of fire.

Suirenshi 燧人氏	make fire by drilling on wood 钻木取火
woodpecker 啄木鸟	apotheosize 神化,奉为神明
Prometheus 普罗米修斯	Zeus 宙斯，众神之王
emblem 徽章,象征	

In the classical mythology of the ancient Greeks and Romans the most familiar equivalent of Suirenshi is the Titan and culture hero **Prometheus**. Before fire was bestowed, humans lived in darkness and coldness, ate uncooked food, and were threatened by wild animals. Sympathetic with the miserable lives of humans, Prometheus went to **Zeus**, the king of Olympian Gods, and pleaded for fire. But Zeus refused in fear of losing power and control over humans if they were given fire and thus they could develop civilization. Prometheus defies Zeus by stealing fire and giving it to humanity. The punishment of Prometheus as a consequence of the theft is a major theme and a popular subject of both ancient and modern culture. Zeus, sentenced him to eternal torment for his transgression. The immortal was chained to a rock, where each day an eagle, the **emblem** of Zeus, was sent to eat Prometheus' liver, which would then grow back overnight to be eaten again the next day. In addition to the gift of fire, Prometheus also taught the human race various skills such as building houses, taming animals, planting crops and forging metal. So in a sense Prometheus is regarded as the creator of mankind.

Part V Reflection and Presentation

1. How do you understand superstition and its connection with folk belief? Do you believe that people are communicating with their ancestors on the Qingming Festival?

2. What role do myth, legend and fairy tales play in social life? For example, what is the folklore significance for people, especially the children to believe in the Kitchen God in China and the Santa Clause in Western culture?

Part VI Mini-pedia

1. Nüwa and Fuxi

In another version of the creation of humanity, Nüwa and Fuxi created humans together. According to the *Classic of Mountains and Seas*, Fuxi and Nüwa lived on the mythological Kunlun Mountain. They used clay to create offspring, and with the divine power they made the clay figures come alive. These clay figures were the earliest human beings.

Fuxi and Nüwa used to be brother and sister and later got married. With the marriage the two were representative of *Yin* and *Yang*; Fuxi symbolizing *Yang* and masculinity while Nüwa symbolizing *Yin* and femininity. Fuxi was credited with establishing marriage ritual. This version of creation was a symbolic story of having a larger family structure that included the figure of a father which mostly represents the significant change from a matriarchal society to a patriarchal one.

2. Number 666

Among the prophecies in the *Book of Revelations* "Apocalypse" is one about a "Great Beast" who will rule the earth and mark his followers on the brow or hand with the "number of his name", which is 666. Clearly, the original allusion was to the pagan Roman Empire, its statues and its coinage; with some forcing, 666 can be matched to the numerical value of "Nero Caesar" written in Hebrew letters. In the 17th century, some feared Doomsday would come in 1666. In current popular imagination, 666 is regarded as Satanic. There have been many press reports of "unlucky" cars with 666 as the licence number. Phone numbers with 666 in them may be rejected, or regarded as a joke.

References

1. 林国平. 关于中国民间信仰研究的几个问题[J]. 民俗研究, 2007(1).
2. 刘春芳, 杜晓, 杨银玲. 中西文化对比教程[M]. 北京:中国人民大学出版社, 2017.
3. 王焱, 赵牟丹. 中西文化比较(英文版)[M]. 北京:清华大学出版社, 2017.
4. 钟敬文. 民俗学概论(第二版)[M]. 北京:高等教育出版社, 2010.
5. 朱海滨. 民间信仰——中国最重要的宗教传统. 江汉论坛, 2009(3).
6. Fenggang Yang & Anning Hu. *Mapping Chinese Folk Religion in Mainland China and Taiwan*. https://www.jstor.org/stable/41681808.
7. Jacqueline Simpson & Steve Roud. *A Dictionary of English Folklore*. New York: Oxford University Press Inc., 2000.
8. Scott Draper, Joseph O. Baker. *Angelic Belief as American Folk Religion*. https://www.jstor.org/stable/23027303.
9. https://en.wikipedia.org/wiki/Dragon.
10. https://en.wikipedia.org/wiki/Fuxi.
11. https://en.wikipedia.org/wiki/Nüwa.
12. https://www.ancient.eu/mythology/.
13. https://www.bbc.co.uk/religion/religions/paganism/history/spiritualhistory_1.shtml.

Unit 10
Chinese and Western Folk Literature

Pangu

Robin Hood

Learning Objectives

- To be familiar with the different genres of Chinese and Western folk literature
- To get one's own understanding of the differences between Chinese and Western mythology, ballads and fables
- To identify and recognize the development of thematic and aesthetic features in folk literature

Lead-in Questions

- Creation myths vary from country to country. Are you familiar with any of them? Share it with your classmates.
- Which folk story do you like most? Why?
- Have you heard of Cinderella? Do you know any stories similar to Cinderella? Discuss their similarities and differences with your classmates.

Folk literature, also called oral literature or folklore, is created by the working people, and spreads among them. It includes all the myths, legends, fables, folktales and ballads passed down through the generations. Traditionally, folk literature works have no written forms and they are handed down through oral teaching. The authors of these literature works are usually unknown or unidentifiable.

Part I Chinese Folk Literature

Chinese folk literature not only expresses the suffering and hopes of the working people, but also shows their exemplary personalities and lofty qualities. It contains and radiates the lofty thoughts and virtues of the people's heroism, patriotism, optimism, humanitarianism and dedication. Chinese folk literature includes myths, legends, folk tales, fables, ballads, poetry, couplets, etc. In the process of circulation and spreading, folk literature often varies with time, region, ethnicity, the subjective thoughts and feelings of the communicator, and the emotional changes of the audience. It often tells stories of deities, historical events, legendary people and the supernatural beings. Natural phenomena and distinctive landmarks are explained in folk literature, too. The same motif may appear in different regions. A number of collections, such as *The Classic of Mountains and Seas*, *Anecdotes About Spirits and Immortals*, *Strange Stories from a Chinese Studio*, now remain popular.

The Book of Songs (*Shi Jing*) which is viewed as the first poetic anthology of China contains some folk songs. *Ospreys* (Some translate it into *Fish Hawks*) might be the most famous one. "There is a maiden fair whom a young man is wooing"① from *Ospreys* has become an idiom that shows a man's adoring to a

① 许渊冲译。

pretty woman. The other notable collection of folk songs is *The Music Bureau* (*Yue Fu*). The flourishing of study on Chinese folk literature started from collection of Chinese folk songs after May 4th Cultural Movement.

1. Chinese Mythology

China is a huge country with a long history, which contains all kinds of geographic areas like craggy mountains, lush river valleys, dense forests, wild deserts and broad grasslands. The varied land gave birth to one of the most diverse and lively collections of myths.

Like many other mythologies, Chinese mythology has been viewed as, at least in part, a factual recording of history. Creation of the world, creation of human beings, cosmology of the universe, deities, the origin of things, inhabitants and culture, the origin of the Chinese state and chronology of prehistoric times are involved in the mythology. Many of these involve a cultural hero who taught people how to build houses, how to cook, how to weave, how to cultivate, or who was the ancestor of an ethnic group or a dynastic family. Mythology is intimately related to ritual acts, such as dances, ceremonies and sacrifice.

1.1 Chinese Creation Myth

Creation myths in China vary from region to region. As for the creators, the Han people have Pangu, the Yao people have Miluotuo, the Hani people have golden fish, the Li people have Giant God, etc.

1.1.1 Chaos

The ancient Chinese believed there was no division between sky and earth before the birth of the universe. There was no light and no darkness, and the world was simply chaos that filled all space.

《庄子·内篇·应帝王第七》，庄子叙"七窍出而浑沌死"故事。原文：南海之帝为倏，北海之帝为忽，中央之帝为浑沌。倏与忽时相与遇于浑沌之地，浑沌待之甚善。倏与忽谋报浑沌之德，曰："人皆有七窍以视听食息，此独无有，尝试凿之。"日凿一窍，七日而浑沌死。

Zhuangzi, a philosopher of the Warring States Period (475-221 BC) wrote a story about Chaos. Chaos was the emperor of the central regions. Unlike men, he had no eyes, no nose, no ears and no mouth. Shu, emperor of the Southern Sea, and Hu, emperor of the Northern Sea, met Chaos who treated them kindly. In order to requite him, Shu and Hu decided to help him by creating him his seven apertures (the eyes, ears, nostrils and mouth). They opened one for him each day and when they were done, on the seventh day, Chaos died. The death of Chaos led to the birth of the universe.

1.1.2 Pangu

Another myth said Pangu was the first living creature and the creator of the world. Among his acts of creation were the separation of the earth and sky, the placement of the stars in the sky, and the shaping of the earth's surface.

徐整《三五历记》：天地浑沌如鸡子，盘古生其中。万八千岁，天地开辟，阳清为天，阴浊为地。盘古在其中，一日九变，神于天，圣于地。天日高一丈，地日厚一丈，盘古日长一丈。如此万八千岁，天数极高，地数极深，盘古极长。后乃有三皇。数起于一，立于三，成于五，盛于七，处于九，故天去地九万里。

At the beginning of time, the universe consisted only of dark chaos, in the form of a cosmic egg. There was a sleeping giant named Pangu within the egg. One day Pangu awoke, saw the darkness and chaotic elements around him, then he held a big axe that no one knew where he brought it from, and split open the egg. The light, pure parts of the egg went up and became the sky, while the heavy, dull parts went down and formed the earth. The earth and sky kept growing.

When Pangu died, different parts of his body were transformed into different elements of the world. According to some stories, his head, arms, feet and stomach became great mountains which helped to anchor the world and marked its boundaries. His breath was transformed into wind and clouds; his voice became thunder; and his eyes became the sun and moon. Pangu's blood became rivers and seas; his veins formed roads and paths; his sweat became rain and dew; his bones and teeth turned into rocks and gems; his flesh changed into soil; the hair on his head became the stars; and the hair on his body turned into vegetation.

Some myths say that humans developed from **fleas** and **parasites** creeping over Pangu's body and beard while in other stories Pangu created humans with clay as Nüwa had done. However, when he left them in the sun to dry, a sudden rain began to fall. Pangu hastily wrapped up these clay figures, but he was in such a hurry that he damaged some of them by accident. That's why some humans are born crippled or disabled.

flea 跳蚤

parasite 寄生生物

1.1.3 Nüwa

According to ***Imperial Readings of the Taiping Era***, Nüwa molded figures from the yellow clay, giving them life and granting them the ability to bear children.

Imperial Readings of the Taiping Era 《太平广记》

Another popular story recounts how Nüwa saved the earth. The water god Gonggong had tried to overthrow the fire god Zhurong. When Gonggong failed, he became angry and rammed **Imperfect Mountain** with his head. The mountain crumbled and tore a hole in the sky. The disorder that followed included fires and floods. Nüwa **smelted** five-colored stones and mended the hole in the sky. She also slew a giant tortoise and used its legs to support the heaven. Nüwa's actions restored the order of the universe and saved the world from destruction.

Imperfect Mountain 不周山

smelt 冶炼

伏羲和女娲故事有很多版本，本书第九单元还有另外一个故事。

The other myth says at the beginning of the universe, Fuxi and Nüwa were brother and sister and they were the only two persons in the Kunlun Mountain. They thought they should marry but felt ashamed. They went to Kunlun Mountain, and the brother said: "If we are destined to be husband and wife, the smoke gets together; if not, the smoke scatters." The smoke got together, so they got married. They used the grass as a fan to cover their faces. Later, Chinese women adopted this custom and used fans, too.

1.2 Chinese Flood Myth

As an ancient farming nation, China has suffered from floods and is still often threatened by floods. Therefore, China has a large number of myths and legends about floods since ancient times.

oracle and omen 神谕和预兆

reclamation 开垦，开拓

The most famous flood myth in China might be the Gun Yu Myth. The father Gun and the son Yu adopted different methods to control the flood. The father Gun tried to block the water while the son Yu channeled the water to the sea. Besides this well-known myth, Chinese flood myth has several sub-types: **oracle and omen**, Leigong and his revenge, the pursuit of the deity's daughter, and **reclamation** by brother and sister. These sub-types are usually associated with the reproduction of human beings.

1.2.1 Oracle and Omen

An old woman or a brother and his younger sister had done something good. To reward them, a deity revealed to them the information of the upcoming flood. Sometimes, the deity also told them the omens of the flood, for example, a stone tortoise had bleeding eyes, the city doors bled, or mortar became wet automatically. When the above-mentioned people saw these omens, they escaped from the great flood. If the survivors were a brother and his younger sister, they would marry each other and thus was the **reproduction** of human beings.

reproduction 繁衍

1.2.2 Leigong and his Revenge

Once upon a time, a farmer was working in his field when he heard thunder. He took his children (in some versions, they were Nüwa and Fuxi) inside their house, prepared an iron cage, and armed with **pitchfork**. When the thunder god Leigong appeared with his thunder axe, the farmer stabbed him and locked him inside the cage. He warned his children not to give Leigong anything to eat or drink. Both kids obeyed their father until they pitied the thunder god who asked them for food and water. After the kids gave him a drop of water, Leigong recovered and freed himself from the cage. He gave the frightened kids his own tooth to be planted, which grew into a **gourd** plant. Leigong leaped into the sky and commanded the rain god to pour the water as heavily as he could.

pitchfork 干草叉

gourd 葫芦

Meanwhile, the farmer came back. He realized what had happened and made a boat, put his children inside the magical gourd, and climbed into the boat. The flood continued to rise until it almost reached the heaven. The farmer knocked at the heaven's gate and pleaded **Emperor Tai** to stop the rain. Emperor Tai did so. The water went away, the boat fell from the sky, crashed to the ground

Emperor Tai 太帝

along with the farmer, but his children inside the gourd were safe because the gourd was flexible.

1.2.3 The Pursuit of the Deity's Daughter

This sub-type of myth appears in Sichuan and Yunnan Provinces.

The ancestors of mankind had three hard-working sons who plowed land everyday. But the deity of the heaven sent the wild boar to destroy their land at night. Later they caught the wild boar. The boar told them there would be a great flood and they should hide in the gold, silver and wooden cabinets. After the flood, all humans drowned, and only the son who hid in the wooden cabinet survived. Later, this son managed to marry the daughter of the deity and returned to the ground to reproduce humanity.

1.2.4 Reclamation by Brother and Sister

Many stories of this sub-type came from the Miao people and the Yi people. The story is a mixture of Leigong' revenge and the pursuit of the deity's daughter.

In ancient times, three children lived together. They found their cultivated land was destroyed every morning. They hid to see what was going on one night. A white-beard man who destroyed their land told them there would soon be a great flood. They hid in a stone cabinet and a gourd. After the great flood, only the couple who hid in the gourd survived. The brother and sister made several tests to see whether the deity wanted them to marry or not. After the confirmation they married and gave birth to a boy. Later the boy married the deity's daughter and human beings reproduced themselves.

2. Chinese Fables

The distinctive feature of the fable is that it contains a moral truth. Chinese fables always tell morals associated with Chinese virtues like **benevolence**, **righteousness**, **courtesy**, wisdom and trust. Many traditional Chinese fables have developed into idioms which are widely used today.

benevolence 仁
righteousness 义
courtesy 礼

The writing of fable has a long history in China. The concept *yuyan* even appeared in Zhuangzi's works. He believed that one could get a satisfactory result by explaining the truth through stories. Many Chinese philosophers had written fables to inform people of their opinions. There are no particular fable books in ancient China. The stories scattered among different books like *Liezi*, *Hanfeizi*, *Mengzi*, *Huainanzi*, etc.

Chinese fable in ancient times can be classified into poetic fable and prosy fable according to the form. Besides, according to the content, it can be classified into philosophical, **exhorting**, satirical and humorous fable.

exhorting 鼓励, 敦促

2.1 *Zhuangzi*

The book *Zhuangzi* consists of a large collection of **anecdotes**, **allegories**, **parables** and fables, which are often humorous in nature. The main themes of *Zhuangzi* are of spontaneity in action and of freedom from the human world and its conventions. Distinctions between good and evil, large and small, life and death, and human and nature were illustrated by the fables and anecdotes in the text. While

anecdote 趣闻轶事
allegory 讽刺诗，讽刺画，寓言
parable 道德小故事；说教性寓言

other ancient Chinese philosophers focused on human morality and personal duty, Zhuangzi preferred carefree lifestyle and developed the philosophy of Laozi to an extreme point. Zhuangzi interpreted the universe as a thing that changed spontaneously and argued that humans could achieve ultimate happiness by living equally spontaneously. His philosophy was illustrated by his fables.

Socratic (与) 苏格拉底(有关)的

The story of "The Debate on the Joy of Fish" is a well-known anecdote that has been compared to the **Socratic** dialogue tradition of ancient Greece.

Zhuangzi and Huizi were walking on the bridge over the Hao River. Zhuangzi said, "The fish are darting about free and easy! This is how they are happy."

Huizi answered, "You are not a fish. How can you say you know they are happy?" Zhuangzi said, "You are not me. How do you know that I do not know the happiness of the fish?"

Huizi said, "I am not you, so of course I know nothing about your thoughts. But you are not a fish, so it's easy to conclude that you know nothing about the happiness of the fish."

Zhuangzi said, "Let's go back to the beginning of this. You said, how do you know the fish are happy; but by asking me this, you already knew that I know it. I know the happiness of the fish right here above the Hao River."

2.2 *Huainanzi*

Huainanzi is a philosophical work written by Liu An and his followers. The book blends Taoist, Confucianist and

Legalist concepts, including theories such as *Yin* and *Yang* and Five-Element Theory. The purpose of *Huainanzi* was to oppose the political reforms Liu Che (Emperor Wu of the Han Dynasty) promoted and the essays were compiled in such a way as to serve as an enlightenment for a **sovereign** and his court.

sovereign 君主

One **dialectic** story from this book is "Saiweng Lost His Horse". The moral behind it is "It can be difficult to foresee the twists and turns which compel misfortune to **beget** fortune, and vice versa."

dialectic 辩证法

beget 引起，导致

There was an old man Saiweng who lived near China's northern borders and was **well-versed** in the practices of Taoism. One day, his horse ran into the territory of the northern tribes. His fellow villagers came Over to **commiserate** with him.

well-versed 精通的

commiserate 表示同情(或惋惜)

"Perhaps this will soon turn out to be a blessing," Saiweng said. After a few months, the horse came back, leading a fine wild horse from the north. The villagers came over to congratulate him.

"Perhaps this will soon turn out to be a cause of misfortune," Saiweng said.

Soon his son became fond of riding and eventually broke his leg falling from a horse. The villagers came over to commiserate with him.

"Perhaps this will soon turn out to be a blessing," Saiweng said.

One year later, the northern tribes invaded Saiweng's nation. All healthy young men were **recruited** and fought against the invaders. As a result, nine out of ten young men

recruit 招募

died in the war. Saiweng's son didn't join the army for he was crippled.

3. Chinese Ballads

Chinese Ballad is a form of verse, often a narrative set to music. The most popular collection of ballads in China is ***The Collection of Poems of Yuefu***.

The Collection of Poems of Yuefu 《乐府诗集》

The Collection of Poems of Yuefu is a collection of Chinese poems composed in a folk song style. The Music Bureau(*Yuefu*) was an imperial governmental organization in charge of the collecting or writing of the lyrics. The word "Music Bureau" came first into being in the Qin Dynasty. Later the term was applied to literary imitations or adaptations of the Music Bureau's poem styles.

The most famous one is *The South of the Yangtze River* which is familiar to Chinese children (translated by Wang Rongpei):

teem 充满，多产

The South of the Yangtze River
The south of the Yangtze River **teems** with lotus seeds.
How dense and flourishing are the lotus leaves,
Around which the fish swims and breeds!
The fish swims to the east of the leaves;
The fish swims to the west of the leaves;
The fish swims to the south of the leaves;
The fish swims to the north of the leaves.

Part II European Folk Literature

1.European Mythology

European mythology is vast and fascinating. Besides the well-known Roman and Greek mythology, there are many other great interesting mythology, such as **Celtic mythology**, **Norse mythology** and **Hebrew mythology**.

Celtic mythology 凯尔特神话
Norse mythology 北欧神话
Hebrew mythology 希伯来神话

1.1 Celtic Mythology

The Celts were a group of people who began to spread throughout European continent in the 1000 BC. At the peak of their authority, they inhabited an area extending from the British Isles in the west to what is now Turkey in the east. Six groups of Celts have survived to modern times. They are the peoples of Ireland, Scotland, **the Isle of Man**, Wales, Cornwall and Brittany.

the Isle of Man 马恩岛(位于英格兰与爱尔兰之间的岛屿)

Celtic mythology is the mythology of **polytheism** and the religion of the Iron Age. Ancient Celts had held a great respect for the nature and the respect continues. All elements and creatures in the nature held a sacred significance. Pre-Christian Celtic beliefs perceived the presence of the supernatural in every mountain, river, coast, spring, lake, **marsh**, tree and rock formation.

polytheism 多神论

marsh 沼泽

In spite of the obvious importance of the Celts in European history, little was known about early Celtic mythology. Prior to Roman or Christian influence, the Celts preferred to pass on their sacred teachings and myths orally, so their **Druidic** priests disdained writing as a means of transmitting sacred text. After the coming of Christianity in the fifth century onwards, the monks helped to record the myths. No myths could survive from Romanized areas, so most of the surviving Celtic myths came from Scotland and Ireland. The greatest body of present Celtic myth came from Ireland, which was not invaded by the Romans, although much of its mythic material was destroyed by Viking **marauders**.

Druidic 督伊德教的

marauder 掠夺者

The Celtic gods were all-powerful local deities rather than gods with specialized power. Each tribe had its own god, who protected and provided for the welfare of that tribe. Some of them had similar characteristics. For example, Dagda, the god of life and death in Ireland resembled Esus, the "master" god of Gaul.

The Celtic goddesses were closely associated with the land, so in this identification, it seemed that they were aspects of a single **all-embracing** goddess. Their link to the seasonal cycles, to fertility and death, might partly account for the fact that a single goddess often took three forms, or aspects—usually maiden, mother and **crone**.Celtic goddesses could be life-giving and sustaining, but were associated with sex and death in their dark aspects. The most powerful Irish goddess was the red-haired shape-shifting Morrigan, said to have coupled with the Dagda.

all-embracing 包括一切的

crone 丑陋的老太婆

1.2 The God Lugh

Though rarely mentioned in inscriptions, Lugh was an

important deity among the Celtic gods and goddesses. Often revered as the **resplendent** sun god, Lugh was also perceived as a dashing warrior responsible for slaying Balor — the one-eyed chief of the **Formorii**.

resplendent 辉煌的，绚烂的
Formorii 爱尔兰的早期统治者

Lugh was additionally associated with thunderstorms, ravens and even **lynxes**. As one of the **preeminent** Celtic gods, he was often portrayed with his armor, helmet and **invincible** spear Gae Assail. Lugh was possibly perceived as the **Gallic** equivalent of Roman god Mercury. In the mythical narrative, Lugh was perceived as the divine father of Cú Chulainn, the most famous Irish heroes, whose character and feats were similar to Greek Heracles.

lynx 猞猁
preeminent 杰出的
invincible 不可战胜的
Gallic 法国(人)的

When young Lugh travelled to Tara to join the court of King Nuada of the Tuatha Dé Danann, the doorkeeper would not let him in unless he had a skill he could use to serve the king. He displayed his skills as a **wright**, a smith, a champion, a swordsman, a **harpist**, a hero, a poet, a historian, a sorcerer and a craftsman, but each time he was rejected as the king already had someone with that skill. Lugh asked if they had anyone with all those skills simultaneously, as a result the doorkeeper let him in. Lugh joined the court and was appointed Chief Ollam of Ireland. He won a flagstone-throwing contest against Ogma, the champion, and entertained the court with his harp. The Tuatha Dé Danann were, at that time, oppressed by the Fomorians, and Lugh was amazed how **meekly** they accepted the oppression. Nuada wondered if this young man could lead them to freedom. Soon Lugh was given command over the Tuatha Dé Danann, and finally the Fomorians were

wright 工匠
harpist 演奏竖琴者
meekly 顺从的

defeated.

1.3 Greek Myth

The religion associated with the ancient Greeks produced one of the world's most complex and sophisticated mythology, one that has particularly influenced the cultures of the Western world. Usually the Greek myths can be read as individual stories. In fact, Greek mythology can be read as a single, gradually composed **saga** of the folk imagination and many talented authors, a saga in which characters and events from the beginning of conceived time are interrelated in a complex web that touches on every imaginable aspect of the human experience.

saga 英雄传奇

1.3.1 Greek Deities

In **Hesiod's *Theogony***, **Chaos** was the first of the **primordial** deities, followed by Gaia (Earth), Tartarus (the nether abyss), and Eros (Love). From Chaos came Erebus (Darkness) and Nyx (Night). Erebus slept with his sister Nyx, and had Aether (the bright upper air), and Hemera (the Day). Nyx's children included the hateful Moros (Fate), the black Ker (Doom), Thanatos (Death), Hypnos (Sleep), Oneiroi (Dreams), Geras (Old Age), Oizus (Pain), Nemesis (Revenge), Eris (Strife), Apate (Deceit), Philotes (Sexual Pleasure), Momos (Blame), and the Hesperides (the Daughters of the Evening).

Hesiod's *Theogony* 赫西奥德《神谱》
Chaos 卡俄斯
primordial 最早的，原始的

Meanwhile, Gaia gave birth to Uranus, the Starry Sky. Uranus became Gaia's husband, surrounding her from all sides. Together, they produced three sets of children: the three **One-eyed Cyclopes**, the three **Hundred-handed**

One-eyed Cyclope 独眼巨人
Hundred-handed Hecatoncheire 百臂巨人

Hecatoncheires, and the twelve **Titans**.

Titan 提坦巨人

Zeus was the son of one of the twelve Titans— Cronus.

1.3.2 Flood Myth

The flood in the time of Deucalion (the son of Prometheus) was caused by the anger of Zeus, **ignited** by the hubris of the Pelasgians. So, Zeus decided to put an end to the Bronze Age. According to this story, Lycaon, the king of Arcadia, had sacrificed a boy to Zeus, who was **appalled** by this savage offering. Zeus unleashed a flood, so that the rivers ran in **torrents** and the sea flooded the coastal plain, engulfed the foothills with spray, and washed everything clean. Deucalion, with the aid of his father Prometheus, was saved from this flood by building a chest which helped him survive the **deluge** with his wife, Pyrrha.

ignite 点燃,使燃烧,使激动

appal 使惊骇

torrent 湍急

deluge 洪水

Once the flood was over and the couple had given thanks to Zeus, Deucalion consulted an oracle of them about how to repopulate the earth. He was told to "cover your head and throw the bones of your mother behind your shoulder". Deucalion and Pyrrha thought that "mother" must be Gaia who was the mother of all living things, and the "bones" must be rocks. They threw the rocks behind their shoulders and the stones turned into human beings. Pyrrha's became women; Deucalion's became men.

1.4 Norse Mythology

Norse mythology is the body of myths of the North Germanic peoples, stemming from Norse **paganism** and continuing after the Christianization of Scandinavia, and into the Scandinavian folklore of the modern period. Norse

paganism 异教信仰

mythology consists of tales of various deities, beings and heroes derived from numerous sources from both before and after the **pagan** period, including medieval manuscripts, archaeological representations and folk tradition.

pagan 异教徒

Perhaps the most popular Norse deities is the thunder-god Thor who wielded his hammer, fought his foes relentlessly and protected humanity. His father, the one-eyed, raven-**flanked** god Odin craftily pursued knowledge throughout the world and bestowed among humanity the **runic alphabet**. The beautiful, feathered cloak-clad Freya is the Goddess of Love, but she is also associated with sex, lust, beauty, sorcery, fertility, gold, war and death. She was sent to the **Aesir** by the **Vanir** as a token of truce. Freya became an honorable member of the Aesir after the war between the Aesir and Vanir ended. God Njord was powerful enough to calm both sea and fire and grant wealth and land. He once married the skiing goddess Skadi. However, their marriage turned out to be a failure for Njord couldn't stand the cold and dreariness of the mountains and Skadi couldn't stand the light and noise of Njord's home by the seashore. Other Norse deities include god Freyr who brought peace and pleasure to humanity; goddess Idunn(also Idun, Ithun) who kept apples that could grant eternal youthfulness and whose absence caused the gods to be old and grey; god Heimdall who could hear grass grow and was born of nine mothers; and numerous other deities.

flank 位于……的两侧

runic alphabet 如尼字母

Aesir 北欧神话中以奥丁为首的神族

Vanir 与奥丁神族对立的一个神族

Besides deities, there were four other creatures: giant, **alfar**, dwarf and man. Most of the surviving mythology centers on the plights of the gods and their interaction with

alfar 精灵

various other beings, such as the friendship, love and hatred between humanity, the giant and family members of the gods. The cosmos in Norse mythology consisted of Nine Worlds that flanked a central tree—Yggdrasil. Units of time and elements of the cosmology were personified as deities or beings. Various forms of a creation myth were recounted, where the world was created from the flesh of the **primordial** being Ymir, and the first two humans were Ask and Embla. These worlds were foretold to be reborn after the events of Fates of the Gods when an immense battle occurred between the gods and their enemies, and the world was **enveloped** in flames, only to be reborn anew. There the surviving gods would meet, and the land would be fertile and green, and two humans would repopulate the world.

primordial 最早的

envelop 覆盖，笼罩

2. Western Fables

The Western tradition of fable begins with Aesop, a legendary figure who contributed a collection of ancient Greek fables to world literature. Modern editions of *Aesop's Fables* contain up to 200 fables, but there is no way to trace their actual origins. The earliest known collection linked to Aesop dates to the 4th century **BCE**.

European fable flourished in the Middle Ages, as did all forms of allegory, and a notable collection of fables was made in the late 12th century by Marie de France. The medieval fable gave rise to an expanded form known as the beast epic—a lengthy, episodic animal story replete with hero, **villain**, victim, and an endless stream of heroic

BCE: Before Common Era 公元前

BC: Before Christ 公元前

CE: Current Era 公元后

AD: Anno Domini 公元后

villain 罪犯

endeavor that parodied epic grandeur. The most famous of these is a 12th-century group of related tales associated with **Reynard the Fox**, a cunning fox who preferred to mock hunters, kings, ducks, etc.

Reynard the Fox 列那狐

Three European fable collections which have affected world literature are *Aesop's Fables*, ***La Fontaine's Fables*** and ***Krylov's Fables***.

La Fontaine's Fables《拉·封丹寓言》

Krylov's Fables《克雷洛夫寓言》

Perhaps the most famous fable collection of European countries is the Aesop's fables. *Aesop's Fables*, or the *Aesopian*, is a collection of fables credited to Aesop, a slave and storyteller believed to have lived in ancient Greece between 620 and 560 BCE. Of diverse origins, the stories associated with his name have descended to modern times through several sources and continue to be reinterpreted in different verbal registers and in popular artistic media.

Jean de La Fontaine (1621-1695) is one of the representative writers of French classical literature and a famous fable poet. La Fontaine's great theme was the **folly** of human vanity. He was a skeptic, not unkind but full of the sense of human **frailty** and ambition. La Fontaine's example gave new **impetus** to the genre throughout Europe. During the Romantic Period, a great practitioner of Aesopian fable was Ivan Andreyevich Krylov. The 19th century saw the rise of literature written specifically for children, in whom fable found a new audience.

folly 愚蠢的

frailty 脆弱，虚弱

impetus 推动

The following is an example from *Aesop's Fables*: "The Ant and the Grasshopper". A grasshopper (in the original, a **cicada**) had spent the summer singing and dancing while the ants worked to store up food for winter.

cicada 蝉

When winter arrived, the grasshopper found itself without food. Being afraid of dying of hunger, it went to the ants and begged for food. However, the ant **rebuked** its idleness and told it to dance the winter away now.

rebuke 指责，斥责

3. English Ballad

Ballads derive from the medieval French **chanson** balladée or ballade, which originally means "danced songs". Ballads were particularly the popular poetry and song of the British Isles from the later medieval period until the 19th century. They were widely used across Europe, and later in Australia, North Africa, North America and South America. Ballads are often 13 lines with an ABABBCBC form, consisting of **couplets** of rhymed verse, each of 14 syllables. Another common form is ABAB or ABCB repeated, in alternating 8 and 6 syllable lines.

chanson 歌曲，歌谣，小调

couplet 对句

Many ballads were written and sold as single sheet broadsides. The form was often used by poets and composers from the 18th century onwards to produce lyrical ballads. In the later 19th century, the term took on the meaning of a slow form of popular love song and is now often used for any love song, particularly the sentimental ballad of pop or rock.

Riddles Wisely Expounded is a traditional English song, dating at least to 1450. In the earliest surviving version of the song, *Between the Devil and the Maiden* (mid-15th century), the "**foul fiend**" proposed to **abduct** a maiden unless she can answer a series of riddles. The woman prayed to Jesus for

foul fiend 魔鬼

abduct 诱拐

wisdom, and answered the riddles correctly. In later versions, a knight put a woman to test before he would marry her (sometimes after seducing her), or a devil disguised as a knight tried to carry her off. The woman knew the answers, and thus either won the marriage or was free of the devil. In the latter case, the last sentence of the riddle is often "what is worse than woman?" (the devil).

The riddles vary, but typical ones include:

What is longer than the way? — love

What is deeper than the sea? — hell

What is louder than the horn? — thunder

What is sharper than a thorn? — hunger

What is whiter than milk? — snow

What is softer than silk? — down

Part III Comparison and Contrast

1. Chinese Thunder God VS Norse Thunder God

The image of Leigong kept changing. In *The Classic of Mountains and Seas*, Leigong had human head and dragon body; in *Lunheng*, he was a giant with magic power while in ***Stories of Immortals*** he became a red monkey with mirror-like eyes and long horns. Some believed Lei Zhenzi in ***The Investiture of the Gods*** was Leigong, however, some argued Lei Zhenzi was the son of Leigong and Dianmu.

It was believed Leigong's major power was thunder and he had capability of producing other types of heavenly climate phenomena. His wife, Dianmu, was the Goddess of Lightning, who was said to have used flashing mirrors to send bolts of lightning across the sky. Other companions included Yuntong, who gathered clouds, and Yushi ("Rain Master") who produced **downpours** with the dragon in his pot. Roaring winds rushed forth from a type of goatskin bag manipulated by Fengbo ("Earl of Wind"), who was later transformed into Feng Po Po ("Lady Wind"). In *Pilgrim to the West*, the one who was in charge of rainfall was the Dragon King.

Stories of Immortals《搜神记》	*The Investiture of the Gods*《封神演义》
downpours 倾盆大雨	Thor 托尔(北欧神话中的雷神)
antagonist 对手,对立者	

In Norse mythology, **Thor** was a hammer-wielding deity associated with thunder, lightning and storms. He was the symbol of strength, the protection of mankind and fertility. Thor's name was the Germanic word for thunder. His main weapon was a short-handled hammer, Mjolnir, with which he could smash the skull of his **antagonists**. This hammer, could return to him like a boomerang. One of his best-known adventures described his pulling the cosmic serpent Jormungand, which surrounded the world, out of the ocean.

Thor was a great warrior represented as a red-bearded, middle-aged man of enormous strength. He was an implacable foe to the harmful race of giants but benevolent toward mankind. His figure was generally secondary to that of the god

Odin, who in some traditions was his father; but in Iceland, and perhaps among all northern peoples except the royal families, he was apparently worshiped more than any other god. Thor was the god of the common people. Peasants worshiped him because he brought the rains that ensured good crops; warriors trusted him because it seemed that he was with them everywhere. Thor has inspired numerous works of art and references to Thor appear in modern popular culture.

2. Ye Xian VS Cinderella

Ye Xian was a pretty, considerate and gentle girl, who was gifted in many skills such as pottery and poetry. Her mother died many years ago and her father married another woman who was cruel to Ye Xian. She **befriends** a fish which **embodies** the spirit of her mother, but the fish was killed by her stepmother.

Ye Xian hid the fish bone which was magical. On New Year's Eve the fish bone created her a gorgeous gown for the gathering where the king fell in love with her. She was recognized by her stepmother and stepsister. While running away from them, she lost one of her shoes. The king found the shoes and saved her from the cruelty she lived in.

The story of Ye Xian which appeared in Guangxi of China around 860 BC is viewed as one of the oldest documented versions of the story *Cinderella*.

befriend 对……友好	embody 附体	heroine 女主人公
reversal 反向，挫折	token 标志，象征	coda 结尾，尾声

Cinderella is the **heroine** of a European folktale, the theme of which appears in numerous stories worldwide. More than 500 versions of the story have been recorded in Europe alone. The essential features of the story were a young girl who was mistreated by her jealous stepmother and elder stepsisters or a cruel father; intervention of a supernatural helper on her behalf; and the **reversal** of fortune brought about by a prince who fell in love with her and married her.

Usually, the supernatural helper was the girl's dead mother or an animal agent sent by her. The prince's recognition of the cinder maiden by the **token** of a "glass" slipper is unique in Perrault (The one who translated the English version Cendrillon which was the version familiar to common people). In other versions of the story the test of recognition was often a golden or silver slipper or a ring.

The first written European version of the story was published in Napoli (Naples), Italy, by Giambattista Basile, in his *Pentamerone* (1634). Another well-known version was recorded by the German brothers Jacob and Wilhelm Grimm in the 19th century. The tale is called *Aschenputtel* (*Cinderella* in English translations). In this version Cinderella's father did not die and the stepsisters mutilated their feet to fit in the golden slipper. There was no fairy godmother, help came from a wishing tree that the heroine planted on her mother's grave. In the second edition of their collection (1819), the Grimms supplemented the original 1812 version with a **coda** in which the stepsisters suffered a terrible punishment for their cruelty.

3. Yue Lao VS Cupid

Yue Lao, also known as the "old man of the moonlight", is the Chinese god of love and marriage. His story originated from the Tang Dynasty. There was a young man named Wei Gu who encountered an old man who was reading a book under the moonlight. Out of curiosity, Wei Gu asked him what he was reading and the old man replied it was the Book of Marriages. The old man told Wei Gu that man and woman who were tied by his red string would be husband and wife. Wei Gu **promptly** inquired the old man who his life partner would be, and the old man pointed to a three-year-old daughter of a blind woman and told Wei Gu that this girl would be his future wife. Years passed and after a series of incidents, Wei Gu came to realize that his wife was actually the daughter of the blind woman whom he had tried to kill years back. He was finally convinced by the words of Yue Lao. Since then, believers began to worship Yue Lao as the God of Marriage. When Yue Lao ties a red string to a couple, they will definitely be husband and wife regardless of their social status. Hence there is a Chinese saying, "marriage of a thousand miles is bonded by a string".

promptly 迅速地，敏捷地	counterpart 对应的人或者物
audacious 放肆的，鲁莽的	unleash 释放，放开
nymph 女神，仙女	aversion 厌恶，反感

Cupid is the ancient Roman god of love in all its varieties. The **counterpart** of Cupid in the Greek mythology is Eros. According to myth, Cupid was the son of

Mercury, the winged messenger of the gods, and Venus, the goddess of love. His image is a winged infant with a bow and some arrows. His golden arrow symbolized love and his lead arrow meant denying.In one tale, Venus asked Cupid to punish the mortal Psyche, only to have Cupid fall in love with Psyche and made Psyche his immortal wife.

Although some literature portrayed Cupid as callous and careless, he was widely accepted as beneficent, on account of the happiness he imparted to couples both mortal and immortal. Sometimes he was mischievous in his matchmaking. Once Cupid decided to take his revenge on the **audacious** Apollo. He **unleashed** two arrows: one sharp and gold-tipped and another blunt and lead-tipped. The gold-tipped arrow pierced the heart of Apollo while the lead-tipped arrow struck a **nymph** named Daphne and created an intense **aversion** for love in her heart. Daphne rejected Apollo. When Apollo pursued her, Daphne prayed to her father to rescue her, whereupon she was transformed into a laurel. Apollo appropriated the laurel for poets and, in Rome, for triumphs.

Part IV Reflection and Presentation

1. Collect the creation myths from different cultures and analyze their differences and similarities.

2. Compare and contrast Chinese fables with Aesop's Fables. What similarities and differences do you find?

3. Contrast your favorite ballads with those of your parents and grandparents. What changes have taken place? Why?

Part V Mini-pedia

1. Chang'e

Chang'e is the Chinese moon goddess whose beauty is celebrated in many poems and novels. The legends associated with her varied. One legend said she stole the drug of immortality from her consort Hou Yi and lived lonely in the Moon Palace as a punishment; the other said she ate up the drug to prevent it from being robbed by Pang Meng. Her company in the Moon Palace was a jade hare who helped her to pound medicine. It is said Hou Yi's pursuit was hindered by the hare, who would not let the outraged husband pass until he promised reconciliation.

In early legends, Chang'e changed into a toad after she flew to the moon, so on Mid-Autumn Festival many Chinese go outside to view the supposed outline of a toad on the surface of the moon.

2. Lady Godiva and Peeping Tom

You might have seen a luxurious chocolate brand with the Name "Godiva". This brand is associated with a 900-year-old English legend. Lady Godiva was an 11th century noblewoman who married the powerful Earl Leofric. Leofric had levied heavy taxes on the citizens of Coventry.

Lady Godiva asked her husband to lessen the burden and Leofric promised that if she rode naked on horseback through the center of town, he would reduce taxes. To help the citizens, Godiva decided to do it. Before leaving, she asked the people of Coventry to remain inside their homes and not peek, but one man named Tom peeped through a small hole and he was struck blind immediately. True to his words, Leofric reduced the people's taxes. Today "Peeping Tom" refers to a person who obtains sexual gratification by observing others surreptitiously.

References

1. 陈建宪. 中国洪水神话的类型与分布——对 433 篇异文的初步宏观分析[J]. 北京:民间文学论坛, 1996.
2. 何其亮, 张晔. 英释中国传统文化[M]. 杭州:浙江大学出版社, 2006.
3. 李惠芳. 中国民间文学[M]. 武汉:武汉大学出版社, 2012.
4. 刘春芳,等. 中西文化对比教程[M]. 北京:中国人民大学出版社, 2017.
5. 束定芳. 中国文化英语教程[M]. 上海:上海外语教育出版社, 2016.
6. 王焱,等. 中西文化比较[M]. 北京:清华大学出版社, 2017.
7. E. T. C. Werner. *Myths and Legends of China* [M]. New York: Dover Publications, Inc., 2016.
8. Karen Armstrong. *A Short History of Myth* [M]. Edinburgh, London: Canongate, 2005.
9. Laurence Coupe. *Myth* [M]. London & New York: Routledge, Taylor and Francis Group, 2008.
10. http://blog.sina.com.cn/s/blog_1676007860102xk08.html.
11. https://en.wikipedia.org/wiki/Ballad.
12. https://en.wikipedia.org/wiki/Celtic Mythology.

13. https://en.wikipedia.org/wiki/Myth.

14. https://en.wikipedia.org/wiki/Norse Mythology.

15. http://icollectmedia. com/details/book/themerryadventuresofrobinhood/nocode 20150704200252804/.

16. https://norse-mythology.org/gods-and-creatures/giants/skadi/.

Unit 11

Chinese and Western Folk Expressions

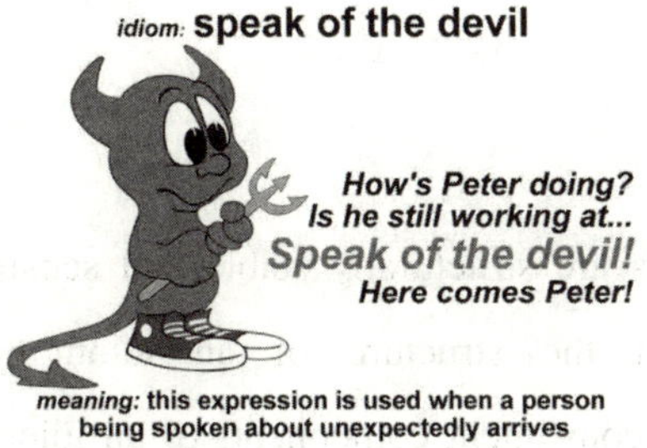

Speak of the Devil

When in Rome, Do as the Romans Do

Learning Objectives

- To get a better understanding of the cultural connotations of commonly-used idioms
- To be familiar with the functions and usages of euphemisms
- To have a basic knowledge of other forms of folk expressions such as tongue twister

Lead-in Questions

- There are many idioms associated with colors.Can you give some examples? Chinese ones and English ones are both welcomed.
- When talking about death, how do people express it euphemistically?
- Which is your favourite tongue twister? Ask your classmates to repeat it.

Folk expressions refer to the expressions used by common people in their daily life. Idioms, proverbs, jargon, slang and tongue-twisters are all folk expressions which come from the wisdom of working people. In this chapter, we focus on idioms, euphemisms and tongue twisters.

Part I Chinese Folk Expressions

1. Idioms

Chinese idioms are structurally stable and semantically united. Quite often the structure of an idiom remains unchangeable. The constituent components of an idiom can't be replaced or omitted. The word order can't be inverted, either. Each single Chinese character in the idiom has lost its individual meaning. Usually it is difficult for people to figure out the meaning of the idiom from the meaning of the individual words.

Categorized as formulaic language, the form of Chinese idioms is fixed. Most of the traditional Chinese idiomatic expressions consist of four characters. Deeply rooted in traditional Chinese culture, many of the Chinese idioms come from famous Chinese fables, folk stories and historical events. Chinese idioms reflect the Chinese traditional philosophical thoughts like "**unity of heaven and human**", "human oriented", "to be **sturdy** and strive to be stronger" and "peacefulness is most valuable". They are widely used in **vernacular** Chinese writing and in spoken language.

"unity of heaven and human" "天人合一"
sturdy 强壮的
vernacular 本地话，本国语

1.1 Classification of Chinese Idioms

Chinese idioms can be classified by structure criteria. Most of Chinese idioms have four Chinese characters, such as “老气横秋，秋高气爽，春华秋实”. Some are of less or more than four characters, such as “敲门砖，空城计，笑面虎，挂羊头卖狗肉，过五关斩六将”.

They can be classified by subjects, too. There are idioms which describe appearance, mood, environment, the taste of food, etc. For example, when people want to say a woman is very pretty, they can use “花容月貌，眉清目秀，倾国倾城”; when people want to describe food and the taste, they can use “唇齿留香，山珍海味，珍馐玉馔”; when people are angry, there are “火冒三丈，怒发冲冠，怒气冲冲”.

1.2 Stories Associated with the Idioms

Chinese idiom “有眼不识泰山” is used to describe a person who is too ignorant or careless to identify an important or capable person. The famous carpenter Lu Ban was very strict with his apprentices. From time to time, he would eliminate those who were not skilled or those who didn't work hard. One of his apprentices named Tai Shan was kicked out because of his poor performance. Several years later, Lu Ban saw lots of **ingenious** furniture in the market. When he was told that the person who made the furniture was exactly Tai Shan, Lu Ban felt so ashamed and sighed: “I was so **arrogant** that I didn't identify Tai Shan!”

> ingenious 精巧的
>
> arrogant 傲慢的

Chinese idiom “南柯一梦” literally means “A Dream in Nanke”, which is a metaphor for an empty dream, an illusory joy. In the Tang Dynasty, there was a scholar named Chun Yufen. One day, he felt depressed and fell asleep under a **locust tree** after getting drunk. He had a dream in which he was invited to the kingdom of Da Huaian. He married the princess, became the major minister and lived a luxurious life. Later when he was appointed the general to fight against Tan Luo's invasion, he was defeated and the princess died. He was removed from his office and went back home **mournfully**. He woke up and realized it was a dream. He found a big ant cave under the tree, in which there was the kingdom of the ants. The ant cave was like a pavilion, a small town. Chun Yufen sighed: Years of glory and wealth turned out to be a dream in Nanke.

locust tree 槐树

mournfully 忧伤地

2. Chinese Euphemism

Euphemism is the use of a word which is thought to be less offensive or unpleasant than another. Because Chinese people are courtly and reserved, they prefer to use euphemism when they have to utter such words. These phrases are used regularly, and there are many examples of euphemisms in everyday language.

Euphemism can be classified into euphemism avoiding taboo words, euphemism reducing or concealing disadvantage and euphemism showing one's respect according to the occasion they are used.

2.1 Euphemism Avoiding Taboo Words

There are many taboos in China, such as death, age,

sickness, etc.

In China, people are afraid of death, and they usually don't say death directly by the very word “死” in Chinese. There are many **substitutions** in Chinese language, such as “走了，逝世，过去了，离开我们，蹬腿，翻白眼，断气儿，不出气了，不醒了，牺牲，殉职，寿终正寝，香消玉殒，溘然长逝，行将就木，一睡不起，长眠，” etc.

substitution 代替，替换

In ancient China, the death of the people of the different social status was expressed separately. People were liable to punishment if the euphemism of death was not correctly uttered or written. For example, the death of an emperor is called *beng*（崩）, the death of a *top official* is called *hong*（薨）, the death of a minor official is called *bulu*（不禄）. When it comes to the death of a monk or a Taoist priest, there are “坐化，圆寂，涅槃，羽化，登仙”.

As for age, there is a set of euphemistic expressions. People in their thirties are “而立”, in their forties are “不惑”, in their fifties are “知天命”, in their sixties are “花甲”, in their seventies are “古稀”, in their eighties are “杖朝” and people of one hundred years old are called “期颐”. “You are sick（你有病）” is not a very good expression in Chinese. The exact meaning of this expression is “you are crazy”, so if somebody is ill, people may say “看起来不太舒服，脸色不好，不适，有恙，身子不爽快”.

（《论语·为政》）子曰：“吾十有五而志于学，三十而立，四十而不惑，五十而知天命，六十而耳顺，七十而从心所欲，不逾矩。”

“厕所” is usually referred to as “卫生间”, “洗手间”, “五谷轮回之所” to avoid vulgarity.

2.2 Euphemism Reducing or Concealing Disadvantage

To avoid embarrassment, some disadvantages are

euphemistically expressed.

When describing a person's appearance, instead of saying someone is "fat", Chinese may say "丰腴, 圆润, 富态, 强壮"; instead of saying "skinny", people use "骨感, 苗条"; instead of using "ugly", people say "长相平庸, 长得有特色".

If someone looks old, people say "成熟"; if somebody is crippled, people say "腿脚不好, 腿脚不便"; people don't say "聋" or "聋子" in Chinese, instead, they use "耳背".

2.3 Euphemism Showing One's Respect

To show one's respect to others, Chinese usually degrade oneself while upgrade others. When people refer to themselves, they may say "在下, 卑职, 愚兄, 鄙人, 小弟, 晚辈". When people refer to others, they may use "阁下, 兄台, 前辈, 台驾, 台甫, 足下". Other people's family members can be referred to as "令堂, 令尊, 尊夫人, 令郎, 令爱", while those of oneself are "家母, 家父, 内人, 犬子, 小女".

People call belongings of themselves "寒舍, 拙作", while they call belongings of others "贵府, 大作". One's own opinions are called "愚见, 拙见", opinions of others are called "高见". While addressing people of senior age or senior authority, people may say "您, 您老". Other person's correction of one's work is called "斧正". To refer to their parents-in-law, people say "泰山, 泰水"; to ask advice from other people is called "赐教"; to read other person's writings is called "拜读".

3. Chinese Tongue Twister

A tongue twister is a phrase that is designed to be difficult to **articulate** properly, and can be used as a type of spoken word game. Some tongue twisters produce humorous results when they are mispronounced. Many language learners practice tongue twisters when they start to learn a new language.

articulate 吐字清楚无误

Many people believe that Chinese tongue twisters are much harder than English ones. They can get super subtle and tricky, even for natives.

Tongue twisters intentionally gather a number of **reduplicated** words or words with the same pronunciation and similar pronunciation together with easily confused words to form simple and interesting rhymes, thus forming a linguistic art which is very tongue-twisting but interesting to read.

reduplicated 重叠的

One famous Chinese tongue twister is "班干部管班干部". When one keeps pronounce this sentence, mistakes are unavoidable and it sounds funny.

Lacking of specific **phonetic** items, some tongue twisters are difficult to people of specific areas, typical examples are "四是四, 十是十;要想说对四, 舌头碰牙齿;要想说对十, 舌头别伸直;要想说对四和十, 多多练习十和四" and "黑化肥发灰, 灰化肥发黑。黑化肥发灰会挥发, 灰化肥挥发会发黑, 黑化肥发灰挥发会发黑".

phonetic 语音的

Part II English Folk Language

1. English Idioms

Like Chinese idioms, English idioms are an essential part of everyday English. They come up all the time in both written and spoken English.

1.1 Classification of English Idioms

criteria 尺度，标准（criterion 的复数形式）

English idioms can be classified by sources and structural **criteria**.

By their sources, many of the idioms come from everyday life, the *Bible*, Shakespeare's plays and fables, myths or legends.

By structural criteria, there can be phrase idioms, clause idioms and sentence idioms.

1.2 Stories Associated with the Idioms

pail 桶

fowl 家禽

dimity 凸花条纹布

frock 女装

"Don't count your chickens before they hatch" came from *Aesop's Fables*. A Milkmaid went to the market with a **pail** of milk on her head. As she went along, she began calculating what she could do with the money she would get for selling the milk. She dreamed of buying some **fowls** from the farmer, selling the eggs they laid and she could buy herself a new **dimity frock** and a chip hat. Then she could go to the market where all the young men would come up and speak to her. Her female friends would be jealous. Thinking of this, she told herself that she would toss her head at that time. As she thought of this, she tossed her head back, the pail fell off it, and all the milk spilt out. So she had to go home and tell her mother about what had occurred.

"Doubting Thomas" came from the *Bible*. One of the twelve **disciples** named Thomas (also known as Didymus) was not with the disciples when Jesus came back. So when the other disciples told him they had seen Jesus, he said, "unless I see the nail marks in his hands and put my finger where the nails were, and put my hand into his side, I will not believe." A week later the disciples were in the house again, and Thomas was with them. Jesus came and spoke to Thomas, "put your finger here; see my hands. Reach out your hand and put it into my side. Stop doubting and believe." Thomas believed Jesus had resurrected. Later people used "Doubting Thomas" as "someone who will not easily believe something without strong proof or evidence".

disciple 耶稣的信徒

Some examples of the idioms and their sources are listed below:

Source	Idiom
Everyday Life	Keep one's shirt on; Go to seed; Be in the same boat with; Speak by the book; Keep the pot boiling

Continued

Source	Idiom
The *Bible*	The blind leading the blind; By the skin of your teeth; Broken heart; Can a leopard change his spots? A thorn in the flesh
Shakespeare's Plays	Flutter the dovecotes; Heart of gold; Lie low; Apple of one's eye; Break the ice
Fables, Myths or Legends	The lion's share; Don't count your chickens before they hatch; Look before you leap; A bird in the hand is worth two in the bush; Out of the frying pan, into the fire

Some examples of the idioms and their structure are listed below:

Structure	Idiom
Phrase Idiom	Black and blue High and mighty Back and forth
Clause Idiom	When it comes to If the worst comes to the worst When one is good and ready
Sentence Idiom	What is sauce for the goose is sauce for the gander Where there's a will there's a way When in Rome, do as the Romans do

2. English Euphemism

English language is rich in euphemisms, too. They serve four basic pragmatic functions: evasion function, indirectness function, politeness function and decoration function. There are euphemisms about old age, unemployment and poverty, menial jobs and professions, etc.

2.1 About Old Age

To many Westerners, old age means worthless and old people don't want to be looked down upon. So no one wants to admit that he is old. People dread about old age so much that the word "old" is viewed as a taboo. "The advanced in age", "the mature", "the longer living", "seasoned man" and "senior citizens" are used to refer to old people.

2.2 About Unemployment and Poverty

Unemployment is still a big social problem in many countries. And once people are out of work, **poverty** is the inevitable result. More and more people get used to be cautious when they mention unemployment and poverty. As a result, expressions or words are created to replace them.

poverty 贫困

When one is unemployed, he is "**laid off**", "eased out" or "given the walking ticket" and he becomes a "lay-off worker". At first he is "out of pocket" and "lives in reduced circumstances (penniless)", then he "lives in difficulties (in debt)", later he has no choice but to "move

laid off 下岗

slum 贫民窟

into a sub-standard housing (**slums**)".

Besides, people don't use "the poor" directly, they use "the have-nots", "the underprivileged" or "the disadvantaged". "Poor countries" are replaced by "developing nations" or "emerging nations". People use these euphemisms to soften harsh reality.

menial 卑微的

2.3 About Menial Jobs and Professions

There were some humble jobs that might be looked down upon by the public in old times. For the sake of politeness, people use **upgrading** euphemisms to "uplift" these jobs by name. The "hair dresser" is replaced by "beautician or hairstylist", the "floor-sweeper" is "**custodian** engineer", the "rat-catcher" is replaced by "pest control operator", and the "wash woman" is "clothes refresher".

upgrading 升级

custodian(公共建筑)的管理人,守卫

2.4 About Shortcomings

When people have to talk about the shortcomings or bad behavior of others, they use **roundabout** ways to avoid hurting others.

roundabout 绕圈子的

2.5 In the Field of Commerce and Industry

Instead of saying "he goes bankrupt", people use "somebody is out of game" or "close one's doors". In Europe "a **compact car**" is equal to "a small car", so "a subcompact" refers to "very small and inexpensive car". As it is inexpensive, it is attractive to people.

compact 小巧的,袖珍的

In industry "cheap" is a taboo word. People don't like

the word "cheap". Its euphemisms are used instead, such as "low-cost", "realistically priced", or "economy priced". In addition, shop owners use "premium-priced" to replace "expensive". "Premium-priced Whisky" in fact is "the most expensive Whisky".

The following are some common euphemisms about shortcomings:

Real Meaning	Euphemism
He is obtuse.	He is a bit slow for his age. He seems to be mentally retarded.
He is lazy.	He needs to raise his ambition a bit. I'm afraid he has to exert himself in his study. He is sure to go far if he can use his resources fully. He'll go somewhere if he is highly motivated.
He has failed a major course.	I'm sorry to find him an underachiever for a major subject.
He lies.	He has difficulty in distinguishing between imaginary and factual information.
He cheats.	He needs help in learning to respect the property right of others.
He must mend his way.	He needs to be brought back into the mainstream.

3. English Tongue Twister

A tongue twister is a specific sequence of words whose rapid, repeated pronunciation is difficult even for native speakers. Often these are similar words which follow one alliteration 头韵

articulation 发音方式

off one's dot 发疯的

stout 肥胖的，强壮的

another but differ in certain syllables. **Alliterations** are also frequent. In addition, some tongue twisters are difficult because of their unusual word composition (sentence structure) and therefore require a high level of concentration.

Some tongue twisters are made for amusement, but on the other hand, professional speakers such as actors, politicians, and television / radio hosts use them as **articulation** exercises.

Some examples are given below:

(1) All I want is a proper cup of coffee,
Made in a proper copper coffee pot
I may be **off my dot**
But I want a cup of coffee
From a proper coffee pot.

Tin coffee pots and iron coffee pots
They're no use to me —
If I can't have a proper cup of coffee
In a proper copper coffee pot
I'll have a cup of tea.

(2) Amidst the mists and coldest frosts,
With **stoutest** wrists and loudest boasts,
He thrusts his fists against the posts,
And still insists he sees the ghosts.

(3) Two tiny timid toads trying to trot to Tarrytown.

Part III Comparison and Contrast

1. Chinese "Dogs" VS English "Dogs"

In ancient China, dogs were viewed as guards to protect the family. Some of them served in rich families and often barked at people, even bit them. So dogs had a bad reputation in ancient China. Many of the idioms criticize or **satirize** dogs. When someone is angry, people say he will "狗急跳墙". When people are not satisfied with the continuation of a story, they think it is "狗尾续貂". When people are serious abused, they are "狗血淋头". When subordinates bully others, they are "狗仗人势". When people are doing something bad, they are "鸡鸣狗盗". When one consorts with his friends who are not very righteous, they are "狐朋狗友". Even though when sometimes people praise others' appearance by saying "人模狗样", it contains some **irony**.

In Chinese history, some emperors killed their followers after they were crowned. This is called "狡兔尽, 走狗烹". When people get in other's way, people joke with them and say "好狗不挡道".

Not all Chinese dog idioms are negative or demeaning, there are "犬马功劳,狗吠不惊,狗吠非主,顾犬补牢" which are positive.

satirize 讽刺, 讥讽　　irony 嘲弄,反话,讽刺

The dog returns to his vomit. 重犯旧日罪恶。

If you want a pretence to whip a dog, say that he ate up the frying-pan. 欲加之罪何患无辞?

In Western countries, even though dogs are viewed as family members, not all dogs are lucky in their languages. "He who lies down with dogs will rise with fleas" means those who flock with the bad guys may follow them. People who return to the old habits are "**The dog returns to his vomit**". People should "beware of the silent dog and still water". When one is alive, he might "lead a dog's life" and when he "goes to the dogs", he will "die like a dog". "A dog in the manger" means an individual who takes or keeps something desired by another out of sheer meanness. If one likes to show off, he "puts on the dog". "**If you want a pretence to whip a dog, say that he ate up the frying-pan**", by doing this, "you give a dog a bad name and hang him".

There used to be dogfighting, the winner is called "top dog" and the loser is called "under dog".

One can eat "hot dogs" when he is "a lucky dog". But most of the time, do remember to "let sleeping dogs lie"!

2. The Color Red in Chinese VS The Color Red in English

Colors in Chinese culture are attached to certain values. Some are considered **auspicious** while the others are **inauspicious**. Red, corresponding with fire, symbolizes good fortune and joy. "Chinese red" is an eternal theme for China, and it is found everywhere during Chinese New Year and other holiday celebrations and family gatherings. In modern China, red remains a very popular color and is affiliated with and used by the government. There are many expressions related to the color red:

To be jealous of others	红眼病
To describe one's appearance	朱唇玉面，朱唇皓齿，唇红齿白
Splendid color	浮翠流丹
Loyalty	赤胆忠心
To have the innocent heart of a child	赤子之心
To be shy	脸红
To become the high-ranked official	纡朱怀金，朱衣紫绶
To be angry	脸红脖子粗

auspicious 吉利　　inauspicious 不吉利　　lavish 慷慨的，大方的

In English language, the color red is associated with celebrations and joyful occasions as well as in China. Red in English can be used to indicate fire, death, anger, and it can also be a particular sign. Many of the English idioms and expressions illustrate these cultural associations.

Days that are important or memorable	*red-letter days*
To give a lavish welcome	*roll out the red carpet for him*
To be angry	*see red, waving a red flag*
To be embarrassed	*red-faced; his face turn red; red in the face; (as) red as a beetroot*
Fact, argument, etc. that leads to attention away from the matter being considered	*red herring*
Over-strict attention to the wording and details of rules and regulations	*red tape*
Be likely to cause strong resentment, anger, violence, etc.	*(like) a red rag to a bull*
Full of vigor or sexual desire	*red-blooded*

3. Chinese Idioms from Buddhism VS English Idioms from Christianity

After **Buddhism** was introduced into China in the first century AD, it brought with it a vast array of new concepts, doctrines and beliefs. Chinese language was affected by Buddhism, too. Many Chinese expressions come from the **sutra**. These words appear not only in daily life, but also in political documents, such as "初心" and "定力". Idioms originated from Buddhism have been integrated with Chinese language and become an important part of Chinese language.

Many of the idioms are associated with Buddhistic stories. One of the famous idioms is "天花乱坠". In the Southern and Northern Dynasties, in the reign of Emperor Wu of Liang, there was a monk called Master Yun Guang who was a very accomplished preacher. Once he explained the sutra so profoundly and subtly that the **Buddha** was moved and sent divine flowers down to earth. Soon the land was covered with flowers.

Other idioms originated from Buddhism include "借花献佛，步步生莲，安身立命，百尺竿头，更进一步，半路出家，本来面目，闭门造车，不即不离，不二法门". Idioms from Buddhism have greatly enlarged Chinese vocabulary.

Buddhism 佛教	sutra 佛经	Buddha 佛陀
Judaism 犹太教	Christianity 基督教	prophecy of the prophet 先知的预言

The *Bible* is the common scripture of **Judaism** and **Christianity** which tells the history of the Jews in ancient times and records the **prophecy of the prophets**. After the introduction of Christianity to England, English language was greatly

affected by the religion. There are many idioms come directly or indirectly from the *Bible*.

"Adam's apple" refers to the protruding part in a man's throat. According to the *Bible*, when deceived by the serpent, Eve and Adam ate the apple and the latter was choked by the forbidden fruit. Since then, there has been a protruding part in man's throat, which is one of the primary physical differences between males and females.

Another example is the "Tower of Babel". People wanted to build a tower whose top would go up as high as heaven and made a great name of themselves. God saw the building of the tower and decided to take away the sense of their language to prevent people from united together. The "Tower of Babel" refers to castle in the air.

Some idioms reflect the wisdom of man, such as "Wisdom is a defense", "Truth will make you free", "No lie is of the truth", "A good name is better than riches". Some idioms come from the parables in the *Bible*, such as "poor as Job", "a grain of mustard seed".

Part IV Reflection and Presentation

1. List the Chinese and English idioms associated with animals, and compare their similarities and differences.

2. Give some examples of Chinese and English euphemisms. Try to explore their origins.

3. Have you heard of climate proverbs? Are they useful in your daily life?

4. Talk about confusion caused by misunderstanding of idioms. For example, "eat one's words" in English and "食言而肥" in Chinese?

Part V Mini-pedia

1. Chinese Kinship

In English, people mainly have to keep track of two things when it comes to kinship: generation and gender. For example, "grandma" is used for both grandmothers on one's mother 's side or father's side. To make things even easier, "cousin" can cover any family member who is a son or daughter of one's parents' siblings.

In Chinese, things become a lot more complicated than in English. In addition to generation and gender, other factors like maternal, paternal, age, by law or by blood, all should be considered. Therefore, the term "cousin" can be split into eight different relations based on mom's side or dad's side, gender and relative age. The Chinese family tree is really complicated even to native Chinese speakers.

For example, there is a joke in *The Dream of the Red Chamber* which displays the complexity of Chinese kinship. 王熙凤说:"一家子也是过正月半,合家赏灯吃酒,真真的热闹非常,祖婆婆、太婆婆、婆婆、媳妇、孙子媳妇、重孙子媳妇;亲孙子、侄孙子、重孙子、灰孙子、滴滴嗒嗒的孙子、孙女外孙女、姨表孙女、姑表孙女,嗳哟哟真好热闹。"

2. Don't Use "Fine, Thank You, and You" Any More

When people ask you "how are you" or "how are you doing", what's your answer? Quite often Chinese people may answer "fine, thank you, and you?" But this is not very common among Westerners. If with acquaintances and strangers, the appropriate answers can be "not bad", "good", "all right", "I'm doing quite well", etc. When talking with a close friends, you can say, "exhausted", "okay", "frustrated", "busy", "stressed out", "I've been better", "great", etc. It's okay to tell them how you really feel. Maybe you'll answer "I'm fine" with a sigh at first, and then your friend will ask you "what's wrong?" You can tell him or her exactly what's bothering you.

After you give your quick answer, it's polite to add a "thanks" afterwards. After that, you can ask the other person "How are you?" You don't have to say "thanks" first, but it's always nice. It's polite to ask the person how they are in return.

References

1. 曹雪芹. 红楼梦. 北京:人民文学出版社, 2013.
2. 邓炎昌,刘润清. 语言与文化——英汉语言文化对比[M]. 北京:外语教学与研究出版社, 1997.
3. 顾明栋. 英语委婉语初探[J]. 济南:山东外语教学, 1981.
4. 林承璋. 英语词汇学引论[M]. 武汉:武汉大学出版社, 1987.
5. 许海琪. 从委婉语看中西文化差异[J]. 戏剧之家, 2019(6).
6. 章旋. *A Brief Study of Similarities Between English and Chinese Euphemisms*

[J]. 海外英语,2012(2).

7. Richard A. Spears & Betty Kirkpatrick. *NTC's English Idioms Dictionary* [M]. 北京：中央编译出版社, 2008.

8. http://blog.tutorming.com/mandarin-chinese-learning-tips/family-tree-relatives-in-chinese.

9. https://en.wikipedia.org/wiki/Euphemism.

10. https://en.wikipedia.org/wiki/Idiom.

11. https://en.wikipedia.org/wiki/Tongue-twister.

12. https://www.britannica.com/art/fable.

13. https://www.britannica.com/topic/Tower-of-Babel.

14. https://www.learnreligions.com/the-tower-of-babel-700219.

Unit 12

Inter-cultural Communication and Sino-foreign Cultural Exchanges

Xu Guangqi and Matteo Ricci Were Preaching

Learning Objectives

- To gain a knowledge of possible barriers and efforts we should make in intercultural communication
- To familiarize yourself with some great events in the history of Sino-foreign cultural exchanges
- To gain better understanding of cultural diversity by analyzing examples of Chinese and Western folklore integration

Lead-in Questions

- Why is inter-cultural communication often frustrating, even for people with a good command of a foreign language? What are the possible barriers that cause misunderstanding? What can you do to achieve successful communication?
- Do you know the stories of those pioneers (like Zhang Qian and Matteo Ricci) in the history of Sino-foreign cultural exchanges? What can you learn from them to become competent intercultural communicators?
- Do you have any idea of Sino-foreign folklore integration? Give one example to illustrate the importance of cultural integration and diversity.

Part I Inter-cultural Communication (ICC)

1. Significance of ICC

accelerating 加速

The early 21st century has witnessed various breakthroughs in science and technology, leading to the process of global economic integration **accelerating** on a daily basis. Frequent exchanges between countries in politics, culture, science and technology, trade and other aspects have greatly changed the world pattern and people's way of life. All these exchanges are typical inter-cultural communication. With communication we can absorb the essence and nourishment of other cultures and promote the progress of our civilization. Otherwise civilization will go to decline.

Today, ICC can happen anytime anywhere and become universal in a globalized environment, though not all communications go as smoothly as expected. The development of modern technology has narrowed the physical distance between peoples in time and space, but it's not easy to close their mental distance. That's why smooth cross-cultural communication is of vital importance to mutual understanding and cooperation between countries.

A good command of a target language is not sufficient to ensure successful communication, for each country or ethnic group has its unique social customs, value orientation, mode of thinking and cultural background, which may cause misunderstanding and even become barriers in the process of ICC.

2. Barriers in ICC

As a practice, ICC dates back to thousands of years ago. Wandering **nomads**, religious **missionaries** and conquering warriors have encountered people from different ethnic groups since the beginning of human civilization. A typical example is the famous "Silk Road" in Chinese history through which peoples of Asia, Africa and Europe interacted with each other. Today, with the rapid development of science and technology, ICC can happen every second at home in a global village. So it's of great significance to recognize the key problems or obstacles in ICC in order to improve intercultural communication competence.

nomad 游牧民
missionary 传教士

2.1 Going to Extremes

Two extreme phenomena may occur in cross-cultural communication: one is the extreme worship of Western culture, or the total Westernization, and the other is the absolute maintenance of Chinese traditions, or prevention of Western cultural invasion. It's very important to take a positive attitude in ICC. Remember: the essence of culture is to spread and borrow from each other. The future peace and development of mankind depend on the coexistence and integration of diverse cultures. Only by drawing on strengths from each other and enhancing exchanges can cultures increase vitality and coexist in the world.

2.2 Ethnocentrism

ethnocentrism 种族优越感，本族中心主义
intrinsic 固有的
cognitive 认知的

It means people think of their own culture as being the center of the world, or they consider their own social norms or behaviors as natural and others as strange. People with **ethnocentrism** evaluate other cultures according to their own cultural background and believe in the **intrinsic** superiority of the nation, culture, or group to which they belong, often accompanied by feelings of dislike for other groups. This is a serious **cognitive** barrier, which reveals one's ignorance of other cultures and leads to misunderstanding or communication failure.

2.3 Assumption of Similarities

Even they have some knowledge of other cultures, people still assume there are more similarities instead of differences in communication. They fail to notice that each culture is unique in some way. Without awareness of the cultural differences, they will do as they would in their own culture, which results in inappropriate or ineffective communication.

2.4 Stereotyping

stereotype 定式思维，成见

Stereotypes are perceptions or beliefs people hold about groups or individuals based on second-hand information. People with stereotypes tend to organize their images into fixed and simple categories to represent an entire collection of people. Stereotypes are over-generalized beliefs which may interfere in objective observation and are not applicable to any individual situation. They persist mainly because they can reduce anxiety and satisfy psychological need for people living in a foreign land.

3. Efforts for Successful ICC

Culture is the eternal treasure created by human beings and enjoys everlasting charm. The formation of culture is like a stream flowing from its source together with other branches. In the process, small **tributaries** join in, merging into a mighty river, then into an ocean. It can't be unchangeable. Chinese culture and Western culture have their own peculiarities but change in the meantime with continuous communication and **integration**. It is an inevitable requirement of cultural development to adopt an integrative attitude towards the study and application of culture so as to promote mutual understanding. Efforts should be made to achieve successful cross-cultural communication and cultural integration.

tributary 支流

integration 融合

3.1 Learning the Native Culture and the Foreign Cultures

It is necessary to develop cultural awareness required for effective intercultural communication. For this reason, we have to know our native culture very well. Without a good knowledge of it, we may lack confidence and cannot tell a good story about our motherland in ICC. And knowing ourselves can help to reduce ethnocentrism and guard against prejudice.

On the other hand, it is vital to learn foreign cultures rather than only foreign languages. A good command of a foreign language is of course indispensable. But language alone does not ensure successful communication. Learning more about a foreign culture and comparing with your native culture will contribute to a better understanding of both and do good to effective communication.

3.2 Being Tolerant of Differences and Developing Empathy

ICC requires us to appreciate similarities and respect differences. Remember that two cultures may be as different as chalk from cheese. Tolerance for differences is the only way we can survive. When encountering differences, it's advisable to be tolerant and develop **empathy** instead of immediate evaluation from our own cultural background. As cultural competence requires some adaptation to the cultures by both parties of communication, either party has to make a certain **compromise**. If we try to see things from the other's point of view, or stand in the other's shoes, we are more likely to gain better understanding and effective communication.

empathy 感同身受

compromise 妥协

3.3 Keeping an Open Mind

As intercultural communicators, people should be tolerant of other cultures and learn from them, developing a strong awareness of international cooperation with an open mind to different cultures. The more different resources an ethnic group has, the more potentials it has for adapting to life challenges.

To sum up, people prefer to live in a world of biological diversity as well as of cultural diversity. A colorful life with more choices is definitely better than a **monotonous** life with only one culture. Actually cultural diversity implies the progress of mankind in the long process of civilization evolution. In today's globalized world with peace and development as the main themes, cultural diversity or multiculturalism becomes a **mainstream**, which requires us to take different cultures as equals. Monoculturalism or cultural **imperialism** should be abandoned as cultural diversity is the basis for possible **fusion** of different cultures contributing to a global culture in the future.

monotonous 单调的

mainstream 主流

imperialism 帝国主义

fusion 融合

Part II Great Events in the History of Sino-foreign Cultural Exchange

Eastern and Western civilizations are two major systems in the development of human history, whose communication and integration have always been generating an important spiritual force for human progress. The major inventions and progress in human history are the products of mutual inspiration and cooperation between the two civilizations. The following are some great events in the history of Sino-foreign cultural exchange. It is wise to learn from these historical events, for history is the past reality and reality is the future history.

1. Silk Road

The Silk Road is a historically important international

Mediterranean 地中海

silk fabric 丝织品，绸缎

overland 陆上的

spinning 纺线

ideological shackles 精神枷锁

trade route between China and the **Mediterranean**, which enjoyed a history of some 1,600 years from the time Zhang Qian pioneered the Road during the Han Dynasty to the breakdown of the Yuan Dynasty. It was so named in 1877 by a famous German geographer for two reasons: China was the first country in the world to breed silkworms and produce **silk fabric** with a fairly advanced level in the Zhou Dynasty (1046-256 BC) and silk was a major export to Europe along the road.

In a narrow sense, the "Silk Road" refers to an ancient **overland** trade route formed in the Western Han Dynasty (206 BC-25 AD), stretching 4,350 miles from Chang'an (today's Xi'an) to western China, central Asia, and even to Europe, enabling these regions to have better communications in diplomacy, business and culture.

The road is not only an ancient international trade route, but also a splendid cultural bridge linking China and the West, bringing about mutual benefits and progress.

For example, the Chinese Four Great Inventions (paper making, printing with movable type, gunpowder and compass) as well as the skills of silkworm breeding and silk **spinning** were transmitted to the West. The use of gunpowder and firearms destroyed the **ideological shackles** of medieval Catholicism in Europe; the introduction of the compass to European navigators made it possible for them to discover America and sail round the world; and printing provided an important basis for the rapid development of European science and the emergence of the Renaissance. All these greatly sped up the development of the entire world.

Many great events happened along this ancient road, making the trade route historically significant. It is now included in the World Heritage List of UNESCO.

In 2013, Chinese President Xi Jinping proposed the "**Belt and Road**" **Initiative**, which created the world's longest and most promising economic development zone based on the ancient trade route. With this initiative, the old Silk Road once again displays its vitality in promoting economic cooperation and cultural communication among **Eurasian** countries.

"Belt and Road" Initiative "一带一路"倡议

Eurasian 欧亚的

2. *The Travels of Marco Polo*

Marco Polo (1254-1324) was an Italian **merchant**, explorer and writer, famous for exploration in China and his book *The Travels of Marco Polo*.

merchant 商人

He learned the mercantile trade from his father and his uncle, who travelled through Asia and met **Kublai Khan**. In 1271, the three people began a long journey to Asia and Marco Polo stayed in China for nearly a quarter of a century. During the period Marco Polo performed a lot of tasks for the emperor, which gave him chances to travel widely throughout China and became familiar with the land and its people.

Kublai Khan 忽必烈(元朝皇帝)

In 1295, Marco Polo returned home only to find his country was in war. He was captured in battle and thrown into prison. He killed the time in prison by telling stories of his travels and adventures to a **cellmate**, who then **transcribed** them. After his release in 1299, Marco Polo became a wealthy merchant, married, and had three

cellmate 同牢难友

transcribe 转录,抄写

children.

Marco Polo's travels are recorded in *The Travels of Marco Polo*, a book that paints a vivid picture of Chinese civilization in the 13th century, a civilization probably more advanced than that of Europe. The book covers the emperor Kublai Khan, his palace, the wealth and great size of China, its capital **Dadu**, and other Asian countries. The book gave Europeans their first comprehensive insight into the inner workings of the Far East, including China, India, and Japan.

Dadu 大都(元朝首都)

Though he was not the first European to reach China, Marco Polo was the first to leave a detailed **chronicle** of his experience. His travels had some influence on the development of European **cartography**, ultimately leading to the European voyages of exploration a century later.

chronicle 编年史

cartography 地图制作

3. Zheng He's Voyages

Zheng He (1371-1433), the "Columbus of the East", was a Chinese navigator and diplomat during the early Ming Dynasty. He was originally born in what is now Yunnan Province as Ma He in a Muslim family. He won Emperor Yongle's recognition and trust with his art of war, strategic wisdom and adventure. It was the Emperor who **conferred** the surname Zheng to Ma He to mark his military achievement.

confer 授予

Emperor Yongle's ruling period witnessed prosperity with the recovery of agricultural economy and development of industry and commerce. It seemed natural and necessary to develop overseas transportation and trade, with all the necessary conditions provided—the development of shipbuilding, the use of compass, the **accumulation** of navigating knowledge and experience. The emperor sought to heighten the country's presence as a global power and impress neighboring nations by sending forth seven **expeditions**. Between 1405 and 1433, Zheng He led seven sea ships to different parts of the world — India, Africa and the Middle East, bringing many Chinese goods like silk and medicine to the foreign kings or to sell for local products. He returned from each trip with boats filled with expensive things such as gold and jewelery, foreign guests and strange animals like a giraffe.

accumulation 积累

expedition 远征

These voyages opened up the sea route from the western Pacific Ocean to the Indian Ocean and other oceans, predating Columbus's discovery of America by 87 years, creating a miracle in the history of world navigation.

Zheng He's fleet demonstrated the political and military superiority of the Ming Empire. And the voyages not only expanded overseas trade but also improved domestic production with the introduction of new material and technology. Most importantly, they strengthened the Sino-foreign cultural exchanges.

4. Matteo Ricci (Li Madou, Chinese Name)

Matteo Ricci (1552-1610), was an Italian **Jesuit** priest, a scholar and one of the founding figures of the Jesuit China missions. His studies covered a wide range of

Jesuit 耶稣会信徒

theology 神学
cosmology 宇宙学

subjects: philosophy, **theology**, mathematics, **cosmology** and astronomy.

Matteo Ricci came to China as a preacher during the Ming Dynasty. He arrived at the Portuguese settlement of Macau in 1582, where he began learning Chinese language and customs, trying to start his **missionary** work with the help of Chinese. He was one of the first Western scholars to master **Chinese script** and **Classical Chinese**.

missionary 传教士

Chinese script 中文手写体
Classical Chinese 文言文

Matteo Ricci then moved to different cities in China: Canton, Zhaoqing, Shaoguan, Nanjing, Nanchang and so on. He stayed in Zhaoqing for six years, where he and Ruggieri compiled a Portuguese-Chinese dictionary.

Matteo Ricci came to Beijing in 1598 and became the first European to enter the Forbidden City of Beijing in 1601 with the invitation of the **Wanli Emperor**, who sought his services in matters such as court astronomy and calendrical science. He converted several prominent Chinese officials to Catholicism, such as Xu Guangqi, who assisted in translating **Euclid's *Elements*** into Chinese as well as the Confucian classics into Latin for the first time.

Wanli Emperor 明神宗

Euclid's *Elements* 欧几里德《几何原本》

Matteo Ricci's book *The True Meaning of the Lord of Heaven*, is written in the form of a dialogue, originally in Chinese, in which he argues that Confucianism and Christianity in fact share notable similarities in key aspects instead of opposition.

His map of the world, named ***Great Universal Geographic Map*** in Chinese characters, is the first map of the world in Chinese history, which introduced the findings of European exploration to East Asia.

Great Universal Geographic Map《坤舆万国全图》

Matteo Ricci was one of the earliest pioneers of Catholic mission in China and the first Western scholar to read Chinese literature and study Chinese **classics**. With his identity of "Western monk" and ability to speak and write in Chinese, Matteo Ricci achieved a great success in spreading Catholicism in China. At the same time, he transmitted Western astronomy, mathematics, geography and other scientific knowledge to China. His writings not only made important contributions to Sino-Western communication but also helped Japan and the Korean peninsula countries gain a better understanding of Western civilization.

classics 典籍

Part III Examples of Sino-foreign Folklore Integration

1. *Shikumen* Architecture

Shikumen 石库门

Shikumen is a traditional architectural style in Shanghai, a mixture of Western and Chinese elements that first appeared in the 1860s during the **Taiping Rebellion**. *Shikumen* is classified as one type of ***lilong*** residences, or "lane houses" in English. It is so named because its door frame is made of stone (stone gate) and the **door leaf** of black **lacquer** solid wood.

Taiping Rebellion 太平天国起义

lilong 里弄

door leaf 门扇

lacquer 漆

Shikumen buildings are of two- or three-story structures resembling Western **terrace** houses or townhouses, distinguished by high brick walls enclosing a narrow front yard. Each residence **abuts** another and all are arranged in

terrace 排屋

abut 毗连

alley 小巷

straight side **alleys** called *longtang*. On the top of the entrance to each alley stands a stylistic stone arch.

British concession 英租界

ventilation 通风

Shikumen is a cultural blend of the elements found in Western terrace with Chinese traditional courtyard along the lower Yangtze River. It was first built in the **British concession**, but quickly became popular throughout the Old City and Chinese zones. Yet it was much smaller due to its urban nature and provided an interior place of peace against the noisy disturbance in the streets, allowing for raindrops to fall and vegetation to grow freely within a residence. The courtyard also allowed sunlight and improved **ventilation** into the rooms.

From the 1910s, various innovations were made to the *Shikumen* in response to social change, such as increasing the width of lanes between terraces and decreasing the width of each dwelling, more elaborate decorations.

As a blending product of Sino-Western architecture, *Shikumen* is one of the most representative residential buildings in Shanghai and considered as one of the symbols of modern urban civilization in Shanghai.

2. Loanwords

loanwords 外来词

Loanwords refer to words adopted from one language and incorporated into another language without translation. They have entered many languages (especially English and Chinese) from different sources as a natural result of frequent communication.

English enjoys the largest vocabulary in the world. With

a strong openness and inclusiveness, English enriches its own vocabulary by constantly absorbing useful words from foreign languages such as Latin, German, French, Greek, Italian and Chinese. It is said that 70 percent of its vocabulary are borrowings. With the ever-increasing Sino-foreign exchanges, Chinese has contributed more and more to the new English words. The following two types of words can be used to show the contribution of Chinese.

Chinese food culture is world-famous and there are a wide variety of words about food in Chinese. English borrows quite a few words of Chinese origin, like dim sum, spring rolls, chow mein, jiaozi, wonton, tea, oolong, Peking duck, **longan**, **lychee**, **ginseng**.

longan 龙眼
lychee 荔枝
ginseng 人参

China's long history and rich culture have great impact on English. This type of words are popular in English, to name only a few: Confucianism, Taoism, *yin-yang*, *fengshui*, kowtow and china.

On the other hand, Chinese borrowing has a long history, dating back to the Qin and Han Dynasties. Chinese words of English origin have become more common in Chinese mainland with its reform and opening-up policy.

A lot of words used in our daily life come from English: humor, coffee, sofa, chocolate, beer, intel, clone, and so on. English **acronyms** are borrowed into Chinese and become widely used—"IT", "PPT", "GDP", "APP" and the like.

acronym 首字母缩略词

Loanwords symbolize more contact between different languages and cultures. With the increasingly frequent communication between the Chinese and English-speaking nations, there will be more and more loan words and expressions from the two languages, thus further promoting their internationalization and diversification.

3. *Turandot*

Turandot《图兰朵》
act 幕

Turandot is an opera of three **acts** adapted in 1924 by Giacomo Puccini, a famous Italian composer. It's a legendary story about an imaginary Chinese princess named Turandot.

The story is taken from a Persian collection of stories called *The Book of One Thousand and One Days*. The original work is a short story titled *The Tale of Calaf and Chinese Princess*.

suitor 求婚者
exiled 流放的

Turandot—a cold-hearted but beautiful princess who challenges her **suitors** to a deadly game of wits: any prince seeking to marry her must first answer three riddles and those who fail must die. Many princes thus become victims of the game. Only the last suitor Calaf, the **exiled** prince of Persia, uses love to conquer her icy heart.

Actually, Turandot is not cold-hearted by nature. It turns out that her beautiful grandma was brutally killed by a conquering prince. In revenge, Turandot has turned against all men and determined that none shall ever possess her.

Turandot's three riddles and answers go as follows:

"What is born each night and dies each dawn?" "Hope."

"What flickers red and warm like a flame, yet is not fire?" "Blood."

"What is like ice but burns?" "Turandot!"

The story itself is cross-cultural in that it is a love story between a Chinese princess and a Persian prince. More interestingly, the story was written by a Persian and adapted into an opera by an Italian. Cultural diversity and blending are definitely inevitable and also eye-catching.

In the opera, Giacomo Puccini uses three of Chinese melodies, including the most memorable folk melody *Molihua* (*Jasmine Flower*). There are other Chinese or oriental elements like the traditional **facial makeup**, or the costumes worn by ancient Chinese officials, and wedding **sedan chair**. The blend of folk arts from different sources makes the opera more expressive and international.

facial makeup 脸谱

sedan chair 花轿

Part IV Reflection and Presentation

1. Chinese history is full of many cross-cultural events, either of conflict or of integration, active or passive. Choose one you're interested in to gain more details from various sources. Then share with your partners and discuss the influence of the event.

2. It is widely accepted that cultural exchanges can serve as a lubricant in bridging differences and resolving disputes between countries. How do you support the argument?

Part V Mini-pedia

1. Four Great New Inventions

As is known to all, the Four Great Inventions—compass, gunpowder, paper-making and printing—are celebrated in the Chinese culture for their historical significance and as symbols of ancient China's advanced science and technology. These four discoveries had a profound impact on the development of civilization throughout the world, serving to highlight the technological interaction between the East and the West.

Interestingly, some modern Chinese scholars argue that other Chinese inventions are perhaps more sophisticated and have a greater impact. In August 2017, Xinhua News Agency described high-speed rail, electronic/mobile payments, bike sharing and online shopping/e-commerce as China's "Four Great New Inventions". It's true that none of the four were actually invented in China, with modern high-speed rail originating in Japan in 1964, e-payment systems originating in the United States in the 1990s, bike sharing invented in Europe in the 1960s and online shopping invented by an Englishman named Michael Aldrich in 1979. But these four are developed to the full and widely used by Chinese for their convenience and efficiency, which serves as a good case of Sino-foreign interaction and integration.

2. Arabic Numerals

Arabic numerals or Hindu-Arabic numerals, are a set of 10 symbols—1, 2, 3, 4, 5, 6, 7, 8, 9, 0—that represent numbers in the decimal number system and are used internationally. They were first invented by the ancient Indians in the 6th or 7th century and introduced to Europe by the Arabs through the writings of Middle Eastern mathematicians, especially al-Khwarizmi and al-Kindi, around the 12th century. Those numerals were later modernized by the Europeans. It is the Arabs who spread the figures and thus the name "Arabic numerals" came into being.

Arabic numerals use the bit-value method, with the high order in the left and the low in the right, writing from the left to the right. With the help of simple mathematical symbols (decimal, negative, percent, etc.), the system can explicitly represent all rational numbers.

The invention of Arabic numerals represented a profound break with previous methods of counting, such as the abacus, and paved the way for the development of algebra.

References

1. 董晓波,编译. 跨文化交际（*Cross-cultural Communication* 第八版）[M]. 北京:北京大学出版社, 2017.
2. 何芳川. 中外文化交流史(上下卷)[M]. 北京:国际文化出版公司, 2008.
3. 王蓉, 张爱琳. 跨文化交际(第四版)[M]. 重庆: 重庆大学出版社, 2018.
4. 张晓立. 世界文化史[M]. 北京:对外经济贸易大学出版社, 2014.

5. 左飚. 冲突 · 互补 · 共存:中西文化对比研究[M]. 上海:上海外语教育出版社, 2009.

6. Oliver A. Johnson & James L. Halverson. *Sources of World Civilization*(The 3rd Edition)[M]. Beijing: Peking University Press, 2004.

7. https://baike.so.com/doc/1718957-1817258.html.

8. https://baike.so.com/doc/5645893-5858528.html.

9. https://en.wikipedia.org/wiki.

10. https://www.britannica.com/topic/Hindu-Arabic-numerals.

11. https://www.travelchinaguide.com/silk-road/.

新时代外国文学与文化系列教材

（丛书主编：王爱菊）

《莎士比亚与西方社会》

《英语诗歌欣赏》

《日本文化漫谈》

《电影中的俄罗斯文学》

《近现代日本社会与文化》

《俄罗斯社会与文化十讲》

《中西民俗文化对比赏析》

《中日文化交流史话》

《英国历史文化要览》

《跨文化交际礼仪》

《国外新闻业与新闻英语导读》